Homes for the 1980s
An Energy & Construction Design Aid

Homes for the 1980s
An Energy & Construction Design Aid

by C. Keeler Chapman & John E. Traister

TAB **TAB BOOKS Inc.**

BLUE RIDGE SUMMIT, PA. 17214

FIRST EDITION

FIRST PRINTING

Copyright © 1982 by TAB BOOKS Inc.

Printed in the United States of America

Library of Congress Cataloging in Publication Data

Chapman, C. Keeler.
    Homes for the 1980s.

    Includes index.
    1. House construction. 2. Power resources.
3. Dwellings—Energy conservation.
I. Traister, John E. II. Title.
TH4811.C48   1982   690'.837   82-5929
ISBN 0-8306-1425-7 (pbk.)   AACR2

Contents

Introduction

The cost of Land is escalating out of control and Land restrictions are becoming more severe but that old American Dream of home ownership is still a dominant goal of many Americans. As society becomes more and more bureaucratic, technological and just plain crowded, people are turning towards the past when life was "simple" for relief from present woes. Early American life was slower paced and had a charm about it (at least that is how we tend to imagine it) regardless of the struggle that life required.

This book is an attempt to deal with such nostalgia for the new home builder. The authors feel that very little has been published to help the layman obtain a home design that renews the past and brings it up to modern thermal and energy requirements.

Energy is the word that is on everyone's mind today. All of us must learn to use less energy, live in smaller, easier-to-heat homes requiring less material and labor to build. At the same time we must build with today's products which in many cases aren't even close counterparts of Early American originals.

Wood siding has almost been eliminated from today's house and replaced with aluminum or hardboard and wood shakes have been replaced by the fiberglass shingle. However, many such materials should not be considered poor alternatives. There are many fine aluminum finishes and colors on the market and the maintenance is considerably less. The fiberglass shingle has a good texture and is much more resistant to fire. Most failures of modern applications of "Early American" is in the detailing and proportioning rather than the modern products themselves.

Don't expect great results if there is a lack of personal compromise. Building products, labor and mortgage rates are at their highest. Keep the home plan simple, even boxy like some of ours. If the Early American look is desired, scale down areas and lower ceiling heights a bit. This will give coziness in winter and coolness in summer without underwriting the utility company. Solar heat, windmills and additional insulation add to the cost of the home, but remember their payback may be sooner that you think.

I Site Examination

He rubbed his eyes - it was a bright sunny morning.
— Washington Irving's Rip Van Winkle

Rip Van Winkle woke up after many years of sleep to a changed world. Today we are waking up to realities of the depletion and expense of the world's energy resources. As a result great significance is being placed upon "natural energy" in site design. This is the energy benefit derived from the natural features of a site. Hardy plant life for erosion control or screening and strong wind for direct windmill power are examples of "natural energies." Every practical use should be made of them to obtain an energy-efficient home.

Almost anyone can quickly learn to investigate a potential building site and draw sensible conclusions about it. One must set aside ample free time and wait for a congenial afternoon to begin a visual examination. Walk over the entire site—observe and listen carefully to discover its qualities.

Even before a site visit, close examination of its qualities on paper (surveyor's plat with land contours) can set a great deal of criteria on home and site development.

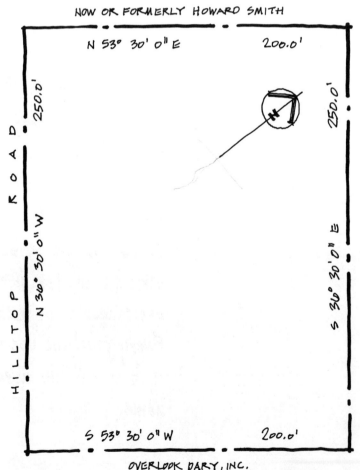

NOW OR FORMERLY HOWARD SMITH

N 53° 30' 0" E   200.0'

HILLTOP ROAD

250.0'

N 30° 30' 0" W

250.0'

S 30° 30' 0" E

S 53° 30' 0" W   200.0'

OVERLOOK DARY, INC.

The plan form of a sample deed description. The written description is part of the property deed and must be transposed into a plat as shown. Usually the most information that can be obtained is the boundaries, area and adjacent land owners.

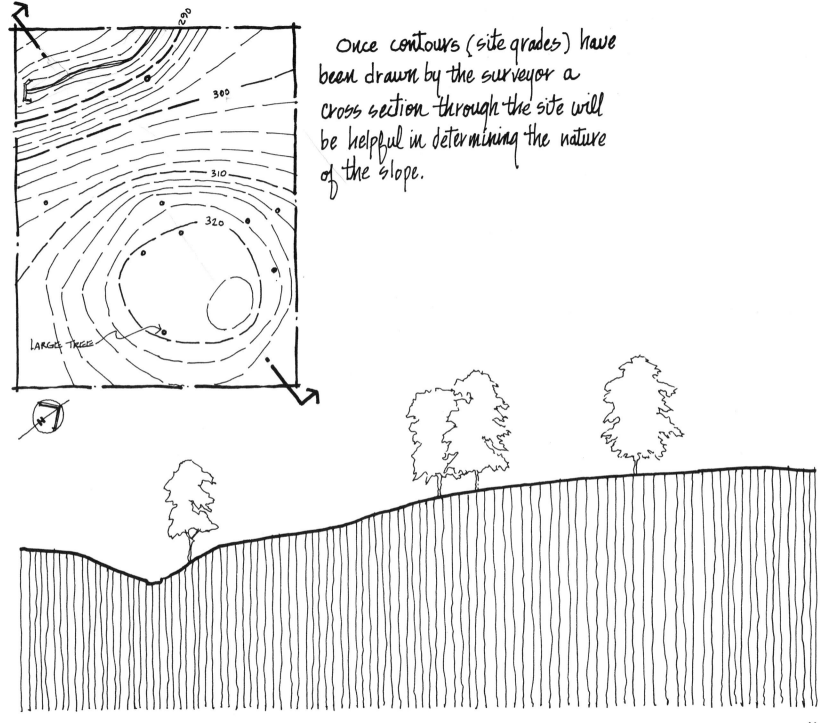

290

300

310

320

LARGE TREE

Once contours (site grades) have been drawn by the surveyor a cross section through the site will be helpful in determining the nature of the slope.

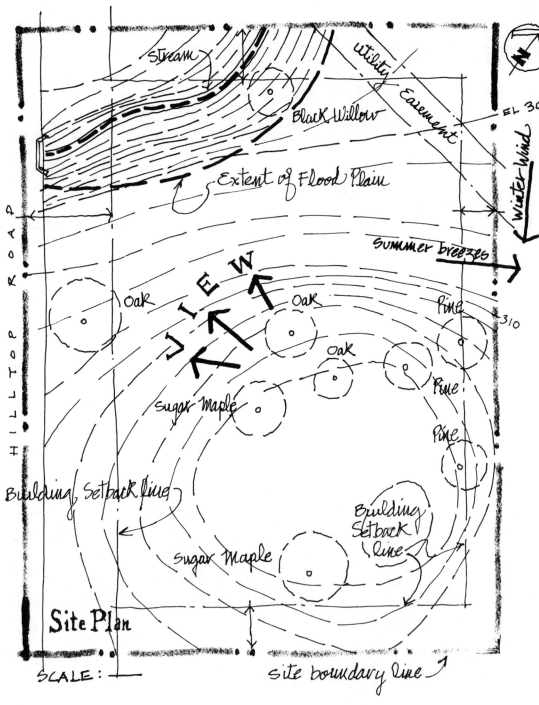

Stream

Black Willow

Utility Easement

EL 300

Extent of Flood Plain

Winter Wind

Summer breezes

VIEW

Oak

Oak

Pine

310

Oak

Pine

Sugar Maple

Pine

Building Setback line

Building Setback line

Sugar Maple

HILLTOP ROAD

Site Plan

SCALE:

site boundary line

The surveyor should indicate land contours at two-foot intervals and locate existing large or speciman trees, buildings, utilities, fences, etc.

Walk the site next and indicate on the plat all other features which might affect your home design or location.

One's home plan should be the result of both room relationships and the site. Draw your home (just the outside walls) on the site plan - don't forget to indicate probable location of the septic field as well. The example to the right has a "summer" wing extending toward the north perhaps to take advantage of cool evening breezes and the view. There is a long southern exposure - maybe for solar roof panels.

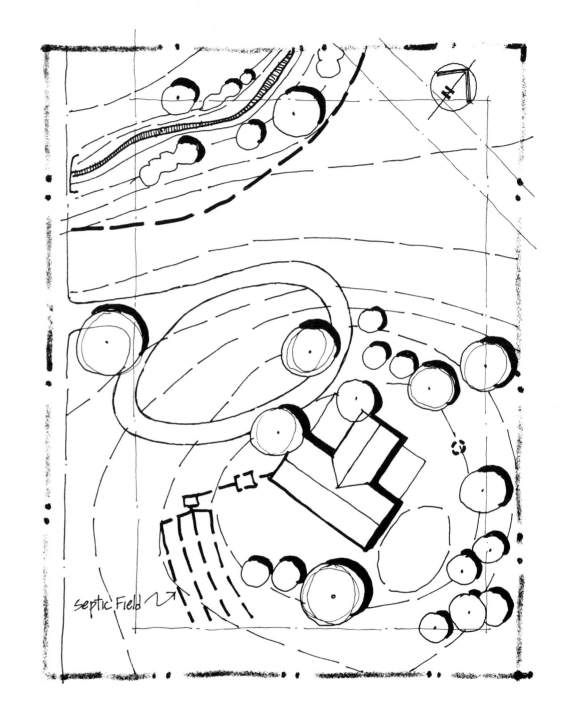

septic Field

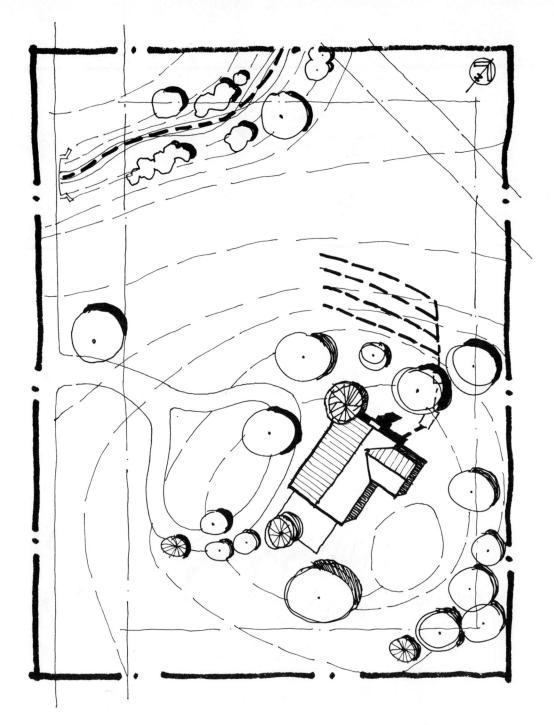

Another solution takes a slightly different form. In this example the orientation of the house is based on the view. A patio on the south end could be used to reflect the sun's heat onto the house in winter and a canopy of grapevines could provide summer shade. Shrubbery could be used to deflect summer breezes onto the patio. The evergreens on the north will help lessen the effect of cold winter winds. The view may be limited a bit in summer due to the large maple and oak in front but the dweller can count on a leafless view in winter.

A closer look at this house will show what the designer had in mind: dense evergreens on the north and a trellis-covered patio and larger window areas on the south. A view to the west means more windows to the winter storms at this site but if one piece of site criteria is overwhelming, then other pieces must take a back seat. Adding evergreen bushes at the front door and providing a closed foyer will add comfort. Also buffering the north end of the house with the closets, bathrooms, bedrooms, utility areas and corridors will make the main living areas more comfortable.

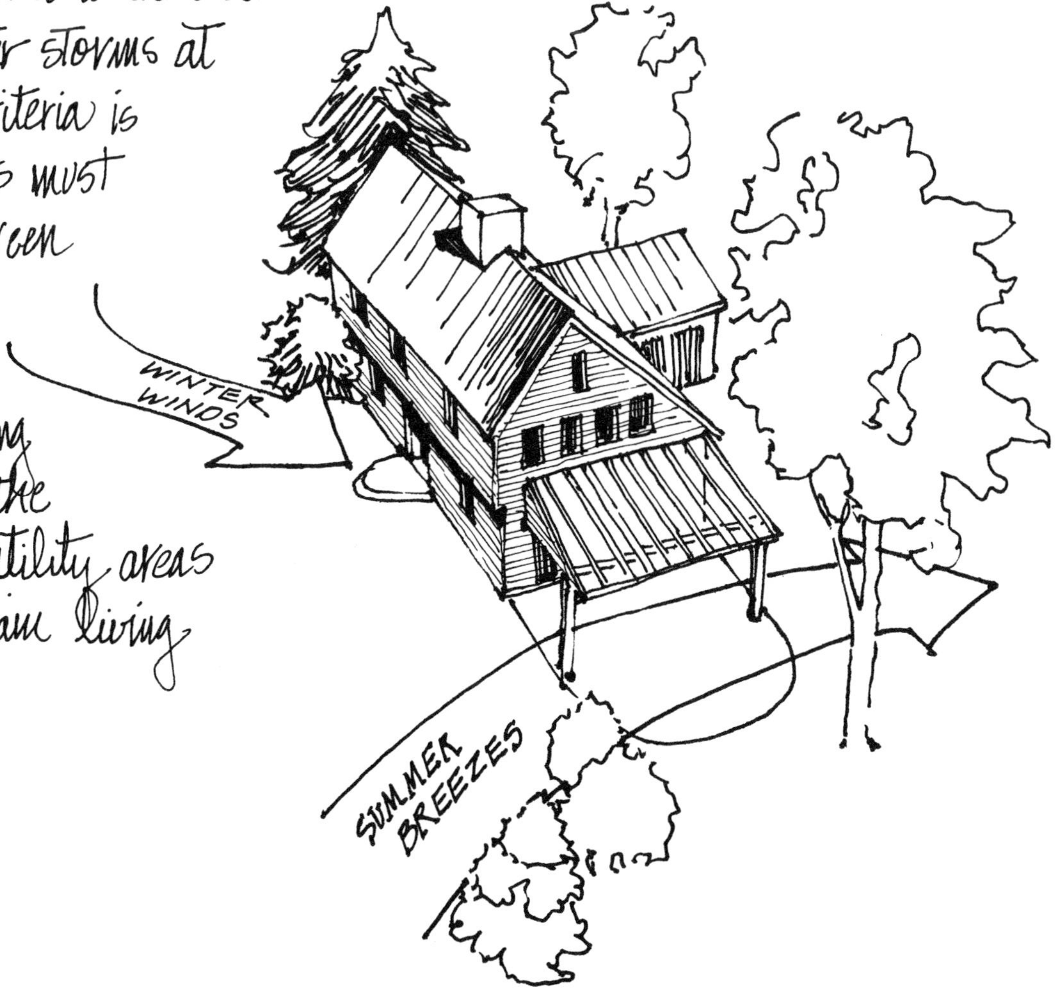

WINTER WINDS

SUMMER BREEZES

A Bird's Eye
Perspective

A Bird's Eye Perspective

   A bird's eye view helps in understanding
how a building will look on a site.
It is difficult to draw such a view but a small site model
would be just as effective. There are many
good books on model making and a rough
basic model is simple to construct.
   The illustration shown on page 16 is helpful
for a number of reasons. The problem of view in the
summer through the large maple
and oak is easier to understand.
The view through a deciduous tree in summer and fall will be
between 4% to 10% of that same foliage area
during the winter. Also, the open ground area
around the house on the south side appears
to be ideal for winter solar exposure but
allows too much summer sun. The high
position of the house will allow good soil drainage
but hillside erosion could be a problem.

Vegetation This sketch depicts a European Beech tree. It is deciduous (loses its leaves in winter) and displays nice coloration in the fall. It is common over most of the eastern United States and the far western edge of the country. Good site planning requires one to be familiar with both the summer and winter profiles of trees and shrubs.

Proper landscaping can distinguish an otherwise nondescript building and give it character. Don't rely on exotic plants - pick those species which are hardy and indigenous to the area.

European Beech
in summer

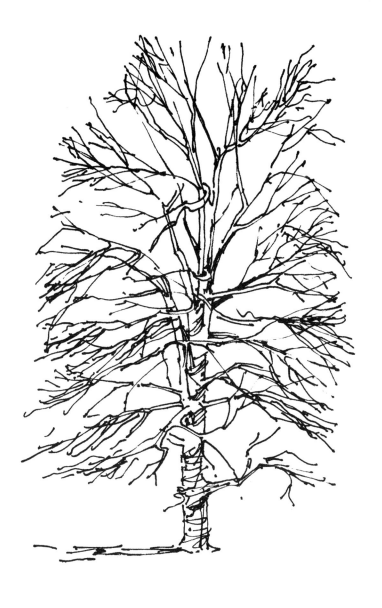

European Beech
in winter

Vines and low-growing plants are also an important site consideration. These plants can be used to prevent erosion on sloping ground as well as to provide shading canopies. Erosion control plans are required in many localities. Changing the natural drainage patterns of a site may tend to erode and destroy the neighboring land. If this happens one could be held liable for damages. A lot of excavation or revamping of grade contours should be done on the advice of a civil engineer or landscape architect. He may have to submit a "soils narrative" to the local government describing how any additional rain "run-off" from the site onto neighboring land will be controlled. If one's home fits into the natural site terrain, many soil problems can be avoided.

Soil Strength

The piece of site data which is perhaps least understood is the soil. Examining the soil, especially for its foundation strength, requires professional skills. However, for most residential situations soil strength is seldom critical. All of the building weight as well as the "live" loads of snow and wind must be transmitted down the building walls or columns to the foundation and finally to earth. The soil stress is determined by total load and footing width. Because of the unknown soil strength (when no professional testing is performed) a footing should be sized to give a large factor of safety.

Uncontrolled erosion can weaken soil strength. Most localities are enacting erosion control codes especially from the farmer's point of view. Erosion tears away his topsoil; it can also destroy homes, especially those on steep slopes. Before beginning any excavation, find out what erosion and sedimentation controls will be required. This information is usually available from county conservation agencies.

Common Soil Types

Sands
- Generally good bearing
- minimal frost problems
- good drainage qualities
- good percolation

Clay
- moldable when moist and may lose strength when wet.
- Poor foundation material
- Susceptible to frost heave
- Difficult to drain.

Silt
- Hard to compact
- very susceptible to frost heaving
- low permeability
- fair bearing capacity

Organic soil (peat, organic silt)
Highly compressible - poor bearing

Hardpan (mixture of various soils)
usually good bearing

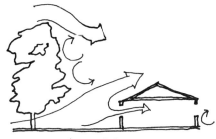

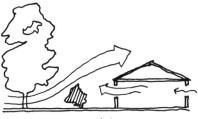

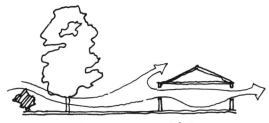

a   Partial Ventilation

b   Partial Ventilation

c   Effective Cross-Ventilation

Diagrams illustrate the
effects of site features
on summer ventilation

The Wind

The influence of the wind is the most commonly ignored site criteria. The velocity and pressure of the wind around a dwelling directly affects heat loss. Strong winds infiltrate a home through cracks and openings in the construction. There is an air "film" which covers a building's exterior surfaces which is also affected by wind velocity. Wind increases the convective heat exchange rate from the wall through the film to the outside air.

In many parts of the United States winter wind direction is different from summer wind. Summer breezes are generally a welcome relief on hot muggy days. Clever site planning and landscaping can protect a home from winter winds while at the same time encourage access to summer breezes.

Strong winds can cause structural damage. Ground contours and man-made development of neighboring areas will affect wind velocity. Familiarize yourself with local wind directions and velocities so that adequate precautions can be taken.

The illustration shows that wind exerting pressure on the windward wall will at the same time cause a negative pressure on the leeward wall and an upward force on the entire roof (low sloping as shown).

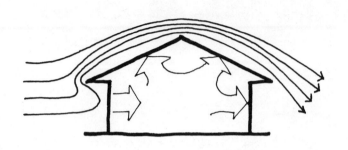

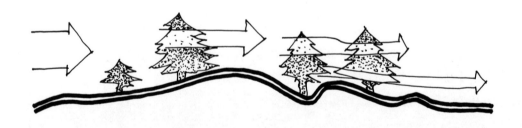

Wind velocity is affected by land and building configuration. Rough ground topography will dampen the wind's velocity. Wind can also be channeled or deflected by site features.

Wind velocity increases at the top of a hill. Houses located on the side of a hill need trees to help deflect cold winter winds and place the home inside the protective cover of the wind's "shadow."

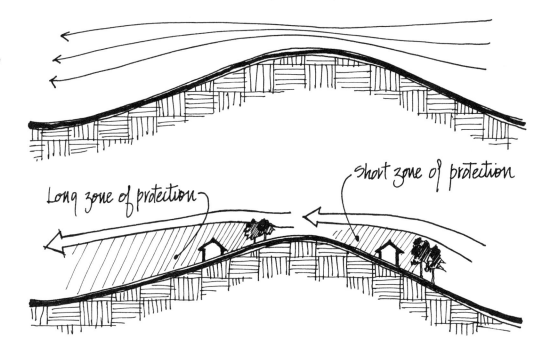

Long zone of protection

Short zone of protection

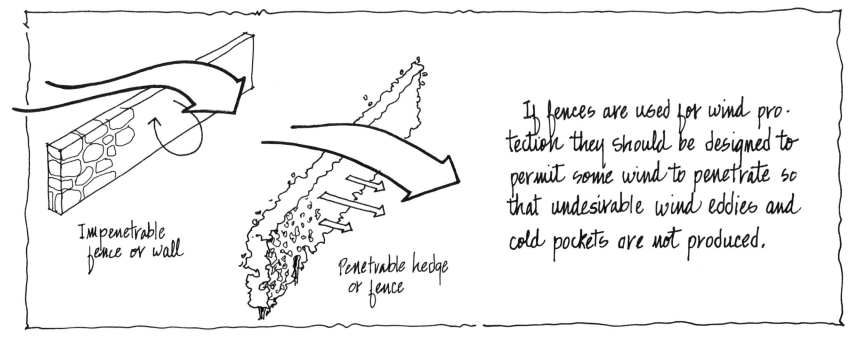

Impenetrable fence or wall

Penetrable hedge or fence

If fences are used for wind protection they should be designed to permit some wind to penetrate so that undesirable wind eddies and cold pockets are not produced.

Earth Sheltering

Earth sheltering by means of earth berming or building into a natural slope is useful in moderating the effects of extreme temperature differences. The earth can be used to both absorb and provide heat. Since the ground below the frost line generally stays moderately cool year round, it can be used to cool hot summer air and to moderate harsh winter cold.

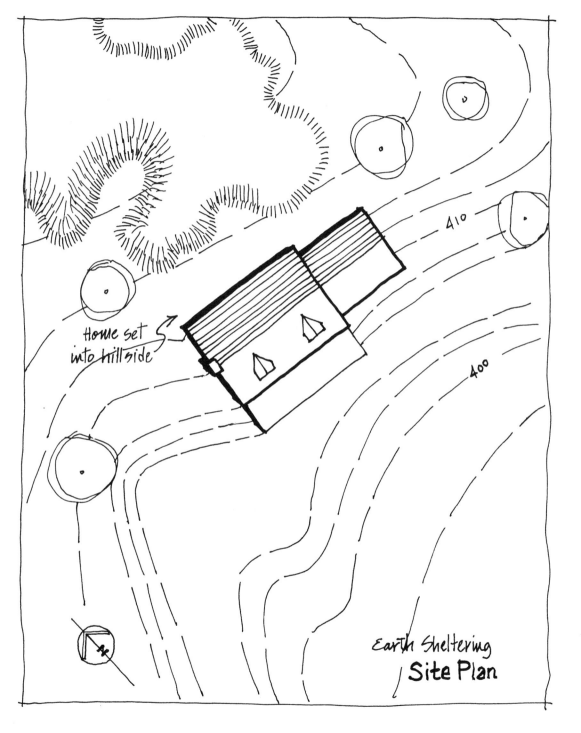

Home set into hillside

410

400

Earth Sheltering
Site Plan

Since the earth in winter will be cooler than the space inside the house, proper insulation must be placed over the entire exterior wall and preferably on its outside face to allow it to act as a thermal storage mass.

Proper moisture-proofing below grade is important. A seasonally high water table may make this design impractical. Effective waterproofing however is usually possible through good site drainage and the use of waterproofing membranes.

Underground areas may have a dampness problem. This can be controlled through the circulation and dehumidification of air.

Some codes are not altogether sympathetic to underground living areas so proper design considerations should be given to ventilation and natural lighting.

Flat Sites

The flat site is potentially the cheapest to build on but is most likely to eliminate quality farm ground. Flat sites are prone to seasonal flooding and general dampness. In such cases one can refer back to the colonial designs of early Virginia which raised the house above a ventilated crawlspace or cellar. In naturally dry areas the flat site allows low, spreading, single-story homes.

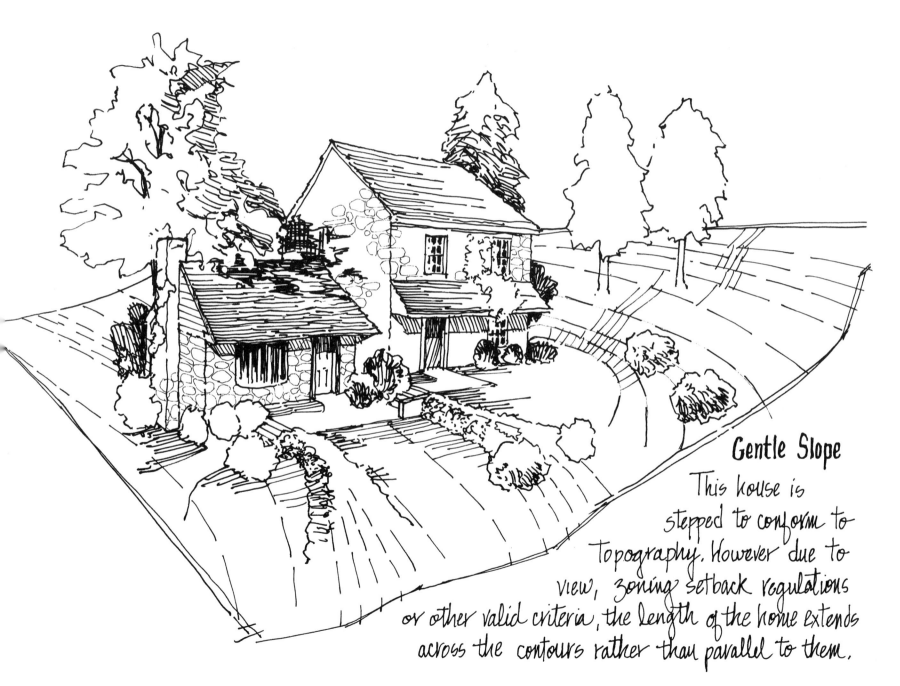

Gentle Slope

This house is stepped to conform to topography. However due to view, zoning setback regulations or other valid criteria, the length of the home extends across the contours rather than parallel to them.

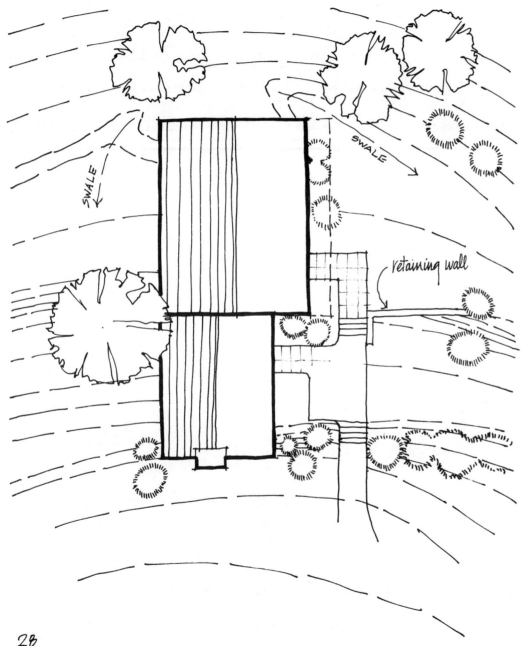

SWALE

SWALE

retaining wall

Gentle Slope
This is the site plan of the home illustrated on page 27. The home is designed on several levels similar to the home on the steep slope so that it harmonizes with the site. On the high side of the house the land is swaled around the sides to promote good drainage. A low retaining wall is used to retain a low bank. This low sloping bank could have been retained with proper vegetation, but a wall was added simply to zone and enhance a terraced lawn area. Another bank farther down the hill is retained by a low-growing ground cover.

Steep Slopes One of the most obvious features of ground is its slope. The site for this house is steeply sloped. Building codes usually discourage development on sloping ground, and building costs are higher. However, proper site design can make the sloping site more desirable than flat areas. Development on slopes and nontillable ground is a great alternative to the destruction of open farm land by subdivisions.

This illustration depicts a south-facing slope. Since there is little chance of trees or ground features obstructing the sun, the steep slope offers good solar heating possibilities.

29

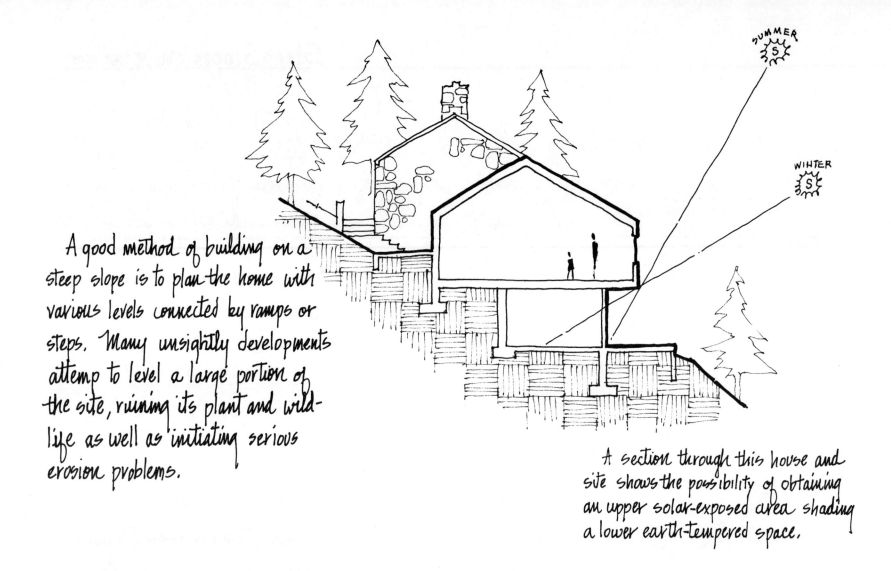

A good method of building on a steep slope is to plan the home with various levels connected by ramps or steps. Many unsightly developments attempt to level a large portion of the site, ruining its plant and wild-life as well as initiating serious erosion problems.

A section through this house and site shows the possibility of obtaining an upper solar-exposed area shading a lower earth-tempered space.

SUMMER
S

WINTER
S

A narrow site
or one without natural
privacy or view can be
designed from the inside out. This
design focuses on an inner court-
yard which could possibly turn
into a summer living room.

A wooded site can be cleared just enough to give a sparse, even scattering of trees. Many wooded sites are cleared extensively to obtain a front and rear yard. Too much clearing causes the house to appear like an intruder.

The site design in this example uses a naturally curving road to allow a variety of views of the house and site between the trees.

Trees between the viewer
and the house help to enliven a
view and give a sense of depth.

Existing site characteristics should play an important part in a final home plan. In this instance a marvelous old tree has been made the focal point of the plan. The two wings of the house have been angled to accentuate the tree. The area around the tree will make a nice patio on which one can sit in the shade and enjoy the distant views.

II Solar Heat

Early Americans were an independent lot. They had to be - there were no large utility companies and no instant telephone communications. They were isolated, a fact reflected in their simple and indigenous architecture. The sun and today's technology offer us a means of becoming more independent or self-sufficient rather than isolated by tapping our portion of sunshine and developing on-site utilities with rates set by ourselves.

The sun's energy in human terms is, of course, forever. It has been shining for billions of years and will continue for billions more. But by the time radiant energy reaches the earth, it is quite diffuse - and when there are obscuring clouds the energy is even less. So it is vital to understand the most efficient techniques for transforming this diffuse energy into a concentrated effective heat source. And the world's dwindling supply of fossile fuels continues to make solar energy more competitive with Arab prices. Early Americans did the best they knew how to take advantage of the sun - we should have no hesitation in doing even better.

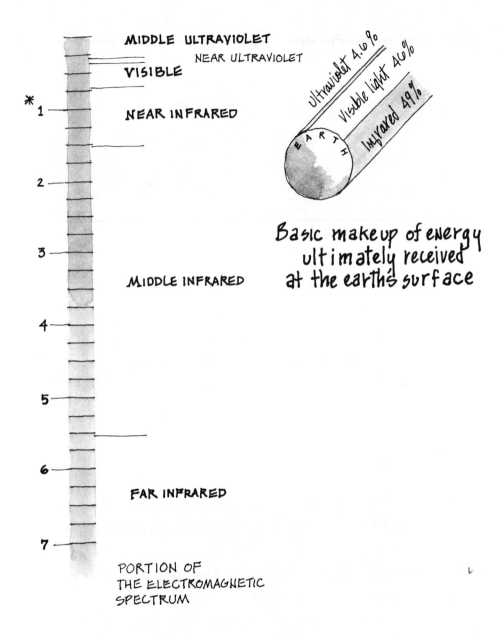

MIDDLE ULTRAVIOLET

NEAR ULTRAVIOLET

VISIBLE

NEAR INFRARED

* 1

2

3

MIDDLE INFRARED

4

5

6

FAR INFRARED

7

PORTION OF
THE ELECTROMAGNETIC
SPECTRUM

Ultraviolet 1.10%

Visible light 40%

Infrared 49%

EARTH

Basic makeup of energy
ultimately received
at the earth's surface

*(UNITS OF WAVELENGTH ARE
MICRONS. ONE MICRON = $\frac{4}{10,000}$
OF AN INCH.)

Scientists refer to the sun's energy in terms of wavelengths and particles. The particles are called photons and are thought of as individual packets of energy. Wavelength refers to energy content and is more important to our basic understanding of solar heating.

The electromagnetic spectrum consists of electromagnetic energy varying extremely in wavelength or frequency of oscillation — and there seems to be no limit at either end of the spectrum. The wavelengths relevant to solar heat extend from ultraviolet (shortwave) through visible light into the infrared (longwave).

Energy emitted from the sun is mostly of short wavelength — the shorter the wavelength the greater is the energy. A solar collector intercepts both the short wavelength sunlight and long wavelength scattered radiation and converts them into usable heat.

The drawings on this page illustrate differences in winter and summer sunshine. The earth rotates once around the sun in a year and once around its own axis in 24 hours. The equator is tilted 23½° off the plane of the earth's orbit (ecliptic) around the sun. This fact is responsible for our seasons. Notice that summer sunshine is more directly overhead resulting in a more intense heating. In winter, the earth has moved through 180° of its orbit since summer and is on the "other side" of the sun. The sun now casts long shadows, and its heat intensity is less in the Northern Hemisphere.

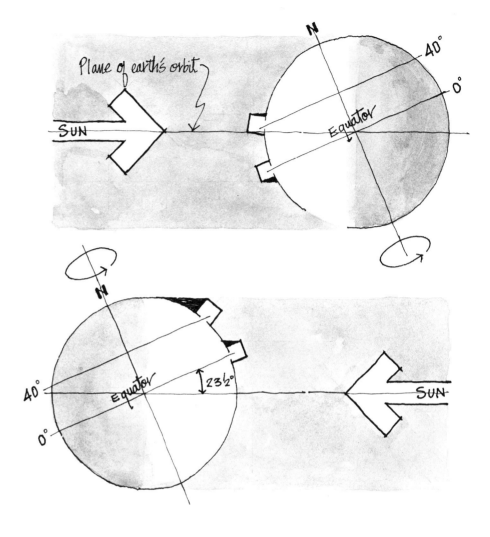

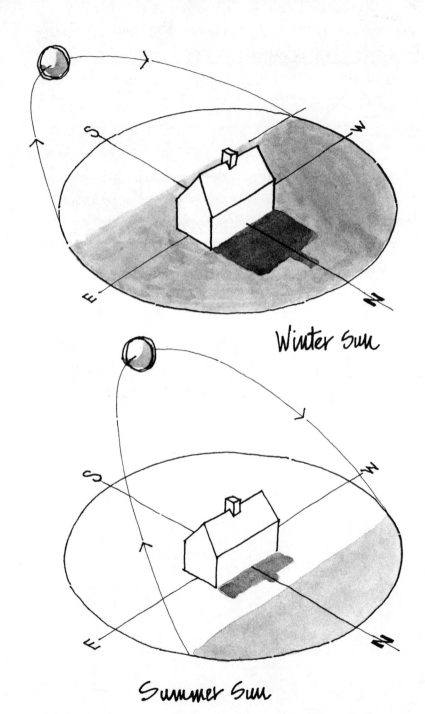

Winter Sun

Summer Sun

Summer solstice occurs on June 21. The sun on this day attains its highest "**altitude**" of the year. The sun will cast its shortest shadow on this day at "solar noon". The longest shadow of the year at solar noon is cast at winter solstice, December 21 (solar noon is that time of day when the sun's altitude is maximum).

Another important solar angle is the measure of "**azimuth**". This is the horizontal angle (bearing) of the sun from "true south". True south is not compass south. A compass points to magnetic north/south and hence locates south based on the earth's magnetic poles. True south is the bearing of the sun at solar noon on any particular day.

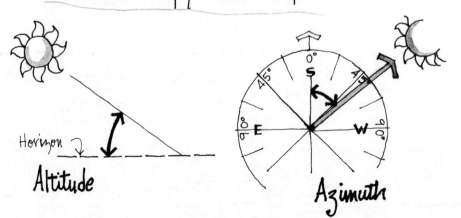

Altitude

Azimuth

The energy emitted by the sun comes to us in the form of electromagnetic radiation. It travels millions of miles to our atmosphere with virtually the same energy it had at its start. Its intensity is less however, because of its diffusion out in all directions. The solar energy reaching our atmosphere is about 429 BTU/FT²/hr. After being scattered, reflected and absorbed by or within the atmosphere, about 50% of this amount is finally absorbed by the earth. Solar energy reaching a particular spot on the earth's surface varies with time of day, time of year, cloud cover, pollution and latitude. Its strength is between 0 and 330 BTU/FT²/hr. The earth's atmosphere is heated more by heat reradiated from the earth than by direct solar radiation.

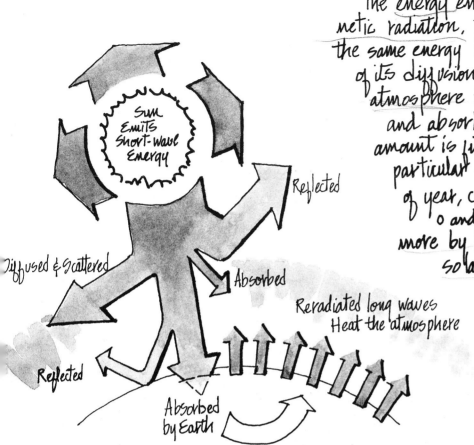

Sun Emits Short-Wave Energy

Reflected

Diffused & Scattered

Absorbed

Reflected

Reradiated long waves Heat the atmosphere

Absorbed by Earth

An important aspect of solar heating is a phenomenon known as the greenhouse effect. Solar radiation in the form of light is a high frequency (short-wave) energy. Light waves will pass readily through glass but longer wavelengths (heat) will not.

Long wavelength energy escapes through glass by being absorbed by it. The absorbed energy raises the temperature of the glass and is eventually reradiated and convected to the colder outside. For this reason it is important to have heavy surfaces on the inside of the greenhouse to absorb the heat and help slow its escape through the glass. At times when the sun is shining there will be a net gain of heat in a south-facing glass wall. However at night more heat will be lost through the glass than was gained during sunshine if movable insulation is not applied.

39

Heat transfer is made by 3 basic processes:

Conduction is the transfer of heat between surfaces which are in contact - heat flow from the warmer surface to the cooler one. Conduction is a very efficient form of heat transfer.

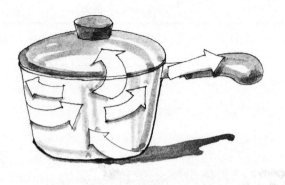

Radiation of heat is similar to conduction but is less efficient and surface contact is not necessary. All materials radiate thermal energy. The wavelength or energy of this radiation depends on the temperature of the material. Thermal energy (heat) is radiated at long wavelengths. Sunlight is short-wave emission,

Convection is the heat transfer which occurs in liquids and gases. If heat is applied to one portion of a liquid or gas, it expands, rises and is replaced with cooler fluid. Likewise a hot fluid in contact with a cold surface will lose heat and sink,

Solar heating systems can be divided into two broad categories: **active** and **passive**. The active system is a forced mechanical collection and distribution of solar heat. This involves pipes, ducts, electric pumps, blowers, etc. The passive system is one in which the heat from the sun is absorbed directly by the home without the use of complicated movable mechanical parts, pumps, etc.

Active system

The basic components of the active system are the collector, distribution system, and storage. The collector is usually a series of sun-facing panels of either the flat-plate or **concentrating** type.

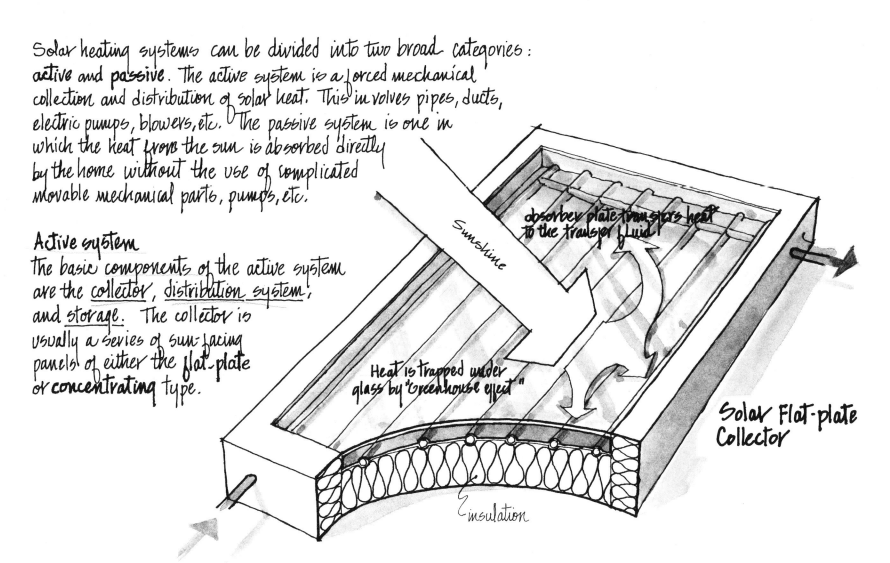

Sunshine

absorber plate transfers heat to the transfer fluid

Heat is trapped under glass by "Greenhouse effect"

Insulation

Solar Flat-plate Collector

The flat-plate version is generally the most satisfactory for domestic use since it can work even on cloudy days. It consists of one or several cover plates (glass or plastic), an absorber plate (metal), and a heat transfer fluid (usually water or air). The collector should face as close as possible to south (azimuth 0-20°) and should be tilted at an "altitude" angle equal to the latitude plus 15° for space heating and at an angle equal to the latitude for domestic hot-water heating.

Solar collectors have, as a basic component, a cover plate of transparent material used to trap heat in a "greenhouse effect" and prevent convective heat losses from the absorber plate. One or two cover plates or more are required to lower conductive heat losses, however, each added plate reduces the amount of transmitted sunlight and increased losses by absorbtion.

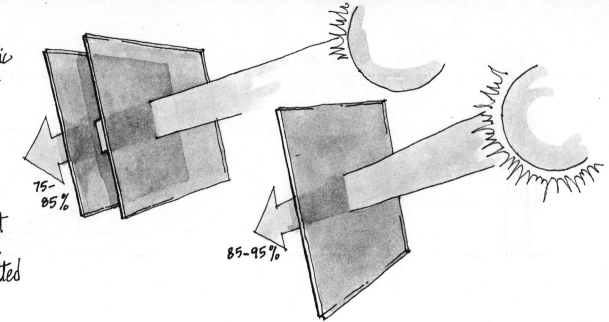

75-85%

85-95%

Glass and Plexiglas are common cover plates. Many types of plastics, however, tend to deteriorate under continuous exposure to ultraviolet light (ultraviolet stable acrylic sheets are expensive). Glass is opaque to long-wave radiation but will absorb and conduct it.

The solar collector must be mounted at the optimum angle to allow the cover plates to face the sun as directly as possible. Glass and plastics will transmit most of the solar radiation that strikes perpendicular (NORMAL) to their surface. Angles off the perpendicular (angle of incidence) will reduce energy transmission increasingly as the angle is widened. Angles greater than 30° begin to reduce transmission dramatically.

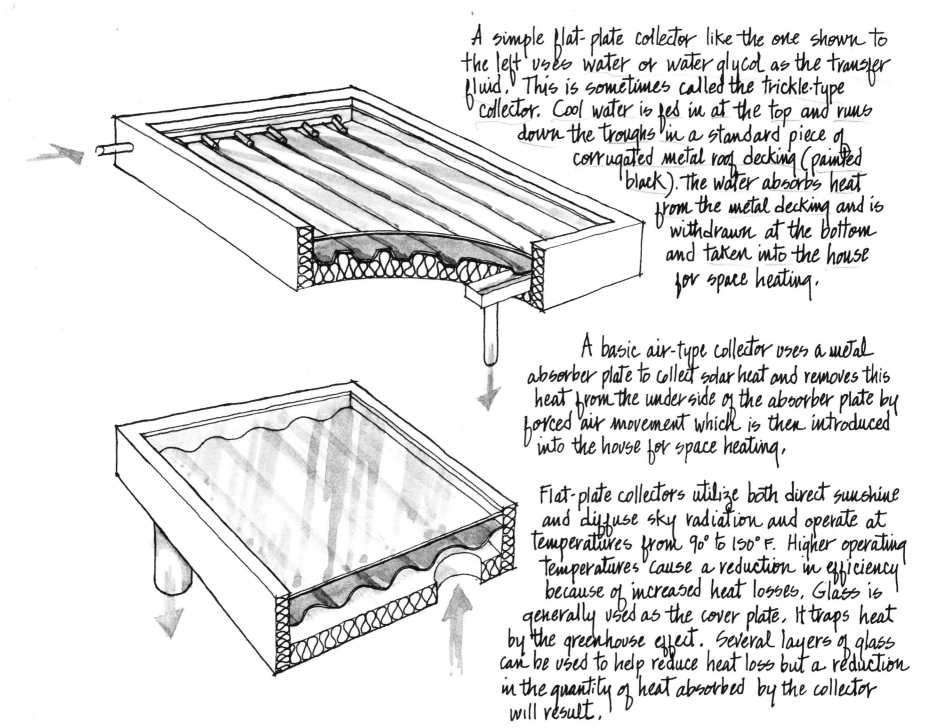

A simple flat-plate collector like the one shown to the left uses water or water glycol as the transfer fluid. This is sometimes called the trickle-type collector. Cool water is fed in at the top and runs down the troughs in a standard piece of corrugated metal roof decking (painted black). The water absorbs heat from the metal decking and is withdrawn at the bottom and taken into the house for space heating.

A basic air-type collector uses a metal absorber plate to collect solar heat and removes this heat from the underside of the absorber plate by forced air movement which is then introduced into the house for space heating.

Flat-plate collectors utilize both direct sunshine and diffuse sky radiation and operate at temperatures from 90° to 150° F. Higher operating temperatures cause a reduction in efficiency because of increased heat losses. Glass is generally used as the cover plate, It traps heat by the greenhouse effect. Several layers of glass can be used to help reduce heat loss but a reduction in the quantity of heat absorbed by the collector will result.

43

A basic active-hot water preheat system

Water flowing through a solar collector is heated and delivered to a heavily insulated preheat storage tank. Heat from the solar collector water is transferred to the water of the preheat tank by means of a heat exchanger. The hot water of the preheat tank is then delivered to the domestic hot-water tank. This system will accommodate drain-down of the solar collectors at times when there is danger of freezing. Using heat exchangers may seem overly complicated, however many solar panel systems use a transfer fluid of water mixed with antifreeze so that no drain-down is required. The antifreeze is of course nonpotable and must be kept separate from drinking water. Even if the system is used for baseboard heat only, an antifreeze mixture is undesirable because of its corrosive qualities.

The plumbing system is relatively uncomplicated.

The valves, pumps and electrical components are standard equipment used on nonsolar systems. Leaks are the potential cause of the worst problems. Close attention should be given to each connecting joint.

Illustrated below is a natural thermosiphoning system:

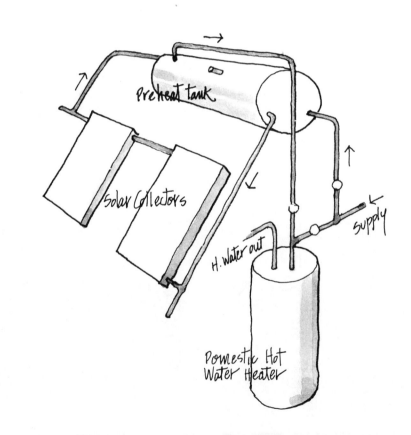

Preheat tank

Solar Collectors

H. Water out

supply

Domestic Hot Water Heater

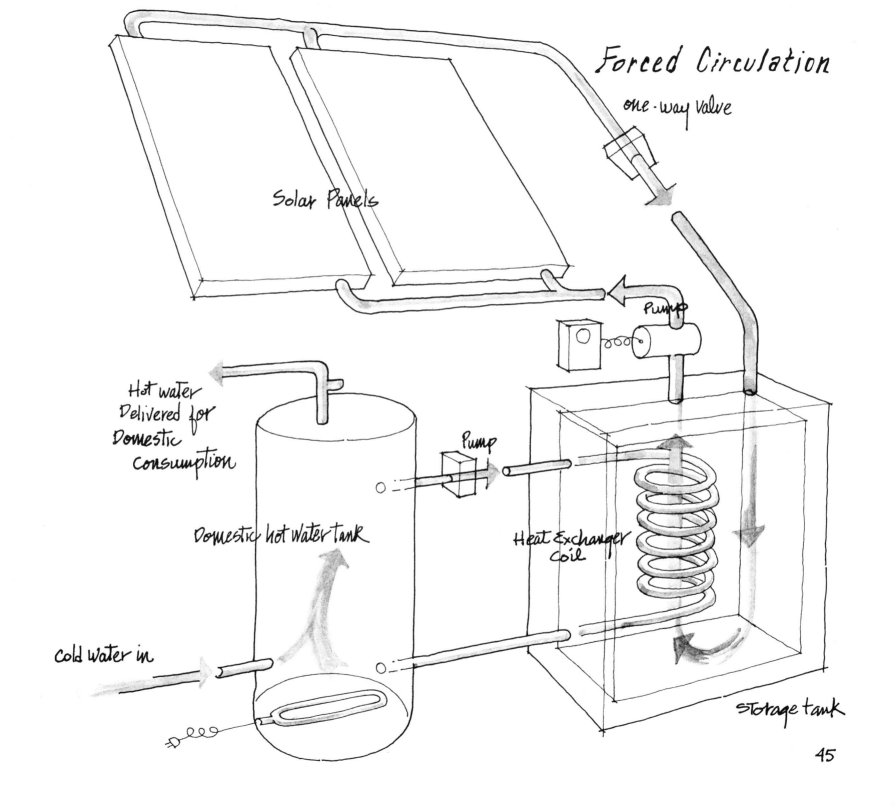

Forced Circulation

one-way valve

Solar Panels

Pump

Hot water
Delivered for
Domestic
Consumption

Pump

Domestic hot water tank

Heat Exchanger
Coil

Cold water in

storage tank

45

The concentrating collector needs bright sunshine in order to work. It is designed to constantly track the sun in its movement across the sky. This requires movement and sensory apparatus. These disadvantages including manufacturing problems of producing highly reflecting curved surfaces have made the concentrating collector generally unsuited to residential applications. Some versions of the concentrating collector like the one illustrated to the right are effective without tracking mechanisms due to a compound parabolic shape which focuses light over a wide range of incident angles.

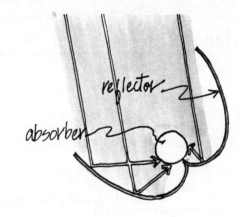

reflector

absorber

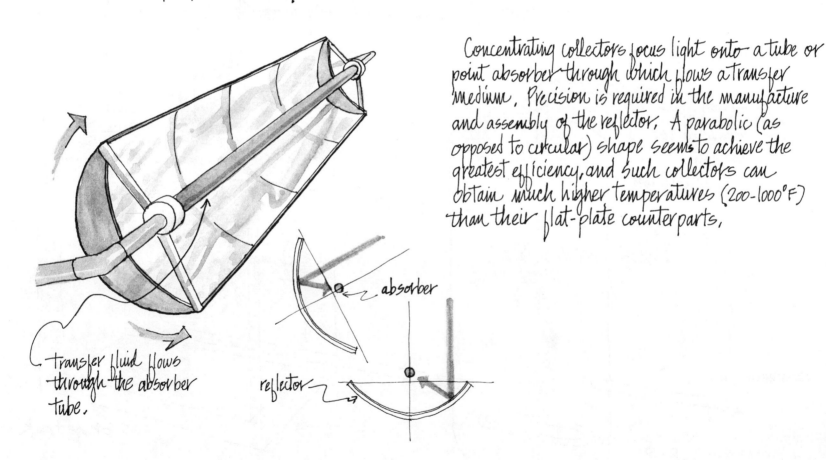

Concentrating collectors focus light onto a tube or point absorber through which flows a transfer medium. Precision is required in the manufacture and assembly of the reflector. A parabolic (as opposed to circular) shape seems to achieve the greatest efficiency, and such collectors can obtain much higher temperatures (200-1000°F) than their flat-plate counterparts.

Transfer fluid flows through the absorber tube.

absorber

reflector

Solar Attic

This idea has been developed and used successfully by a Chicago-based group of architects called the Hawkweed Group.* Fiberglass panels are placed directly over conventional wood roof rafters. A space in the attic facing south is partitioned off and insulated from the rest of the house. The walls and floor of the space are lined with gypsum board painted black. Air is drawn out through the top of the space and delivered to a conventional furnace for redistribution throughout the house. In summer the space is vented to remove heat.

glazing

insulated Duct

solar Attic

Return   insulation

To furnace or storage or direct space heating

Solar Attic Section

*The Hawkweed Group 1981.
Passive Solar House Book.
Chicago, IL : Rand McNally & Co.

Solar Roof

Conventional wood frame roof rafters can become an integral part of a solar collector. Metal pans with inlet and outlet openings are positioned between the rafters. A blackened metal absorber plate is placed on top of the pans and is covered by two layers of glazing. This is a site-assembled flat-plate system which uses air as the transport medium.

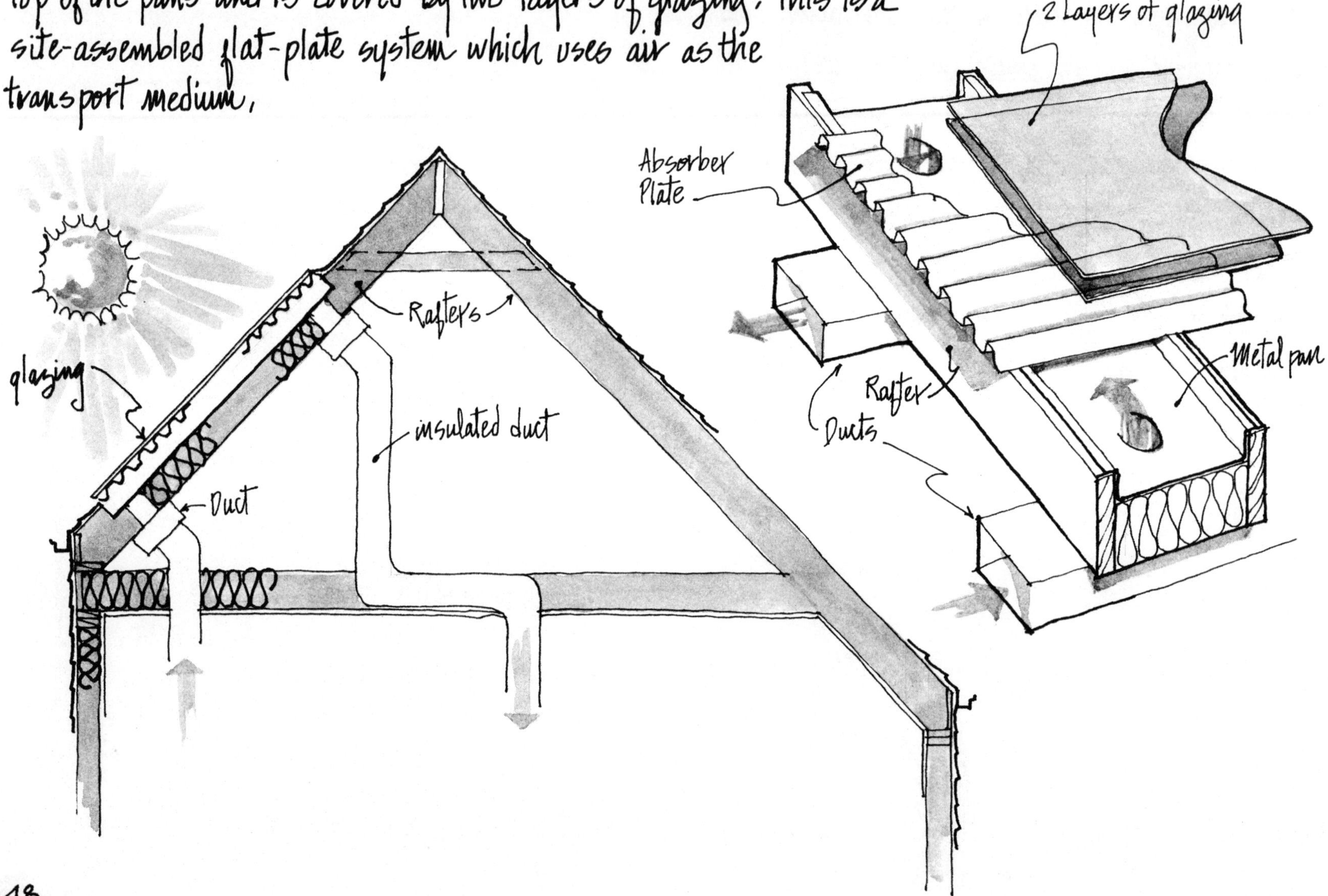

glazing

Rafters

insulated duct

Duct

2 Layers of glazing

Absorber Plate

Metal pan

Rafter

Ducts

Solar Collector Sizing
The Basics

Begin by obtaining a rough idea of the quantity of sunshine available. One of the best references is the ASHRAE data on clear-day insolation for a given latitude. For instance we will examine the month of November for Lancaster, Pennsylvania 40° N latitude by illustrating the quantity of sunshine in BTU's striking a collector (tilted 50°) over the course of an average November day.

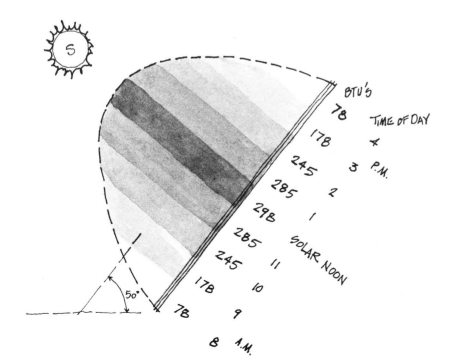

BTU'S
78
178
245
285
298
285
245
178
78

TIME OF DAY

4   P.M.
3
2
1
SOLAR NOON
11
10
9
8   A.M.

S

50°

Note that the quantity of sunshine is symmetrical about solar noon. Also note that the insolation before 8:30 and after 3:30 is of little value. We will dismiss it as useless for solar heat. The sunshine at solar noon is the most intense of all hours - 298 BTU's. The total BTU's striking our collector over a day's time is 1870 BTU's/ft². The useful quantity of BTU's contributing to solar heat is 1870 minus the early morning (78) and late afternoon (78) quantities or 1870 - 156 = 1714 BTU's.

49

We have figured that on a perfectly clear day in November in Lancaster, Pa., 1714 BTUs are available for solar heating. But what about cloudy or partially cloudy days? The cloudiness factor has been figured into maps based on records of the U.S. Weather Bureau. These maps are available from the U.S. Department of Commerce, and they give the mean percentage of possible sunshine for each month (the portion of the month that the sun is likely to shine when clouds are taken into consideration).

The map shown on this page is a partial adaptation of the U.S. weather map for the month of November. Lancaster, Pa., falls between the 40% and 50% lines of sunshine or about 45%. Note that Boise, Idaho, has about the same mean percentage of sunshine.

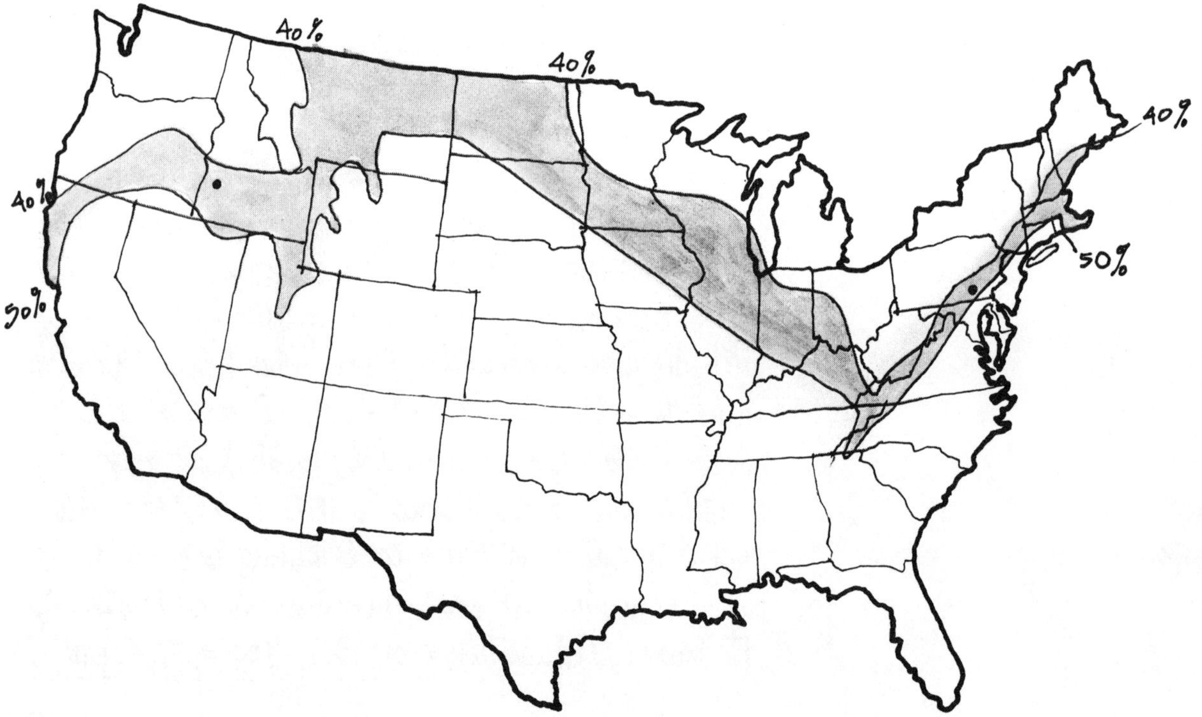

40%

40%

40%

40%

50%

40%

50%

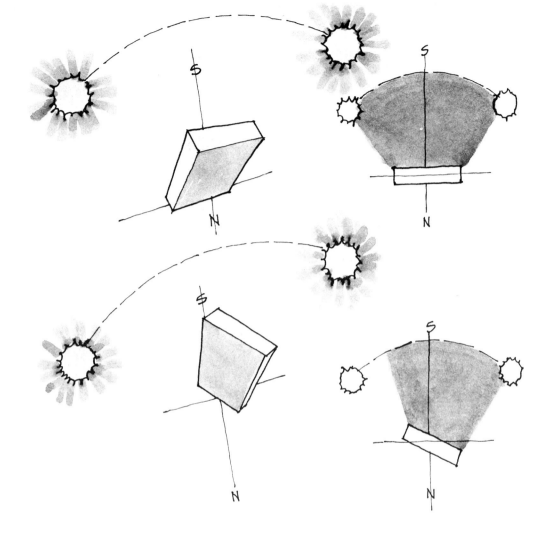

Another factor influencing solar collection is the azimuth orientation. As can be seen from the diagrams to the left, a surface facing true south will receive the greatest sunshine during the course of a day. Deviation from true south changes the percentage of sunshine received roughly in accordance with the azimuth angle chart shown below (to be used for winter months only).

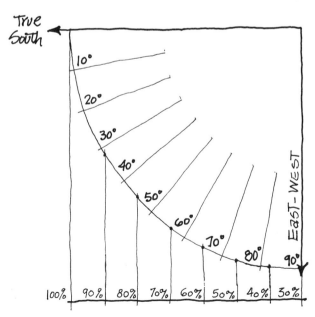

True South

East-West

10° 20° 30° 40° 50° 60° 70° 80° 90°

100% 90% 80% 70% 60% 50% 40% 30%

The collector itself has certain inherent inefficiencies which must be allowed for in sizing. Out of every 100 BTU's received by the collector only 25 to 85 might actually be delivered as space heating. The best determination of collector efficiency might be to accept the figures of the particular manufacturer you plan to use. Naturally you want the collector which offers the greatest efficiency for the money. Remember that the storage and delivery system heat losses are a part of the overall system efficiency.

Now we can set down a formula for collector sizing:

Using your figures for monthly household BTU heat loss (Refer to this book's section on heat loss calculations) chart the square footage requirements you feel are appropriate to your home design and finances.

MONTH	% OF SOLAR HEATING DESIRED	X	MONTHLY HEAT LOSS BTU'S	÷	$\dfrac{\text{BTU OUTPUT}}{\text{ft}^2 \text{ COLLECTOR}}$	=	AREA OF COLLECTOR ft² REQUIRED
NOV	50%		6,000,000		8793		341

Continue charting each month of the heating season; then decide on the square footage that will give a suitable percentage of yearly heat loss.

$$\frac{\text{BTU'S}}{\text{CLEAR DAY}} \times \text{\% SUNSHINE} \times \text{DEVIATION \%} \times \frac{\text{STORAGE/COLLECTOR}}{\text{EFFICIENCY}} \times \frac{\text{DAYS}}{\text{MONTH}} = \frac{\text{BTU'S OUTPUT}}{\text{ft}^2 \text{ COLLECTOR/NOVEMBER}}$$

$$1714 \times 45\% \times 95\% \times 40\% \times 30 = 8793$$

Repeat the calculations for each month containing degree-days to come up with an overall yearly system capacity.

Passive System

Solar collectors which require little technology, few moving parts and extremely low maintenance can be classified as passive. Unsophisticated but knowledgeable use of thermosiphoning effects and the inherent heat storage qualities of building materials characterize the passive collector. Windows on south-facing walls of a home constitutes a simple passive design.

The window-wall collector can be made most effective by adding an absorber/storage medium: dark heavy materials used for floors and walls help store heat and prevent large fluctuations in daily room temperatures. The term **thermal mass** is important to understand. The mass (density) of a material affects its ability to store heat. Heavy masonry will store (absorb) heat and thereby delay its flow through the material! Light weight walls such as those constructed of wood and insulation don't have this inherent storage ability.

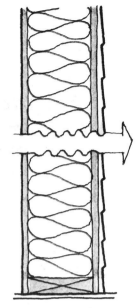

Wood Stud

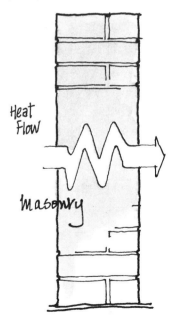

Heat Flow

Masonry

53

Heat Capacity

In addition to thermal mass or density of a material, its heat capacity should also be analyzed for solar applications. Heat capacity is the measure of the ability of a material to store heat. It is the quantity of heat that can be absorbed or released from a cubic measure of a material per degree change in temperature. Even though wood has a high heat capacity, it is a poor conductor and is combustible.

Water has the highest heat capacity of most common materials and is cheap. It is, therefore, an excellent heat transfer and storage medium. Water can provide good thermal lag. It can absorb large quantities of heat and through means of convective currents (natural thermo-siphoning effects) can distribute heat evenly throughout its volume before reradiating it.

Stone, with a heat capacity of 25 BTU/cu ft-°F (when considered as a pile of stones with 30% air voids) is a good storage medium and is economical. Heat distribution within the storage bed should be carefully analyzed because heat will distribute itself mainly at points of contact through conduction if no forced circulation is used.

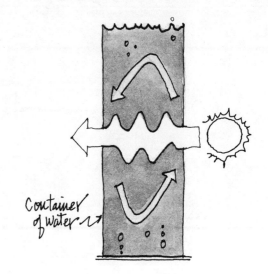

Container of water

Water distributes heat within itself by convective movement of the water molecules thus maintaining a lower surface temperature than the masonry surface under the same direct sunshine. When hidden from the sun masonry will cool (lose its heat) faster.

MATERIAL	DENSITY lb/ft³	HEAT CAPACITY BTU/ft³°F	SPECIFIC HEAT BTU/lb°F
Water	62.4	62.4	1
Ice	57.5	28.75	.5
Steel	490	58.8	.12
Concrete	144	28.8	.2
Stone	95	19	.2
Brick	123	24.6	.2
Air	.071	.017	.24
Wood	47	26.79	.57
Glass	154	27.72	.18
Sand	94.6	18.1	.191

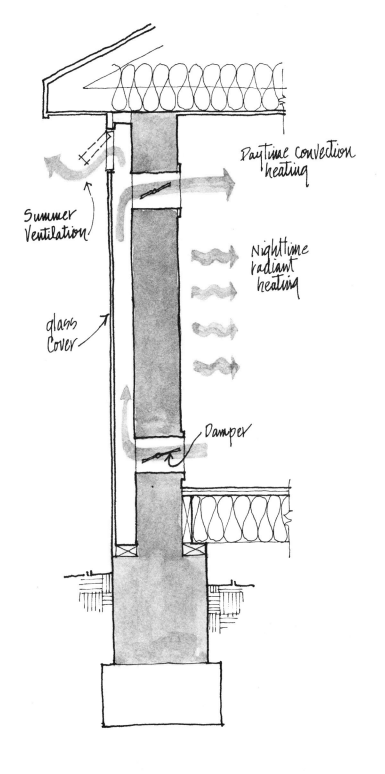

Daytime convection heating

Summer Ventilation

Nighttime radiant heating

glass cover

Damper

The **greenhouse effect** is critical to understanding today's solar heating. Another natural thermal effect called **thermosiphoning** is also important. Thermosiphoning is the transfer of heat through convection and is used in both passive and active systems for both heating and cooling.

French professor Felix Trombe led in the development of simple passive solar wall collectors based on natural thermosiphoning effects. The **Trombe wall** should be heavy masonry with a thickness of 8 to 16 inches and should be painted black on its collector side. Glass or plastic panels are mounted at a distance of 2-24 inches from the wall face so that heat can be trapped similarly to a flat-plate collector. As the heated air rises, it is drawn into the house through top vents while simultaneously being replaced by cooler air drawn in through the lower vents. At night the vents are closed and heat is conducted through the wall and radiated to the house.

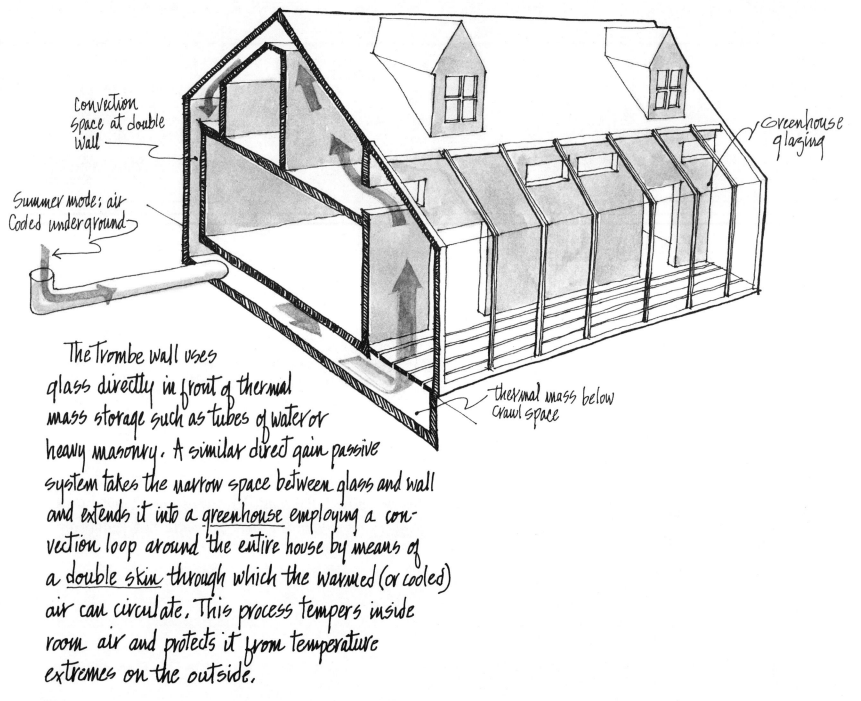

Convection
space at double
wall

Summer mode: air
cooled underground

Greenhouse
glazing

thermal mass below
crawl space

The Trombe wall uses glass directly in front of thermal mass storage such as tubes of water or heavy masonry. A similar direct gain passive system takes the narrow space between glass and wall and extends it into a <u>greenhouse</u> employing a convection loop around the entire house by means of a <u>double skin</u> through which the warmed (or cooled) air can circulate. This process tempers inside room air and protects it from temperature extremes on the outside.

The Thermal Chimney effect is basic thermosiphon-ing. It causes air movement and thus a cooling effect by convecting heat away from the surface of one's body. As the sun heats the top of a building, the inside air warms and rises creat-ing a current whereby lower cooler air moves in to replace the rising warm air. Power ventilators can be used to help propel the air flow.

Air drawn in through ground ducts can also help cool a home. In a temperate region ground temperatures will equal the local well water temperature or roughly 54°.

Because of the earth's large mass, Thermal Lag keeps year-round Temperatures constant. Cool air of the Luray Caverns in Virginia is used to cool buildings on the ground above.

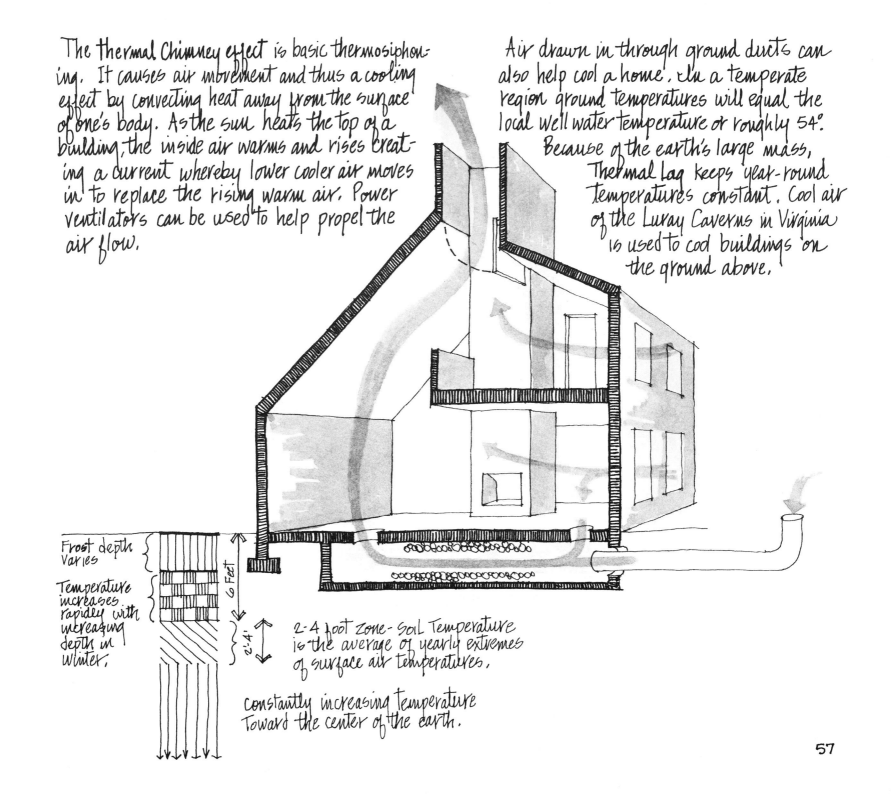

Frost depth varies

Temperature increases rapidly with increasing depth in Winter.

6 Feet

2'-4'

2-4 foot zone - Soil Temperature is the average of yearly extremes of surface air temperatures.

constantly increasing temperature Toward the center of the earth.

57

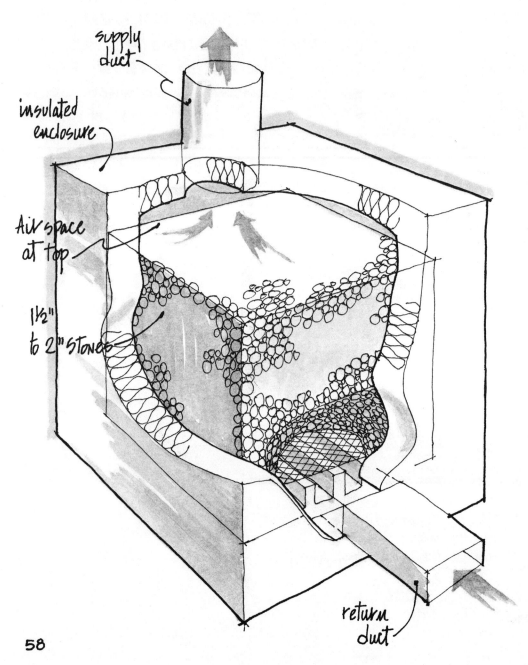

supply
duct

insulated
enclosure

Air space
at top

1½"
to 2" stones

return
duct

Storage of solar heat is necessary for those times when the sun is not shining. One should estimate the most practical amount of storage based on an average sunless period and on the volume and expense of a storage medium. The storage facility should be heavily insulated. The rock storage shown to the left delivers heat through air transfer. Cool return air enters at the bottom through air channels. Over these channels is a wire mesh; the air is pulled up through the rocks, absorbing heat along the way and exits into an upper air pocket and out through ductwork. Rock storage can simply be a rock bed in a crawl-space, or in an insulated bin or in a vertical cylinder adjacent to a heated space.

Water is also a good storage medium. The volume of water storage, because of its higher heat capacity, is less than that of stone. Calculating the volume of storage required is based on heat capacity and is a simple procedure.

Storage Volume Using Water as the Storage Medium

Assumed Data:

Heat capacity of water   **62.4** BTU/ft³/F°

Back-up storage time   **2** Days

Indoor minus Outdoor   **65°-10°= 55°**F
design temperature

Dwelling Heat loss   **50,000** BTU/hr

Degree-days for coldest
month of January   **600** °F-Days

maximum storage temp.   **150°**

minimum useful
storage temperature   **82°**

maximum minus
minimum storage temp.   **68°**

$$50,000 \text{ BTU/hr}/55°F =$$
$$909.1 \text{ BTU/hr}/°F$$

$$600 °F\text{-Days}/\text{month} =$$
$$20 °F\text{-Days}/\text{Day}$$

2-DAY HEAT LOSS (STORAGE REQUIRED) =

$$909.1 \text{ BTU/hr}/°F \times 20 °F\text{-Days}/\text{Day} \times 2 \text{ Days} \times 24 \text{ hours}/\text{Day} =$$

$$872,736 \text{ BTU}$$

BTU'S PER CUBIC FOOT OF STORAGE

$$62.4 \text{ BTU/ft}^3/°F \times 68° \Delta T = 4243.2 \text{ BTU/ft}^3$$

STORAGE VOLUME REQUIRED

$$872,736 \text{ BTU} \div 4243.2 \text{ BTU/ft}^3 = 206 \text{ ft}^3$$

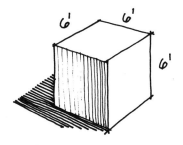

storage volume could
be a cube with 6' sides

III Wind Energy

Sweetly, sweetly blew the breeze—
On me alone it blew.

Samuel Taylor Coleridge —
The Rime of the Ancient Mariner

Not too many years ago, before power companies had extended service to rural areas, almost every farm used windmills for at least part of their energy source. The windmill was used to pump water and to drive a generator. Electricity was stored in batteries where it then powered lights and a few small appliances and motors.

Windmill systems proved adequate (along with engine-driven generators) until the advent of abundant, inexpensive power distribution by public utilities in the 1930s and 1940s. The windmills were left to rust.

Between 1940 and 1970 wind energy took a back seat to other energy sources. Now, because of our nation's dependence on imported fossil fuel, wind energy may soon become quite practical and cost competitive.

Windmills use turbines that can be divided into two broad categories: (1) Horizontal axis and (2) vertical axis. The propeller and bicycle Types are common *horizontal axis* designs. The two-or three-blade propeller design seems to be best suited for deriving power from medium to high winds. The faster the tip speed (speed of rotation of the tips of the blades) the more efficient is the turbine. Water windmills have lots of blades in order to develop high torque from low winds. This is ideal for pumping water at a slow rotation but is ineffective in high winds. The two-or three-blade propeller rotates fast in high winds for greater efficiency.

Turbine with feathering blades:

The blade twists flat in high winds

if the wind velocity gets too high the blades feather-out to slow the rotor rotation

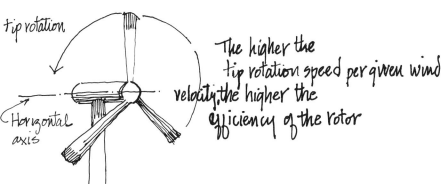

tip rotation

Horizontal axis

The higher the tip rotation speed per given wind velocity, the higher the efficiency of the rotor

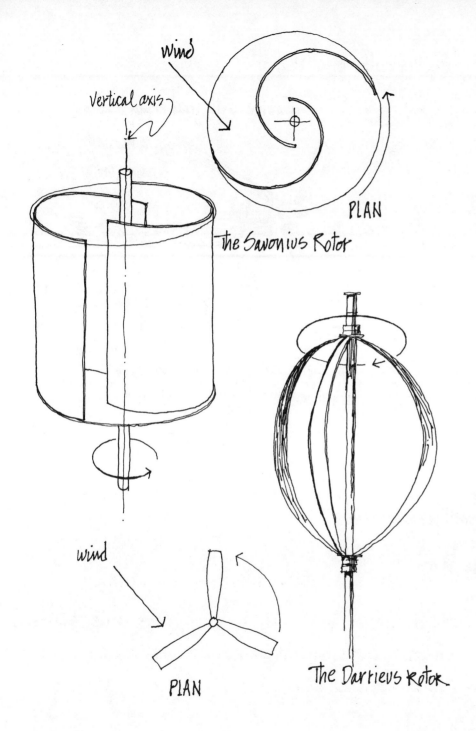

wind

vertical axis

the Savonius Rotor

PLAN

wind

PLAN

The Darrieus Rotor

The vertical axis turbines most often used on modern windmills are of the Darrieus and Savonius designs, named after their inventors. The Darrieus is a 2-or 3-blade high-speed turbine that looks like an eggbeater and requires motorized start up. This turbine is presently being developed for up to a 500-kilowatt output.

The Savonius rotor design is similar in principle to industrial turbines. Rotation is effected by changes in the momentum of the air blowing between the blades. The Savonius (as well as the Darrieus design) allows effective use of the wind blowing from any direction without the necessity of a tail vane. However, the Savonius has severe limitations in both size and wind-speed for proper operation and is probably best suited for pumping water.

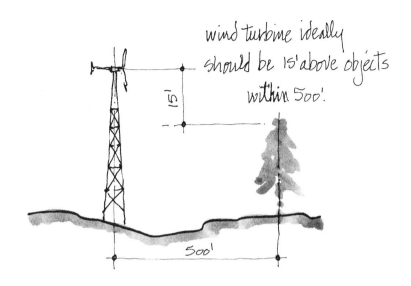

wind turbine ideally should be 15' above objects within 500'.

15'

500'

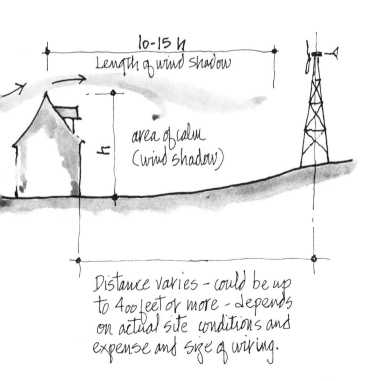

10-15 h
Length of wind shadow

area of calm
(wind shadow)

h

Distance varies - could be up to 400 feet or more - depends on actual site conditions and expense and size of wiring.

Availability of Wind

One of the major criteria for having a feasible wind energy system is the amount and distribution of the wind. The wind varies extremely from day to day and even from moment to moment. This is true for both direction and speed.

An open rounded hill usually provides a good location for a wind turbine. Buildings or trees tend to reduce wind speed as well as make the wind more turbulent (refer to our chapter on "site examination"). When considering an extensive wind energy program, examine the actual wind conditions on the site over a period of 6 to 12 months.

A good source of generalized regional wind information is the Climatic Atlas of the United States printed by the U.S. Government Printing Office, Washington, D.C. 20402.

The Generator

Armature

Lines of Magnetic Flux

S   N

slip rings

Brushes

Elements of
a simple generator

The device which transforms the mechanical energy of the wind into electrical energy is the generator. The current that is produced can be either alternating (ac) or direct (dc). Generators that produce alternating current are called alternators. The blades of a wind rotor rotates relatively slowly (approximately 200 RPMs in high winds) so that a generator that works efficiently at Low RPM is desirable. Most of today's generators are designed for high RPM (1200-3600) so that for wind applications a system of gearing is needed. Efficient Low-speed generators are the best choice.

Automotive alternators have been used successfully in home-built systems, but because of their high-speed design they are generally not practical.

The Battery

The electricity generated by a wind turbine varies with the wind. When the wind dies - so does the current, creating the need for electrical storage. So far the only practical solution is the battery. Since the battery stores and releases only direct current, most wind turbines deliver direct current. Resistance appliances such as toasters will operate on direct current, but induction motors such as the ones used in today's large appliances will not. Direct current can be transformed into 60 cycle alternating current by the use of inverters but at a fair cost. Therefore, it is best to design a wind system using as many direct current appliances as possible.

The best battery for use in the wind system is the type that can be charged and fully discharged thousands of times without damage.

The best ones, of course, are quite expensive, so it boils down to a matter of personal economics. Nickel-cadmium batteries are probably best suited to wind systems but are very expensive. The car battery is not well suited to wind use because it doesn't hold up under constant charge/discharge conditions. The most practical and readily available battery for wind use is the so-called "stationary" type. Batteries with similar characteristics to the stationary type are those used in electric tow carts. These are generally Lead-acid batteries with high efficiency at normal operating temperatures and low efficiency at low temperatures. For this reason, the battery should be housed in a warm area. Batteries produce flammable gases when being re-charged, so they should be kept in a ventilated area.

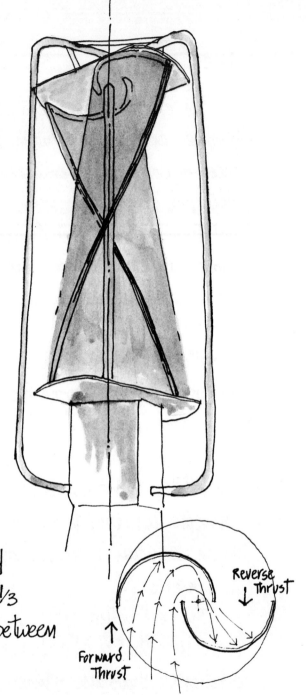

Forward
Thrust

Reverse
Thrust

Example of a Small Commercial Wind Energy System

In this example we will discuss the Helius rotor as manufactured by the Thermax Corporation. The Helius rotor is a different twist of the Savonius design. It is simple, durable and omnidirectional. Because the power output of the Savonius rotor varies as it rotates - the Helius designers twisted the Savonius design into a helix, yielding a smooth output torque with no "dead spots." The best configuration of a small Helius rotor was found to be a 90° vertical twist of two semicircular vanes with a 1/3 crossover ratio (that is, the crossover or width of the gap between vanes is 1/3 of the total frontage width of the vane).

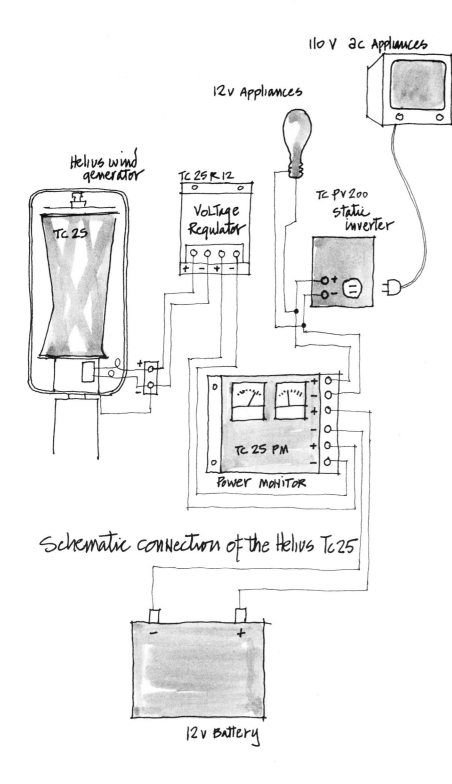

110 V ac Appliances

12v Appliances

Helius wind generator

TC 25

TC 25 R 12

Voltage Regulator

+ − + −

TC PV 200 static inverter

+ −
=

+

Power Monitor

TC 25 PM

Schematic connection of the Helius Tc 25

− +

12v Battery

The Thermax engineers have designed a small inexpensive generator to go with their rotor. It is a compact 3½ pound permanent magnet dc generator, composed of two extremely powerful composite annular magnets, magnetized after assembly to avoid adherence of small metallic particles.

The Helius system delivers electric power proportional to the cube of the wind-speed. Actually very little power is developed by light winds, but each time the wind velocity doubles, the power obtained is increased 8 times. To control such a wide range of power outputs, the generator is connected to a voltage regulator.

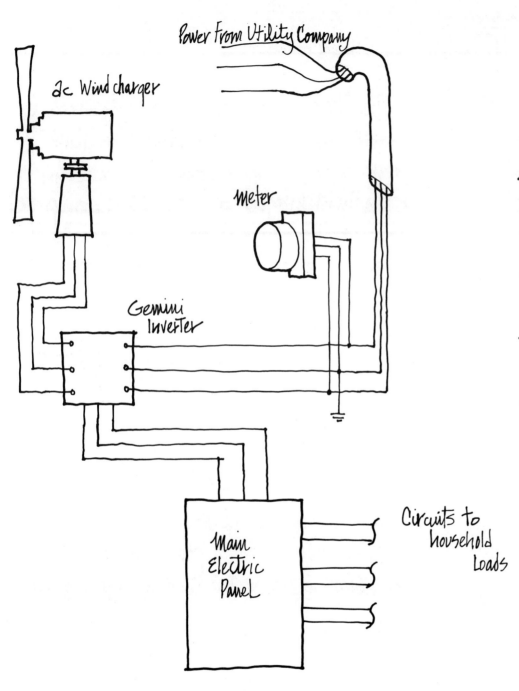

Power From Utility Company

ac Wind charger

meter

Gemini Inverter

Main Electric Panel

Circuits to household Loads

In this system, the Gemini inverter will convert the varying voltage and frequency from the wind generator to the same as the power lines. When the wind charger furnishes sufficient power, no current is drawn from the power company lines. In fact, if the wind charger furnishes more power than needed, all excess current goes into the power company's lines and the meter turns backwards. In other words the consumer will be selling electricity to the power company.

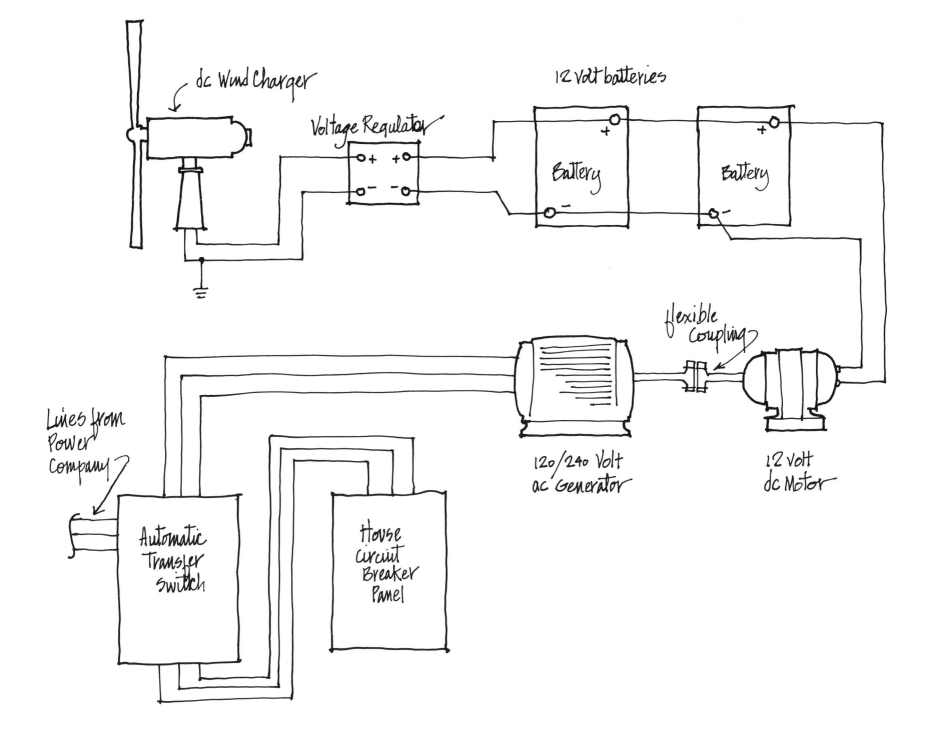

dc Wind Charger

12 Volt batteries

Voltage Regulator

Battery

Battery

flexible Coupling

Lines from Power Company

120/240 Volt ac Generator

12 Volt dc Motor

Automatic Transfer Switch

House circuit Breaker Panel

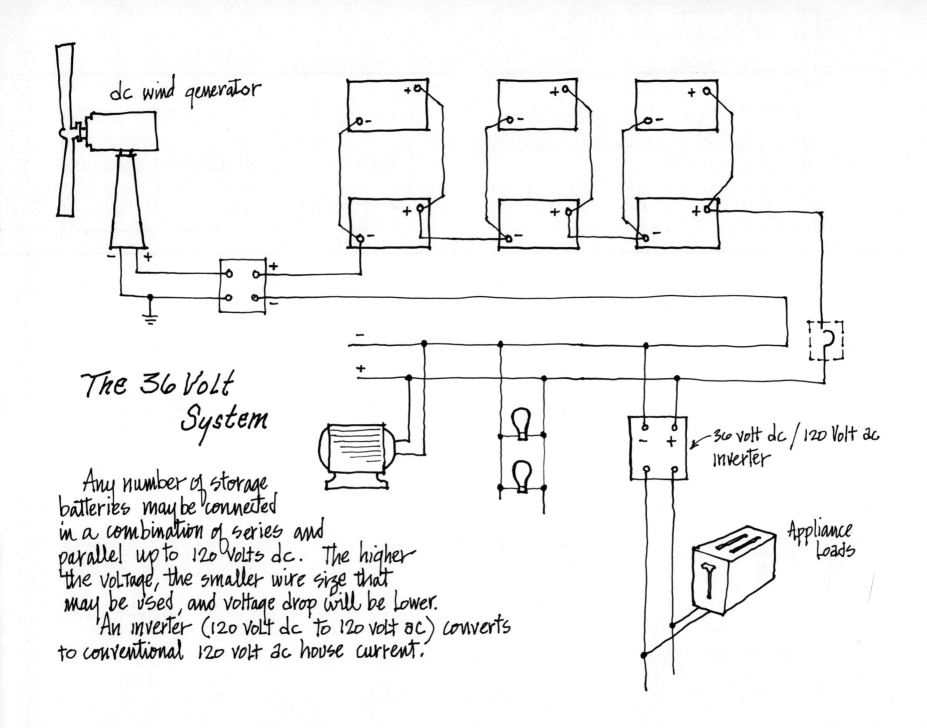

dc wind generator

The 36 Volt
        System

36 volt dc / 120 Volt ac
Inverter

Appliance
Loads

Any number of storage
batteries may be connected
in a combination of series and
parallel up to 120 Volts dc. The higher
the voltage, the smaller wire size that
may be used, and voltage drop will be Lower.
    An inverter (120 Volt dc to 120 Volt ac) converts
to conventional 120 Volt ac house current.

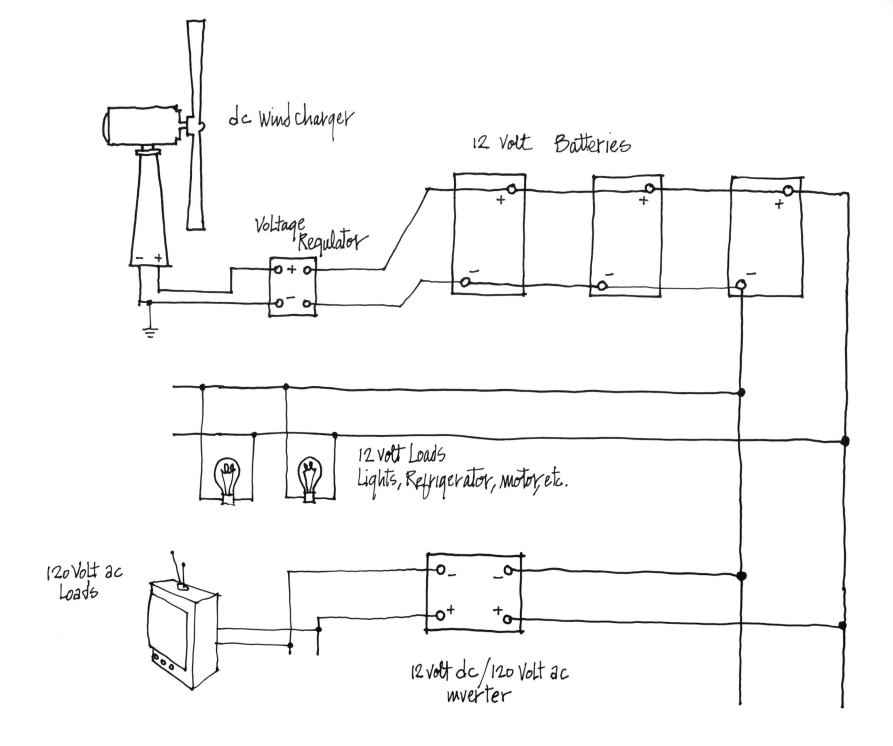

dc Wind charger

12 Volt Batteries

Voltage Regulator

+   +   +

-    -   -

12 volt Loads
Lights, Refrigerator, motor, etc.

120 Volt ac
Loads

-    -

+   +

12 volt dc / 120 Volt ac
inverter

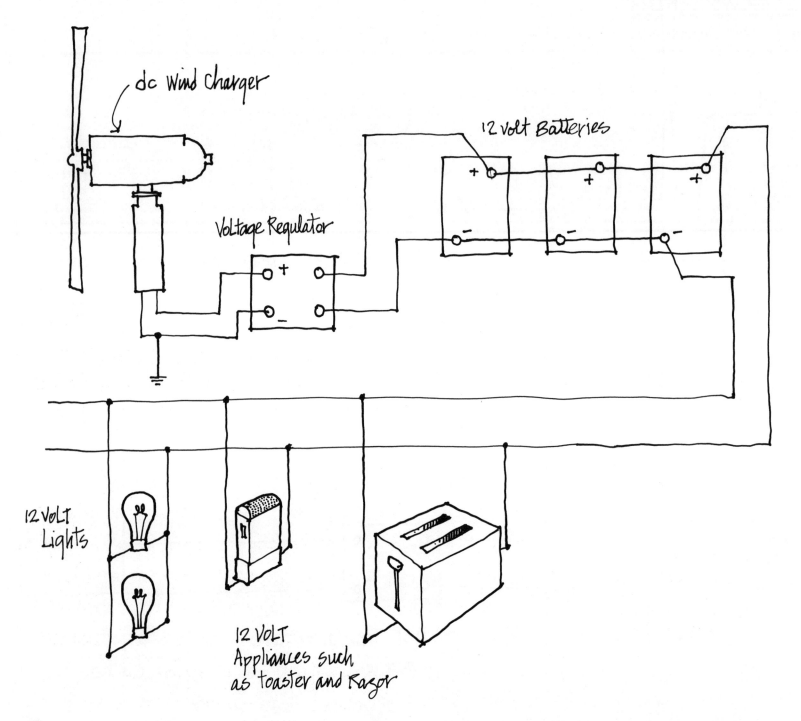

dc Wind Charger

12 Volt Batteries

Voltage Regulator

12 Volt
Lights

12 Volt
Appliances such
as toaster and Razor

IV Heat Loss

Man is unable to live without protection from the environment. Jack London's fictional character exposed himself carelessly to harsh winter elements. Man's home provides shelter and maintains proper temperatures. The faster heat is lost from the interior of a home, the greater is the expense of resupplying heat. For this reason a house should be built "thermally tight." It should be constructed of materials which insulate or restrict the flow of heat and be sealed or weather-stripped properly to reduce cold air blowing into the house from cracks around doors and windows.

All materials resist the flow of heat to some degree. In building construction it is necessary to know the thermal characteristics of each material that makes up the composition of a wall, floor or roof. And just as important is the ability to figure the effect of the total composition.

The final exterior or interior finish material very often offers little resistance to heat flow. Therefore it becomes necessary to fill in the space between inside and out with special insulating products,

Relative heat flow through various materials over the same period of time and temperature difference:

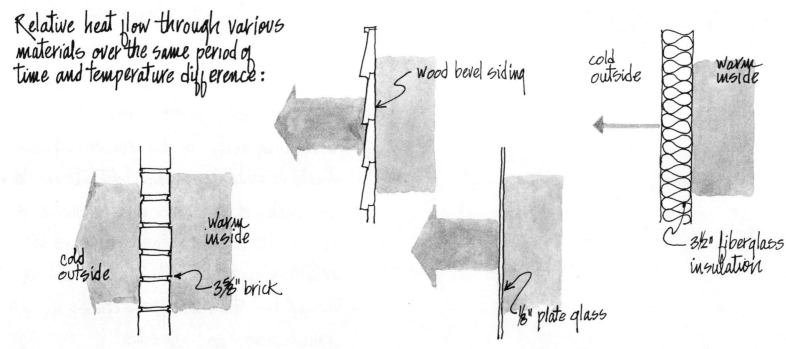

cold outside

warm inside

wood bevel siding

⅛" plate glass

warm inside

cold outside

3⅝" brick

cold outside

warm inside

3½" fiberglass insulation

Thermal Conductance C

Thermal conductance is the measure of BTU's that will seep through one square foot of a material in an hour's time for each degree of temperature difference that exists between one side of the material and the other—indicated by the term $BTU/hr/ft^2/°F$.

R-value

The R-value of a material represents its resistance to thermal movement or heat loss. It is the reciprocal of thermal conductance C for a particular material and is used in determining the overall heat loss of a wall, floor or roof. Many manufacturers list the R-value of their building products. It is a useful rating standard for building materials. And R-values can be added. The R-value of a wall, Roof, etc. is the total of the R-values of the individual components.

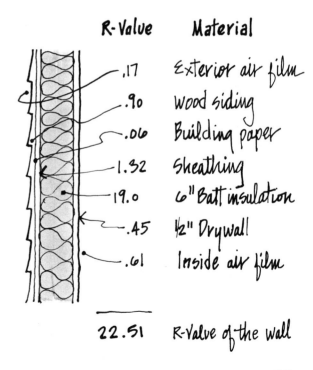

R-Value	Material
.17	Exterior air film
.90	Wood siding
.06	Building paper
1.32	Sheathing
19.0	6" Batt insulation
.45	½" Drywall
.61	Inside air film
22.51	R-Value of the wall

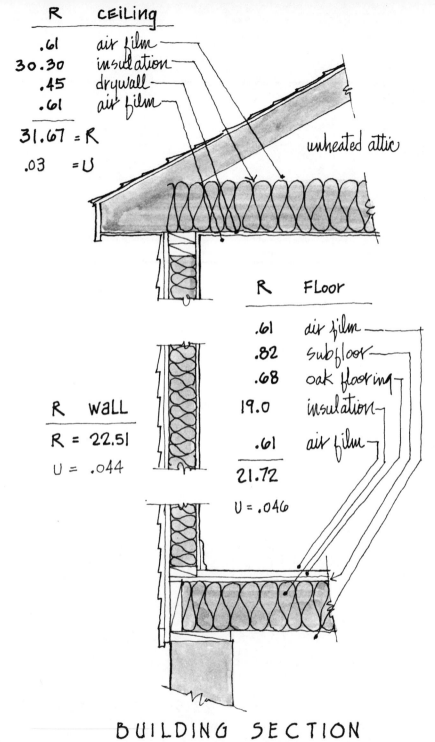

R	CEiLiNG
.61	air film
30.30	insulation
.45	drywall
.61	air film

31.67 = R

.03 = U

unheated attic

R	FLoor
.61	air film
.82	subfloor
.68	oak flooring
19.0	insulation
.61	air film

21.72

U = .046

R WaLL

R = 22.51

U = .044

BUILDING SECTION

U·Value

The U-value is similar to the conductance C except that it applies to the wall, roof or floor assembly as a whole, and it is called the overall coefficient of transmission. It is the quantity of BTU's that are conducted through a square foot of an assembly in an hour's time per degree temperature difference: $BTU/hr/ft^2/°F$.

The U-value is what we're really looking for. One has to figure the overall R-value first, then convert to the U-value. The U-value is the reciprocal of the overall R-value.

Infiltration Heat loss

Heat loss that occurs through cracks around windows and doors, etc. and losses that occur when doors are opened to the outside are called infiltration losses. Some fresh air is necessary at all times of the year. Infiltration losses are considered to supply this air. But all such heat losses during the winter must be figured into the total heating requirements of the home. As a rule of thumb one can figure that infiltration accounts for ½ – 1 complete air change within the house each hour.

The total infiltration heat loss per hour is equal to: $$H = .018 \times \Delta T \times nV$$

.018 is a factor related to the density and heat capacity of air (a constant).

ΔT is the temperature difference (indoor temperature – outside design temperature)

n is the number of air changes per hour.

V is the volume of the home or heated space.

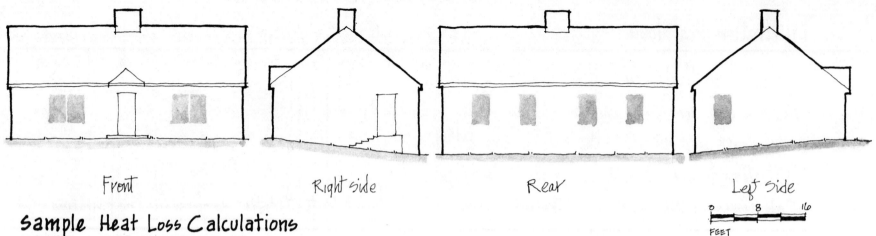

Front   Right side   Rear   Left Side

0   8   16
FEET

Sample Heat Loss Calculations

Using our sample home construction developed thus far:

Section	U-value BTU/ft²/°F/hr	Area ft²	ΔT °F	Heat loss BTU/hr
Wall	.044 ×	884 ×	56° =	21782
Roof (ceiling)[1]	.03 ×	1000 ×	54° =	1620
Floor[2]	.046 ×	1000 ×	30° =	1380

Other exterior wall components are the doors and windows:

Doors	.071 ×	35 ×	56° =	139
Embossed metal door w/ polyurethane injected core				
Windows	.58 ×	121 ×	56° =	3930
with insulating glass				

Infiltration Heat loss H = $.018 \times \Delta T \times m V$

$.018 \times 56° \times 1.8000 = 8064$

Total Peak Load   36915 BTU/hr

Notes

We will assume that our house is located in Harrisburg, Pa., with an outside design temp. of 9°.

We will assume an indoor design temp. of 65°.

[1] We will figure that our attic is slightly warmer than the outdoor design temperature.

[2] Assume that the crawlspace will remain at a constant temp. of 35° during the winter.

Heat Loss Calculations Continued

Next we need to know the total BTU/hr heat loss for our house for an entire heating season. This part of our calculations is based on **degree-days**. Degree-days are a basis for determining both seasonal heating and cooling requirements. Degree-days are figured by finding the average temperature during a particular 24-hour day and subtracting this total from the assumed 65° indoor temperature. Do this each day that the average outdoor temperature is below 65° and add the daily totals to find the degree-days per heating season. The yearly total of degree-days for Harrisburg is 5251.

For our sample home the yearly BTU heat loss is:

Yearly Heat Loss = Hourly Heat Loss × 24 hr/day × °Days/year ÷ ΔT

$$H_y \quad = \quad 36,915 \quad \times \quad 24 \quad \times \quad 5251 \quad \div \quad 56°$$

$$H_y \quad = \quad 83,074,571 \text{ BTU}$$

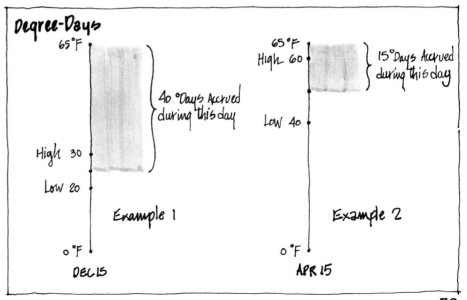

Degree-Days

65°F — High 30, Low 20 ... 40 °Days Accrued during this day — Example 1 — DEC 15

65°F — High 60, Low 40 ... 15 °Days Accrued during this day — Example 2 — APR 15

State - City - Outside design temp. - Annual degree-days

AL - Mobile	25	1560	MT - Billings	-15	7049
AK - Anchorage	-23	10864	NE - Lincoln	-5	5864
AZ - Phoenix	31	1765	NV - Reno	5	6332
AR - Little Rock	15	3219	NH - Concord	-8	7383
CA - Oakland	34	2870	NJ - Newark	10	4589
CO - Denver	-5	6283	NM - Roswell	13	3793
CT - Hartford	3	6235	NY - Albany	-6	6875
DE - Wilmington	10	4930	NC - Charlotte	18	3191
WASH. D.C.	14	4224	ND - Bismark	-23	8851
FL - Miami	44	214	OH - Columbus	0	5660
GA - Atlanta	17	2961	OK - Tulsa	8	3860
HI - Honolulu	62	-0-	OR - Portland	17	4635
ID - Boise	3	5809	PA - Harrisburg	9	5251
IL - Chicago	-8	6639	RI - Providence	5	5954
IN - Evansville	4	4435	SC - Charleston	25	1794
IA - Des Moines	-10	6588	SD - Huron	-18	8223
KS - Topeka	-0-	5182	TN - Memphis	13	3232
KY - Louisville	5	4660	TX - Houston	27	1396
LA - New Orleans	29	1254	UT - Salt Lake City	3	6052
ME - Bangor	-11	8220	VT - Burlington	-12	8269
MD - Baltimore	10	4654	VA - Richmond	14	3865
MA - Boston	6	5634	WA - Seattle	21	5145
MI - Detroit	3	6293	WV - Charleston	7	4476
MN - St. Paul	-16	8382	WI - Milwaukee	-8	7635
MS - Jackson	21	2239	WY - Casper	-11	4410
MO - Kansas City	2	4711			

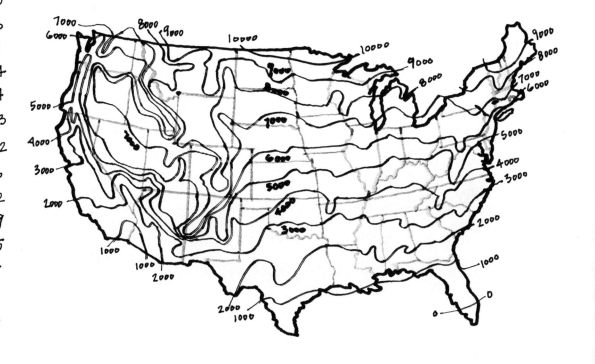

Annual Degree-Days

Heat Gain

Yearly heat loss should not be based on heat loss alone. There are sources of internal heat gain which will reduce the seasonal heating requirements of the furnace. Most all electrical appliances give off heat. People radiate heat, and the sun shining through windows contributes heat.

Appliance heat can be estimated by determining the hours of monthly use and the wattage rating of each appliance; however for our purposes it will be sufficient to estimate a heat gain of 20,000 BTU's per person per day. If, for instance, our heating season covers 240 days then we have 240 × 20,000 or 4,800,000 BTU's per person heat gain per winter.

Direct solar heat gain through south-facing windows will contribute a small portion of heat to our sample house, however because of the small glazing area we will ignore solar gain. For more information on solar gain refer to the chapter on solar heat.

Thus far in our heat loss calculations for our sample home we have found that the furnace must be sized to deliver 36,915 BTU/hr. If we include heat gain for 3 people our figures are adjusted thus:

$$20,000 \times 3 \div 24 = 2500$$

20,000		3	24		2500
BTU/Person/day		people	hours/day		BTU/hour

$$
\begin{array}{l}
36,915 \text{ BTU/hr} \\
-\ 2,500 \text{ BTU/hr} \\
\hline
34,415 \text{ net BTU/hr heat loss} \\
\quad (77,448,499 \text{ BTU/winter})
\end{array}
$$

V Insulation
and Condensation

Insulation and condensation seem to go hand in hand today. If water vapor condenses within insulation, the thermal value is lost (most all insulations transmit heat when wet). Many insulation products can be bought with an integral vapor barrier. Some insulations like the Styrofoam type naturally resist the penetration of moisture.

Most modern insulation products perform their function very well and can be expected to have a long life. A great aspect of the fiberglass variety is the ability to resist combustion (up to certain limits), and rock wool is virtually non-combustible. The urethanes are both toxic and combustible but are safe to use when properly covered and are extremely good insulators.

Insulation

Insulation is manufactured from many materials and in many forms. The homeowner should know the R-value and the proper form of insulation for a particular use. There are six common forms of insulation:

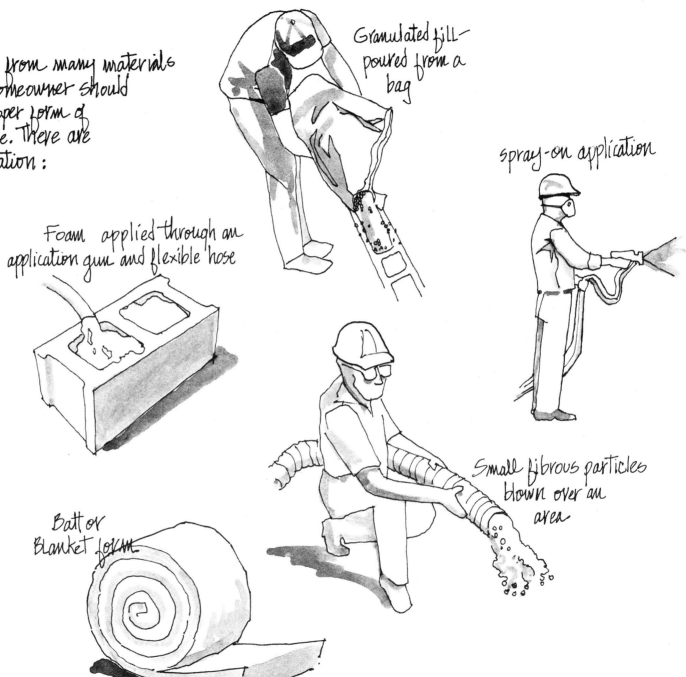

Granulated fill-poured from a bag

Foam applied through an application gun and flexible hose

spray-on application

Small fibrous particles blown over an area

Batt or Blanket form

Board or Sheet form

83

Heat loss through a typical House

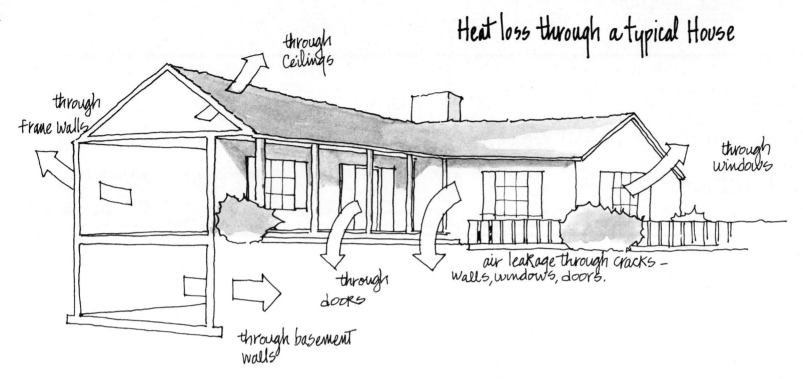

through ceilings

through frame walls

through windows

through doors

air leakage through cracks - walls, windows, doors.

through basement walls

Today, standards of insulation are much higher than in earlier years before the energy crunch. Many utility companies require certain minimum insulation standards before they will allow service connection on new construction. Insulation should be added at all exterior exposed surfaces. If the basement is unheated, apply insulation in the basement ceiling. If it is heated, apply insulation to the walls - especially down to the frostline. Insulate the exterior walls and the ceiling making sure that the attic is well ventilated. Windows should be double-glazed and fitted with storm windows. Storm doors should be installed also.

Batt Insulation

Batt insulation is produced in widths which generally conform to standard wall and floor/ceiling stud or joist spacings.

For instance, studs are commonly 16" on center. Wall insulation can be bought in 16" widths that fit snugly between the studs. It is common today to use 2x6 studs so that a nominal 6½" thick insulation batt can be used. Such insulation will yield an R-value of 19. 3⅝"(for 2x4 studs) thick insulation yields an R-value of 11.

Ceiling joists are commonly 2'-0" on center and are deeper than wall studs. Nominal 9¼" fiberglass batt insulation will yield an R-value of 30.

vapor-resistant
membrane facing

Stud

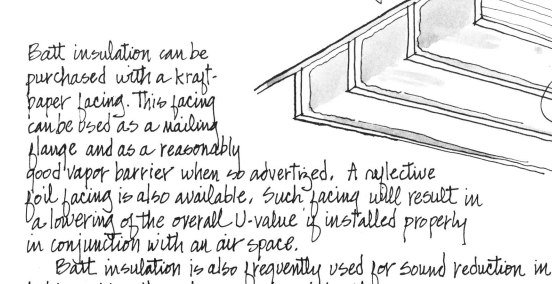

flooring

Floor truss or joist

Batt insulation

Batt insulation can be purchased with a kraft-paper facing. This facing can be used as a nailing flange and as a reasonably good vapor barrier when so advertized. A reflective foil facing is also available. Such facing will result in a lowering of the overall U-value if installed properly in conjunction with an air space.

Batt insulation is also frequently used for sound reduction in lightweight walls and over suspended ceilings.

Blowing Wool

Blowing wool is generally used in existing homes at locations where pneumatic application is the only practical solution such as in attics and sidewalls. The application is made using standard automatic and hand-fed mineral fiber-blowing wool machines. R-value depends on the thickness and density of application. Vapor barriers are recommended with all types of loose fibrous insulation. Common materials used for blown insulation are cellulose, rock wool, and glass fiber.

Foams provide an
effective noise barrier
and are not
highly combustible

An application hose is dropped
to the "bottom" of the cavity and is
withdrawn as the foam rises.

The foam
seals all cracks
and flows easily
around
obstructions

Foam Insulation

Foam insulation is injected into a wall cavity
under pressure. It firms up to create a thermal and
acoustical insulation. The initial setting time is 10 to 60
seconds; within the next 2-72 hours final curing takes
place.

Foam applications are appropriate in filling wall cavities
and the cores of hollow concrete block. Foam applications are
especially good in existing buildings. Small holes are
drilled into stud cavities or into brick wall facings and
the foam is pumped in.

One inch thickness of foam yields an R-value of 4.5 - 4.9.

Studs open on one side can
be foamed. Interior finish should
be immediately applied
with a vapor barrier
to the warm
side.

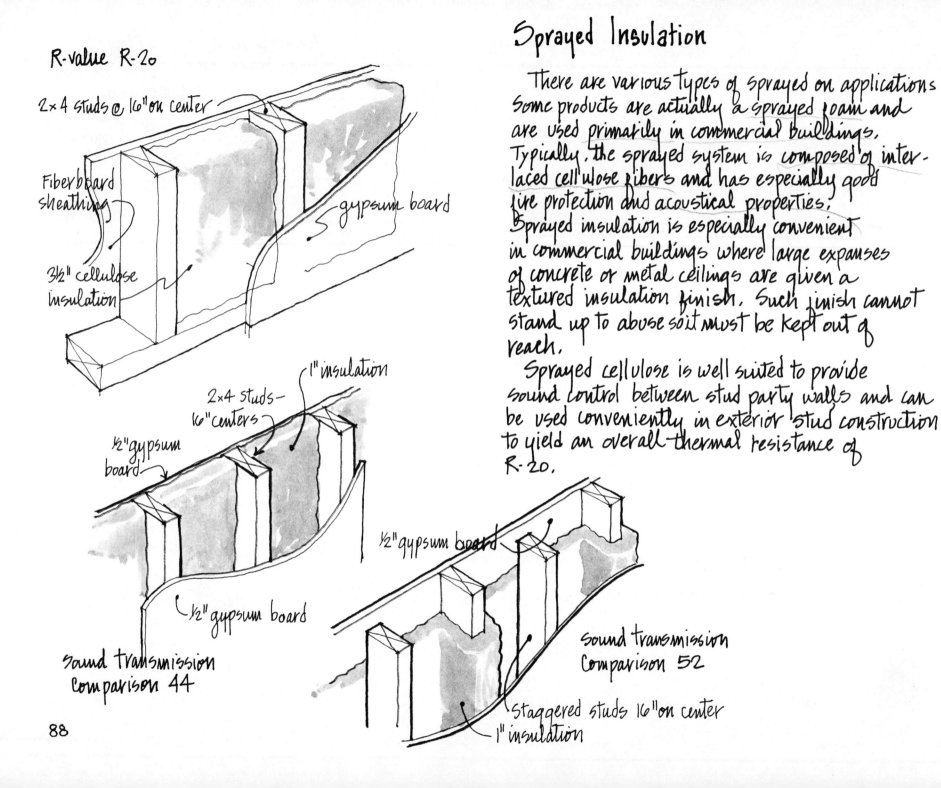

Sprayed Insulation

There are various types of sprayed on applications. Some products are actually a sprayed foam and are used primarily in commercial buildings. Typically, the sprayed system is composed of interlaced cellulose fibers and has especially good fire protection and acoustical properties. Sprayed insulation is especially convenient in commercial buildings where large expanses of concrete or metal ceilings are given a textured insulation finish. Such finish cannot stand up to abuse so it must be kept out of reach.

Sprayed cellulose is well suited to provide sound control between stud party walls and can be used conveniently in exterior stud construction to yield an overall thermal resistance of R-20.

R-value R-20

2 x 4 studs @ 16" on center

Fiberboard sheathing

gypsum board

3½" cellulose insulation

1" insulation

2 x 4 studs - 16" centers

½" gypsum board

½" gypsum board

sound transmission comparison 44

½" gypsum board

sound transmission comparison 52

staggered studs 16" on center

1" insulation

88

Insulative Sheathing - Typical Applications

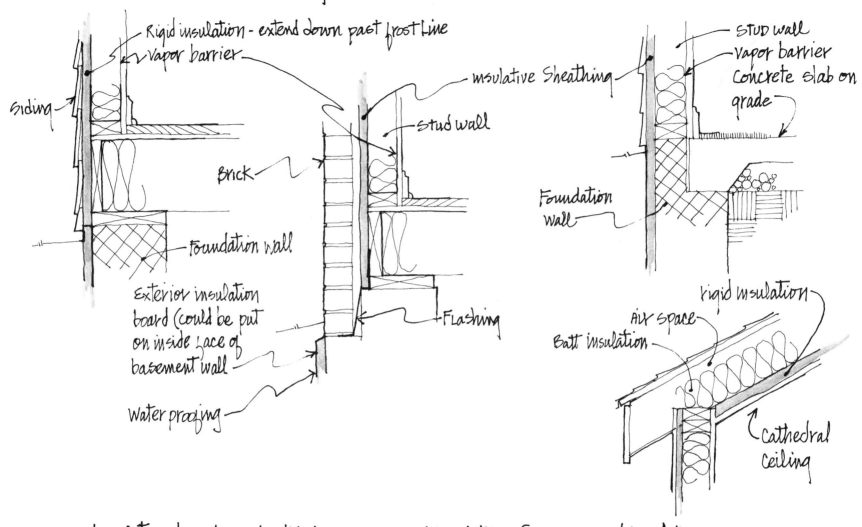

Rigid insulation - extend down past frost line

Vapor barrier

Siding

Brick

Foundation wall

Exterior insulation board (could be put on inside face of basement wall)

Water proofing

Insulative Sheathing

Stud wall

Flashing

Stud wall

Vapor barrier

Concrete slab on grade

Foundation wall

Rigid insulation

Air space

Batt insulation

Cathedral Ceiling

Insulation board or sheet is known as rigid insulation. Common rigid insulations are <u>cellular glass</u>, expanded polystyrene, polyurethane and polyisocyurate. The urethane board is the most expensive and is therefore used less frequently in home construction.

Expanded polystyrene (also used for insulated coffee cups) sheathing board gives a typical R-value of 5.41 for a one-inch thickness.

All of these insulation boards are combustible and must be covered by a suitable finish material to reduce fire hazard.

Granular Fill Insulation

A common application of loose fill insulation is in filling the cores of concrete block. Usually such insulation is an inorganic granular vermiculite treated for water repellency. The insulation is packaged in bags - the mason pours the insulation into the block cores as he lays the wall. Walls 20 feet high can be poured at one time - no tamping or rodding is required.

Block walls filled with granular vermiculite insulation are rated higher for fire resistance. The material will not decay and will not support combustion. Such walls also have reduced sound transmission.

Granular expanded polystyrene is another masonry fill material. Neither polystyrene nor vermiculite will absorb water but moisture can enter the interstices between individual particles by capillary action. Normal precautions must be taken to eliminate water penetration so that the insulation stays dry.

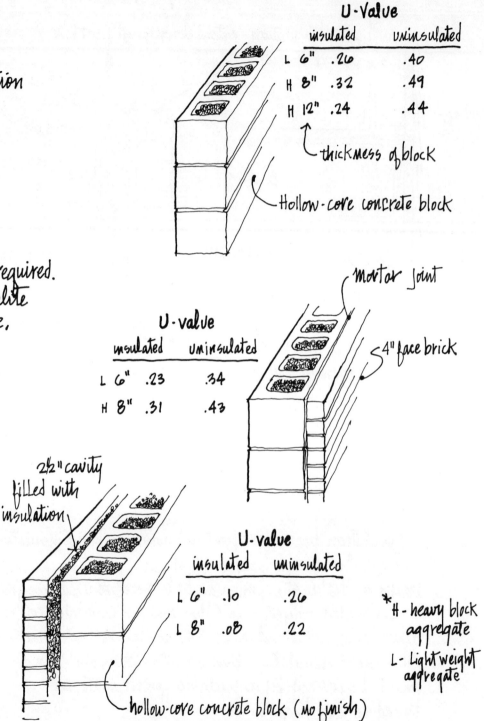

U-Value

		insulated	uninsulated
L	6"	.26	.40
H	8"	.32	.49
H	12"	.24	.44

↑ thickness of block

Hollow-core concrete block

U-value

		insulated	uninsulated
L	6"	.23	.34
H	8"	.31	.43

mortar joint

4" face brick

U-value

		insulated	uninsulated
L	6"	.10	.26
L	8"	.08	.22

2½" cavity filled with insulation

* H - heavy block aggregate
  L - lightweight aggregate

hollow-core concrete block (no finish)

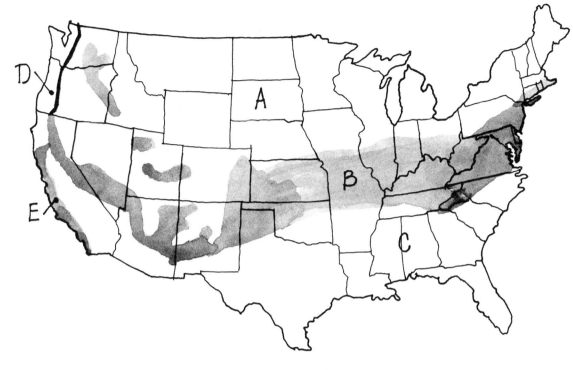

	CEILINGS	Walls	FLOORS
Zone A	R-44	R-19	R-22
Zone B	R-38	R-19	R-19
Zone C	R-30	R-19	R-19
Zone D	R-19	R-13	R-11
Zone E	R-19	R-11	R-11

Insulation standards as developed by Johns-Manville company.

Optimum levels of insulation, of course, vary from home to home depending on microclimate, etc. The chart shown should be checked against federal, state or local municipal and utility requirements. Ceiling values apply to the insulation only. Wall values apply to both the sheathing and cavity insulation. Floor insulation values are for floors over unheated areas. Floor insulation may be installed either between floor joists or applied to exterior walls, such as crawl space walls.

Condensation

Condensation problems in the home are often the result of today's insulation standards which carefully point out the quantity of insulation to be used but give little information on the relationship between insulation and water vapor.

Water vapor has pressure - it moves from moist areas (high temperatures) to dry areas (lower temperatures). Warm moist air inside the home in winter attempts to move through porous building materials to the colder, dryer outside.

Today's homes are built "tight." This means that they are insulated, weather-stripped and sealed so well that water vapor is sealed in as well. In its passage through porous building materials water vapor may condense out of the air. If condensation is allowed to saturate the insulation, then the effectiveness of the insulation is eliminated - wet insulation is no insulation. Such moisture within the walls of a building can also cause mildew and rot.

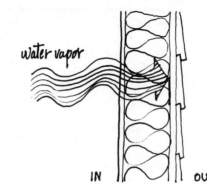

water vapor

IN   OUT

Without a vapor barrier condensation is likely to occur on the inside face of the sheathing.

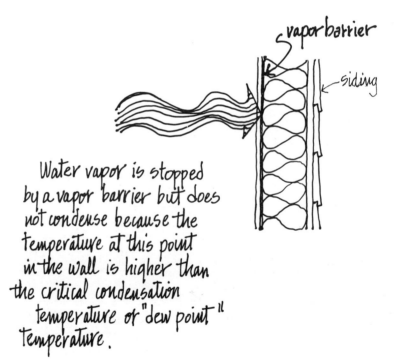

vapor barrier

siding

Water vapor is stopped by a vapor barrier but does not condense because the temperature at this point in the wall is higher than the critical condensation temperature or "dew point" temperature.

Cold-side Venting

In existing walls which are insulated with blown insulation in the stud cavity, "cold-side" venting is employed to prevent condensation. Holes are drilled through the outside wall face into the stud cavity and small round metal vents are placed over the holes. Water vapor moves through the wall and out through the vents.

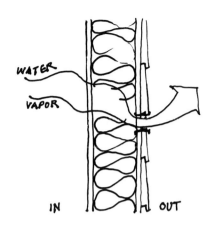

WATER

VAPOR

IN   OUT

Conditions for Condensation

Condensation occurs when the temperature of air (with a fixed amount of water vapor) is lowered to its <u>dew point</u> temperature. This condition raises the <u>relative humidity</u> of the air to its saturation point at which it can hold no more water vapor. Water condenses out on the coolest building surface through which the water vapor is unable to penetrate.

Window Condensation

single pane window - condensation is likely.

Warm | Cold

Double-pane or insulated window - condensation is less likely.

Warm | Cold

Water vapor cannot penetrate glass. Where there is an immediate drop in temperature from one side of a vapor barrier to the other side, condensation is likely. If the warm side is 70° then a relative humidity of about 15% will show up as condensation on the inside face of a single pane window in winter.

Vapor Barriers

Vapor barriers are materials of low permeance. Permeance is the ability of a material to transmit water vapor. The **Perm** is the standard rating unit for vapor barriers. Rather than defining the perm, suffice it to say that a material yielding a vapor transmission rate of one perm or less can be considered as a good vapor barrier. Polyethylene sheets, aluminum foil, certain paints, and asphalt are some good vapor barriers. Always apply vapor barriers on the warm side of a construction assembly.

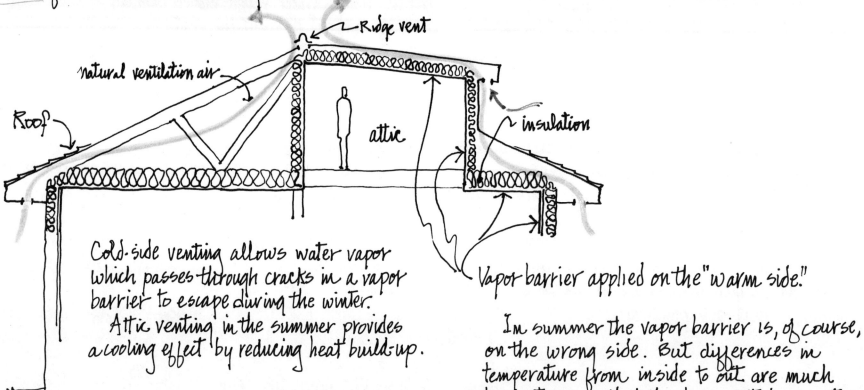

Ridge vent

natural ventilation air

Roof

attic

insulation

Cold-side venting allows water vapor which passes through cracks in a vapor barrier to escape during the winter.

Attic venting in the summer provides a cooling effect by reducing heat build-up.

Vapor barrier applied on the "warm side."

In summer the vapor barrier is, of course, on the wrong side. But differences in temperature from inside to out are much less extreme so that the dew point temperature is seldom reached.

Crawl Spaces

Homes built over crawl spaces are susceptible to floor rot and mildew. In winter, water vapor from the house will collect in the crawl space. A vapor barrier installed above the floor insulation will help prevent this. In summer, the crawl space will tend to stay damp unless wall vents are installed. In order to keep moisture of the earth from collecting in the crawl space a second vapor barrier should be laid on the ground.

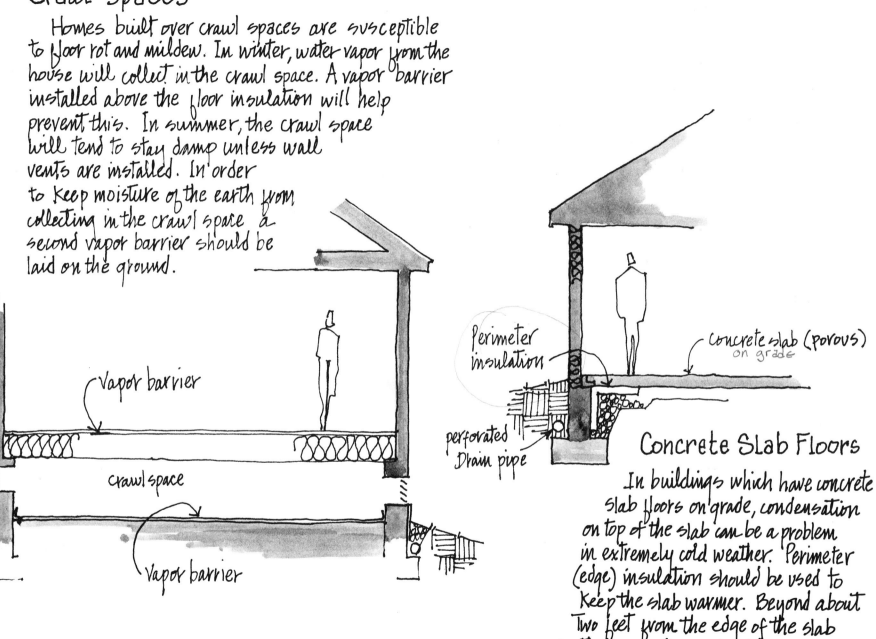

Vapor barrier

crawl space

Vapor barrier

Perimeter insulation

perforated Drain pipe

concrete slab (porous) on grade

Concrete Slab Floors

In buildings which have concrete slab floors on grade, condensation on top of the slab can be a problem in extremely cold weather. Perimeter (edge) insulation should be used to keep the slab warmer. Beyond about two feet from the edge of the slab earth temperatures should stay moderate year-round.

95

VI Water Rams

Finally, water, not merely supplying drink but filling an infinite number of practical needs, does us services which make us grateful...
— Vitruvius, *The Ten Books on Architecture*
Translated by Morris Hicky Morgan

Water rams were once used extensively in rural areas for pumping water. Since our nation is seeking new ways to save energy, many homeowners are once again taking a serious look at the hydraulic ram to solve some of today's energy problems.

For proper operation, water rams must have a source of moving water to enable the mechanism to function. For example, it is necessary to have a fall or "head" of 20 inches or more and a flow of 1½ gallons per minute or more to enable the ram to automatically pump a good volume of water. In general, most rams will pump water to a height of 25 feet for each one-foot fall of water available. Therefore, if there is a fall of, say, three feet, the ram will pump a sufficient volume of water up to 75 feet high!

The basic operation of a hydraulic ram may be briefly expressed as follows: water flows down the drive pipe to the ram and develops a certain amount of power due to its weight and velocity. It first flows through the outside valve of the ram until it reaches a certain velocity, then the valve closes suddenly. The column of water continues on through the inside valve and into the air chamber. When the pressure in the air chamber equalizes and overcomes the driving force behind it, a rebound takes place. This operation is repeated from 25 to 100 times per minute working on a hydraulic principle, building up pressure in the air chamber, which in turn forces water through the delivery pipe.

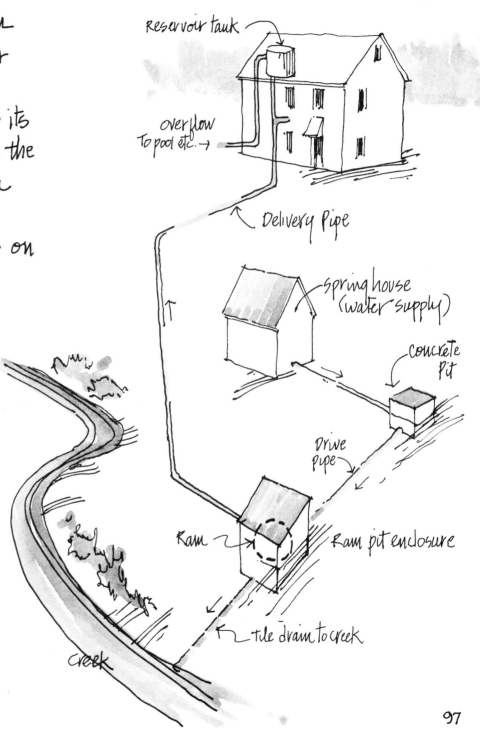

reservoir tank

overflow to pool etc. →

Delivery Pipe

spring house (water supply)

concrete pit

Drive Pipe

Ram

Ram pit enclosure

tile drain to creek

creek

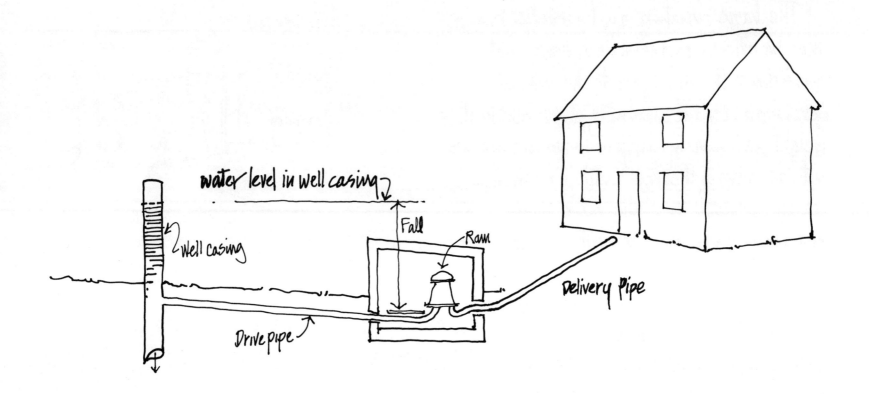

An artesian well provides an ideal source of supply water for operating a ram. The constantly flowing sand in the water from artesian wells rapidly wears bronze or other metal valves. Special composition rubber valves are used in the ram — eliminating damage from this source.

The drive pipe is connected directly to the well casing slightly below ground level. The drive pipe should have as much slope or fall to the ram as the lay of the ground will permit.

The layout above is ideal for a small home installation.

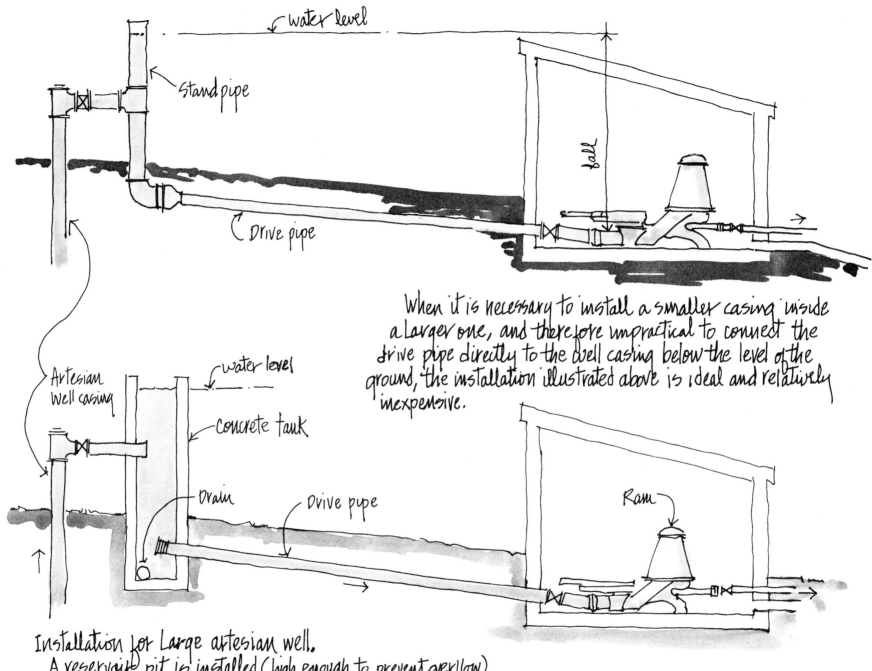

water level

stand pipe

Drive pipe

Artesian
Well casing

water level

concrete tank

Drain

Drive pipe

Ram

ball

When it is necessary to install a smaller casing inside a larger one, and therefore impractical to connect the drive pipe directly to the well casing below the level of the ground, the installation illustrated above is ideal and relatively inexpensive.

Installation for large artesian well.
A reservoir pit is installed (high enough to prevent overflow) which feeds water to the ram or a battery of rams.

99

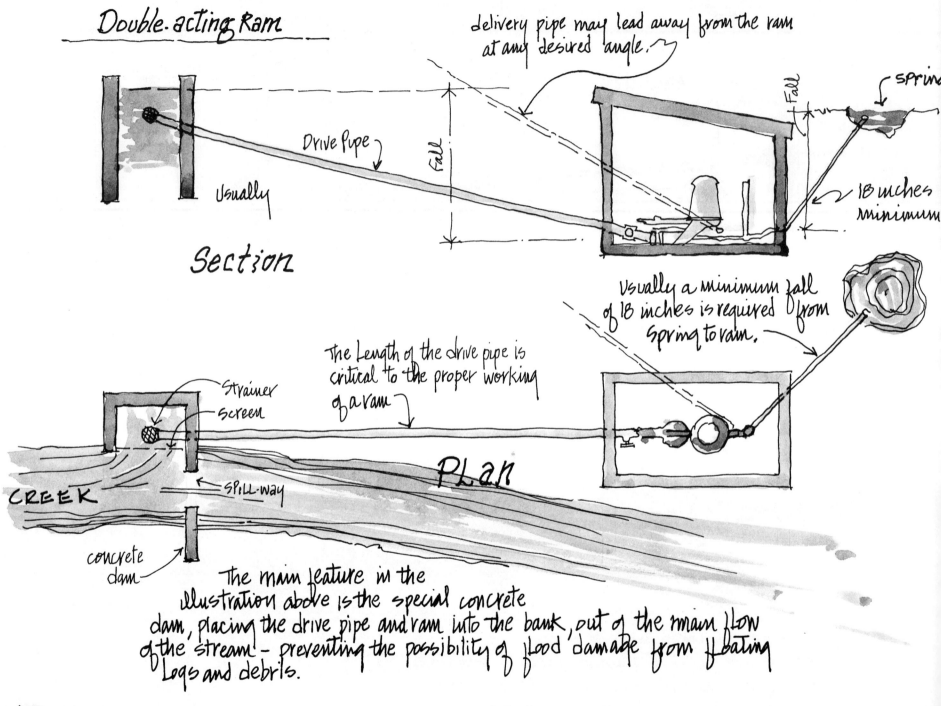

Double-acting Ram

delivery pipe may lead away from the ram at any desired angle.

spring

Fall

Drive Pipe

Fall

Usually

18 inches minimum

Section

Usually a minimum fall of 18 inches is required from spring to ram.

Strainer Screen

The length of the drive pipe is critical to the proper working of a ram

Plan

CREEK

SPILL-way

concrete dam

The main feature in the illustration above is the special concrete dam, placing the drive pipe and ram into the bank, out of the main flow of the stream - preventing the possibility of flood damage from floating logs and debris.

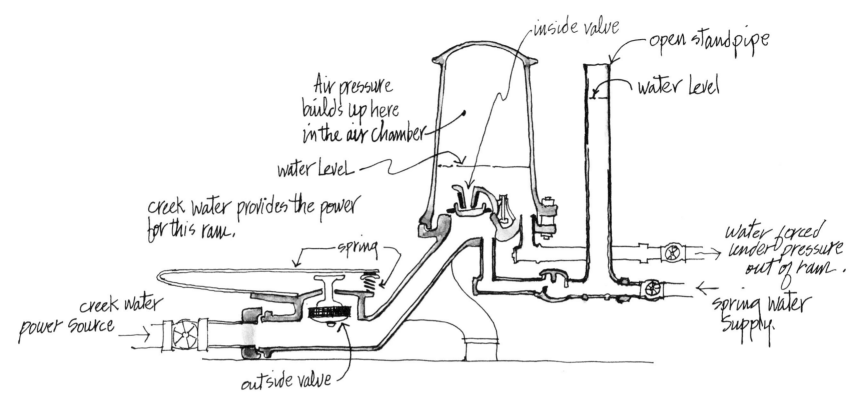

inside valve

open standpipe

water level

Air pressure builds up here in the air chamber

water Level

creek water provides the power for this ram.

spring

creek water power source

Water forced under pressure out of ram.

spring water Supply.

outside valve

Schematic Sectional View
of Double Acting Ram

Creek water provides the power soure to pump spring water. In a single acting ram the water to be pumped is the same water that furnishes power and operates the ram.

Ram and Pressure Tank System

The pneumatic pressure tank water system uses the ram to pump water into an air-tight steel tank. The pressure within the tank forces water to faucets throughout the house. Altering the pressure setting of the relief valve controls the height to which water can be fed above the tank.

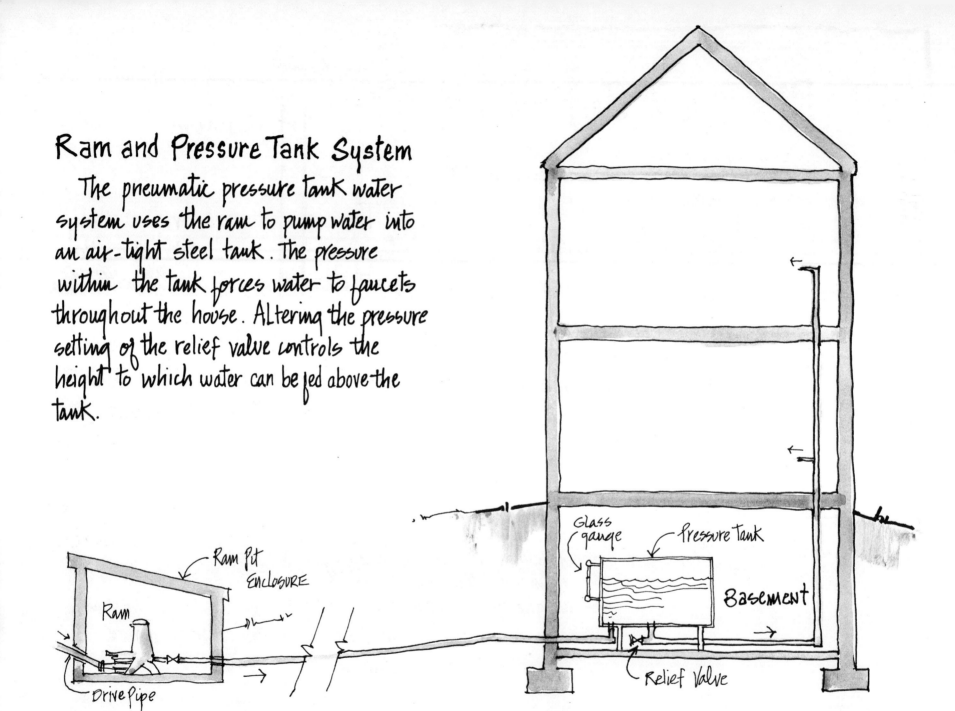

Ram Pit Enclosure

Ram

Drive Pipe

Glass gauge

Pressure Tank

Basement

Relief Valve

VII Plans and Sections

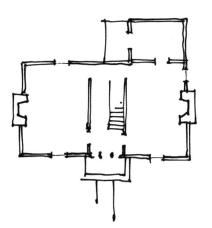

There aren't enough original Early American homes around to satisfy the insatiable American appetite for restoration and the desire to settle into a life style built around the past. The homes that do exist are either much too expensive or are too long neglected for a practical economic recovery. To satisfy such needs we must now build anew but with our eye on the past. The homes herein presented resemble earlier building forms but aren't based on precise historical details or material. They are designed for today's construction standards.

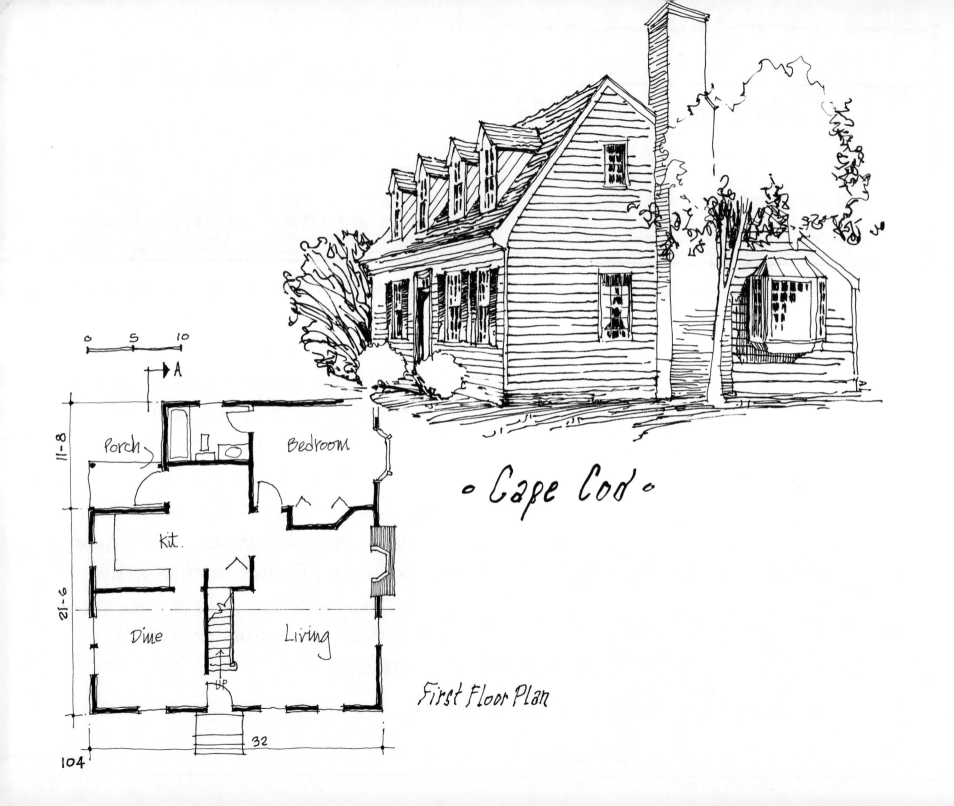

- Cape Cod -

First Floor Plan

0 5 10

A

Porch

Bedroom

Kit.

Dine

Living

UP

11-8

21-6

32

104

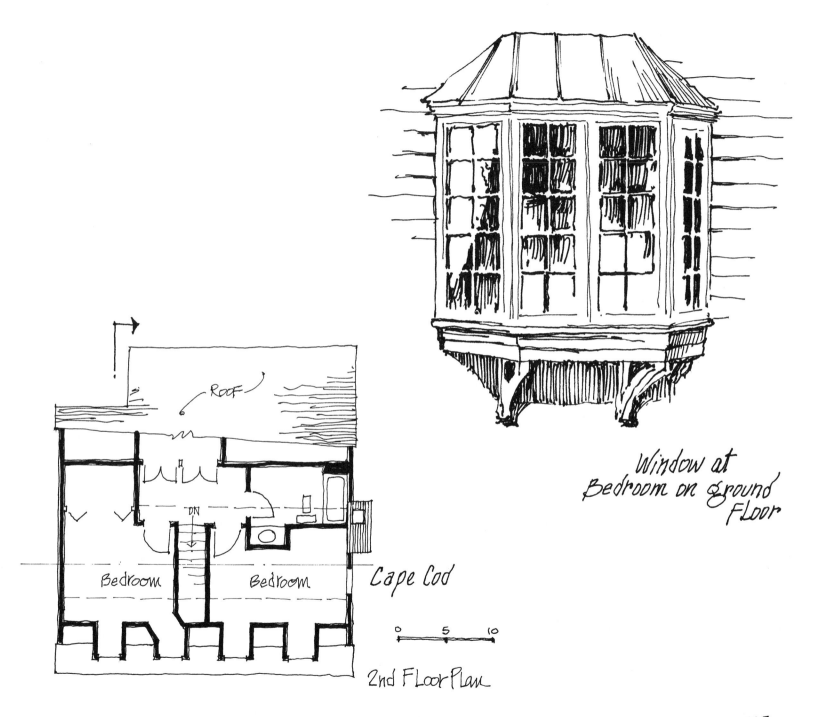

ROOF

Bedroom   Bedroom

DN

Cape Cod

Window at
Bedroom on ground
Floor

0   5   10

2nd Floor Plan

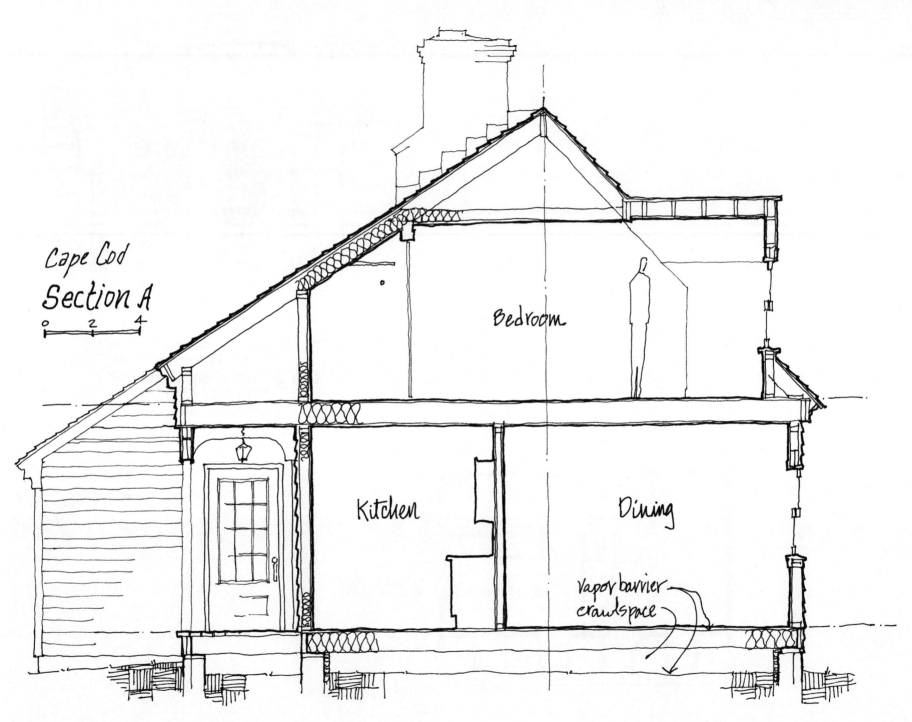

Cape Cod
Section A

0   2   4

Bedroom

Kitchen

Dining

Vapor barrier
crawlspace

106

various Early American Hardware

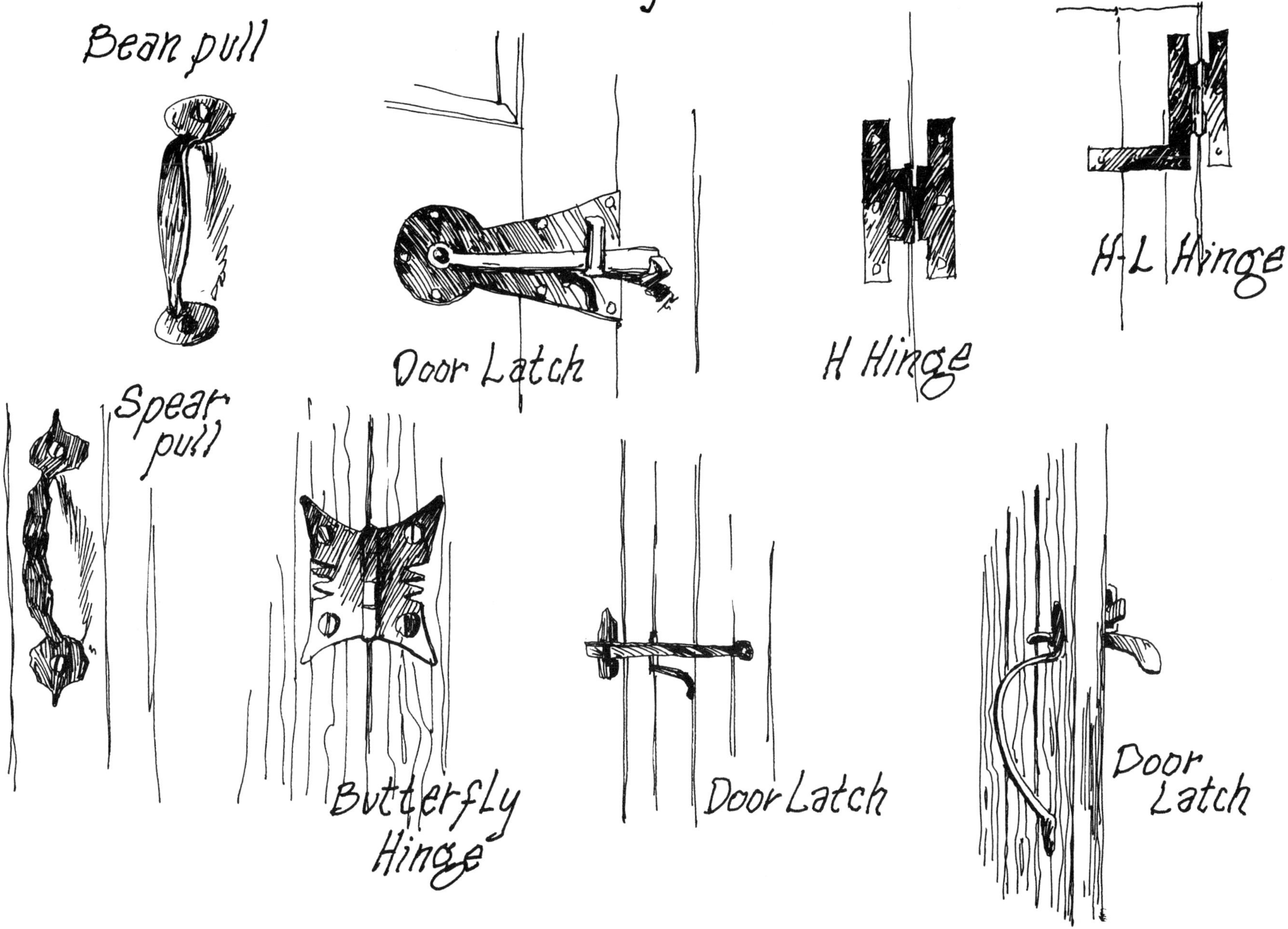

Bean pull

Door Latch

H Hinge

H-L Hinge

Spear pull

Butterfly Hinge

Door Latch

Door Latch

An Old Rim Lock
found on an interior door of an old Virginia home

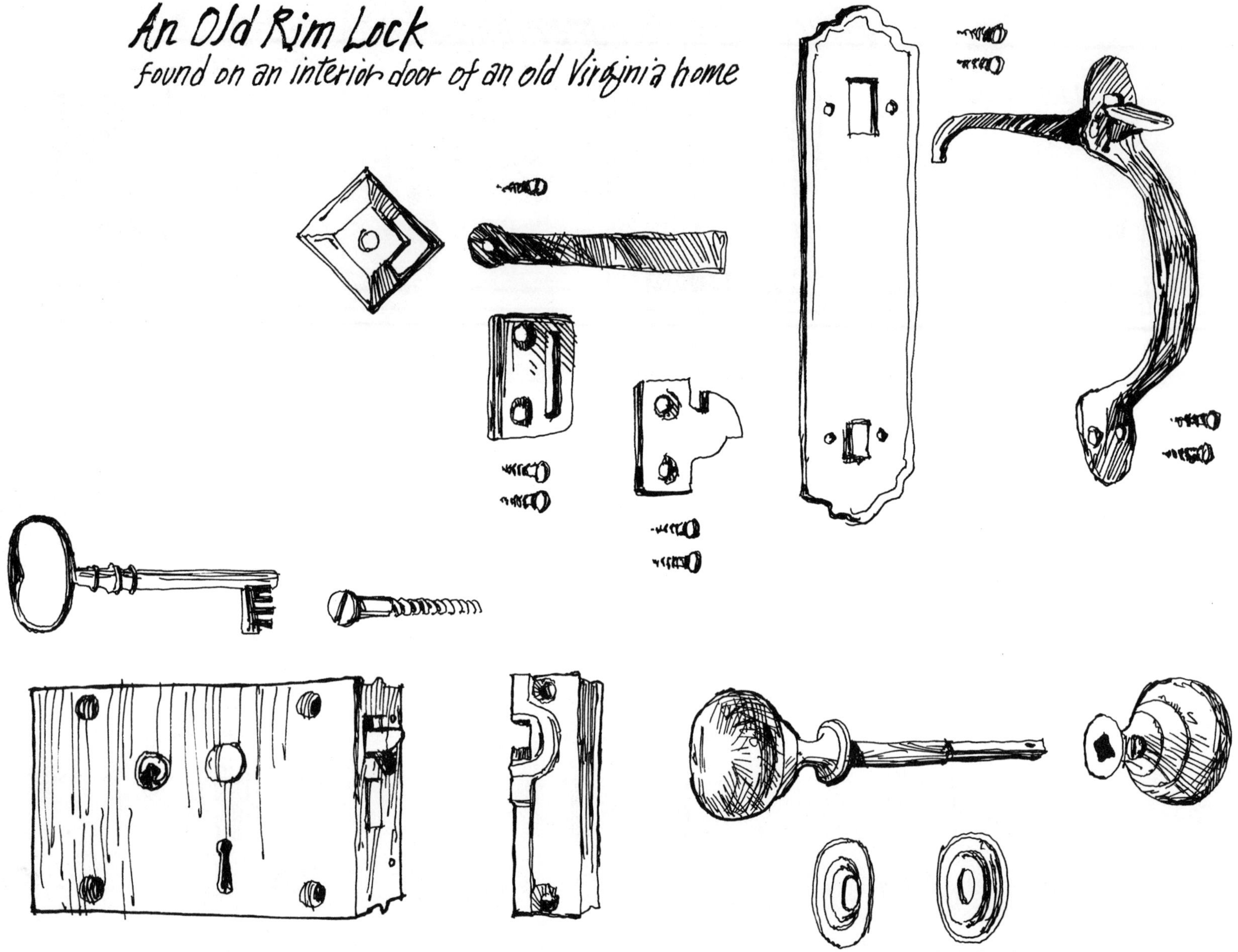

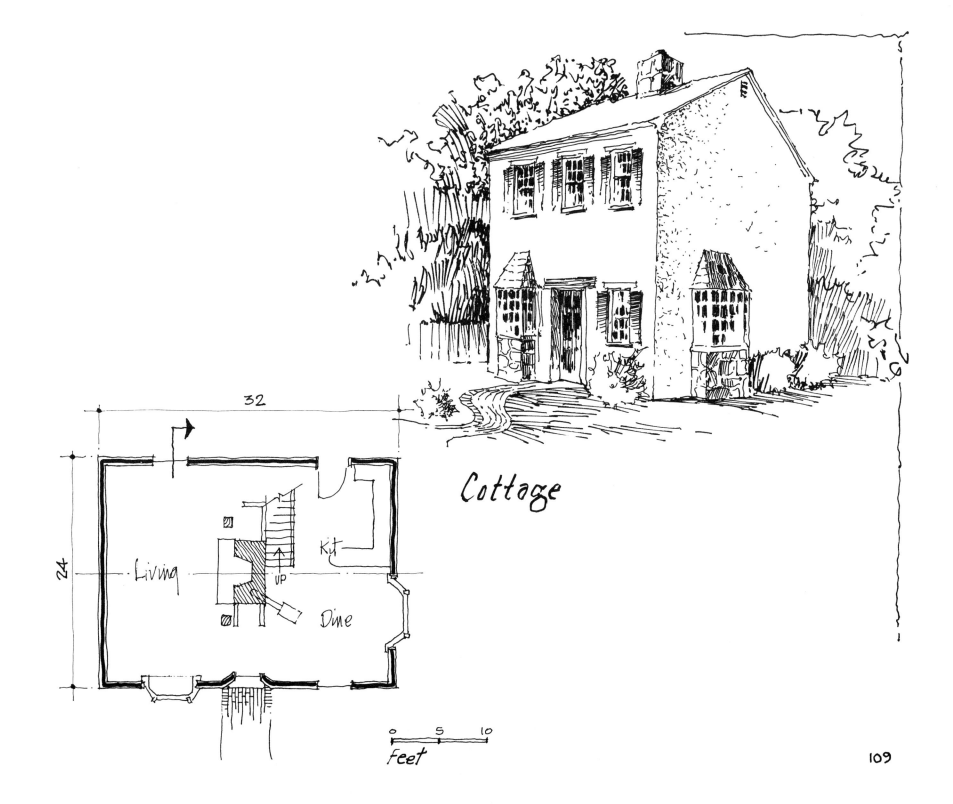

Cottage

32

24

Living

Kit

UP

Dine

0   5   10
Feet

- Fence gate detail -

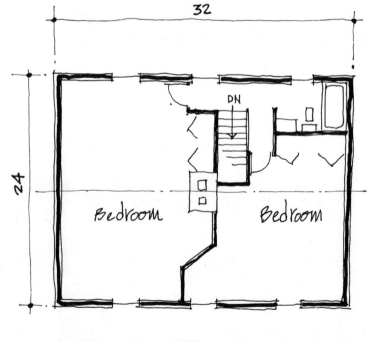

Cottage

2nd Floor Plan

0 2 4 6 8 10

Feet

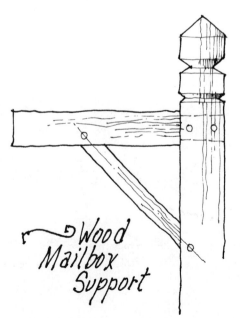

Wood Mailbox Support

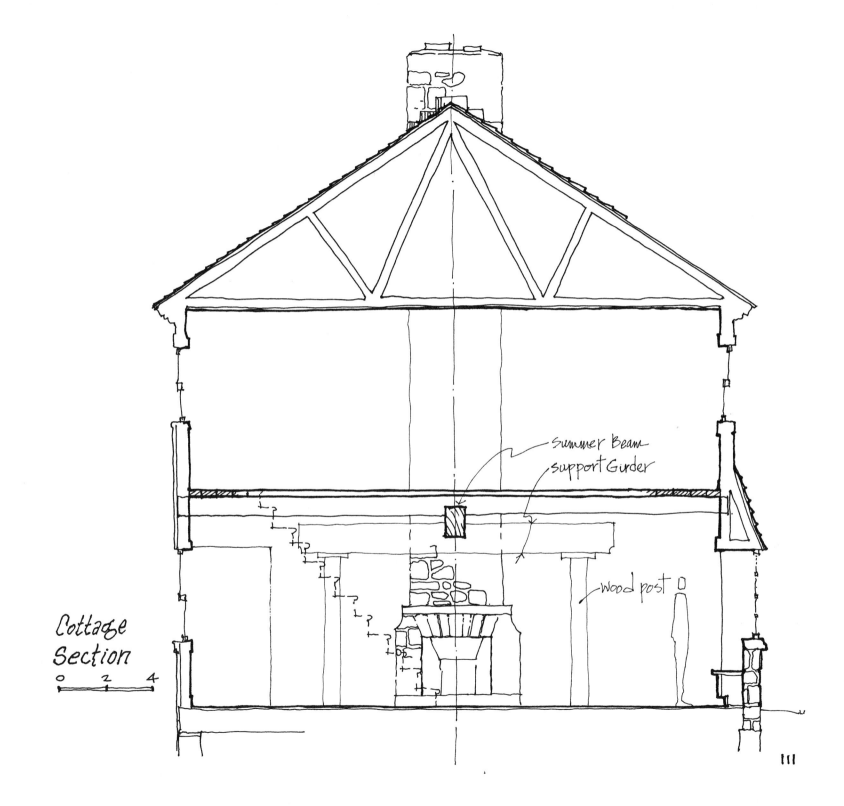

Summer Beam

support Girder

wood post

Cottage
Section

0   2   4

111

The Sconce

Candles were a main source of light in very Early American life. The metal sconce which hung from the wall provided a base, wax catcher and reflective back.

candle sits over metal spear

Decorative Light bulb

Electric Wire

sconces today are made of tin.

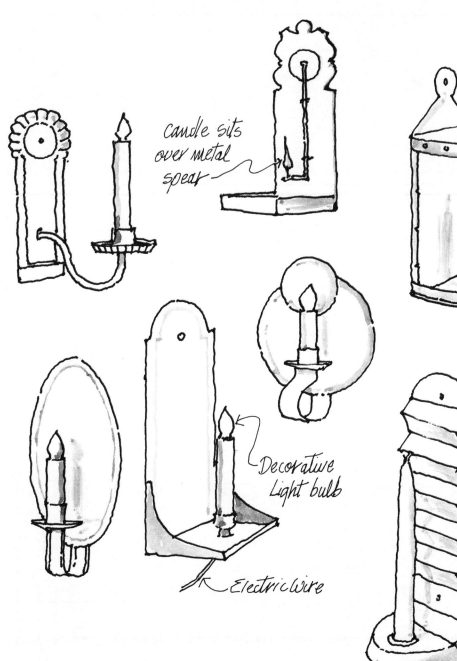

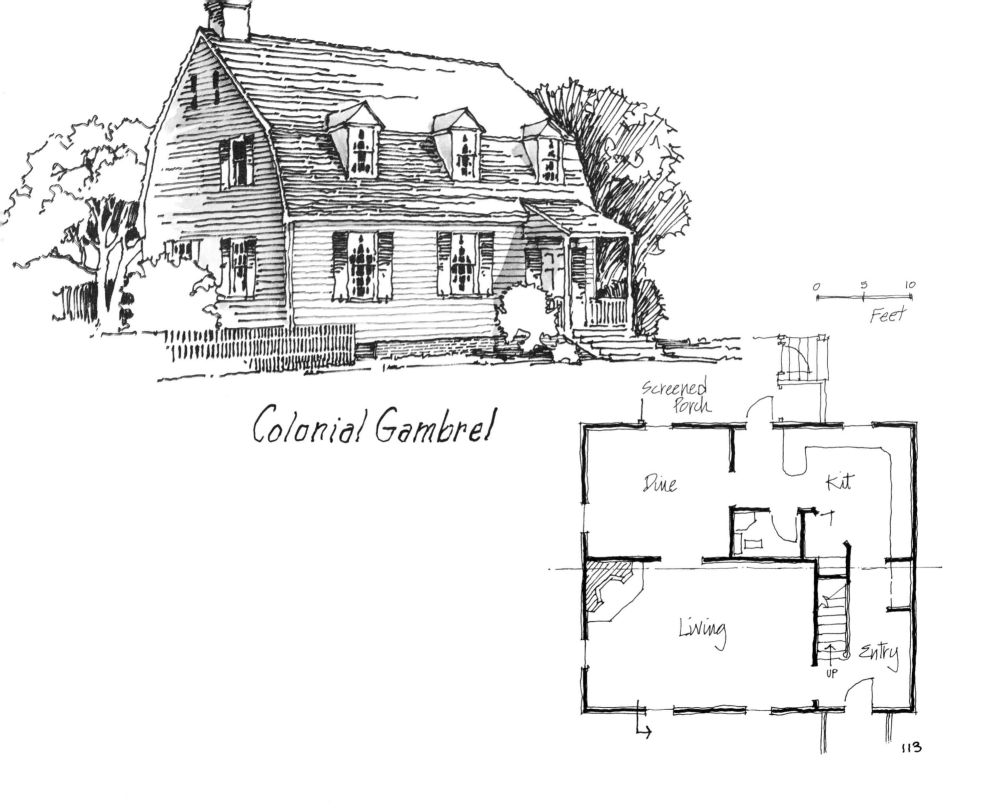

Colonial Gambrel

0   5   10
Feet

Screened Porch

Dine

Kit

Living

Entry

UP

113

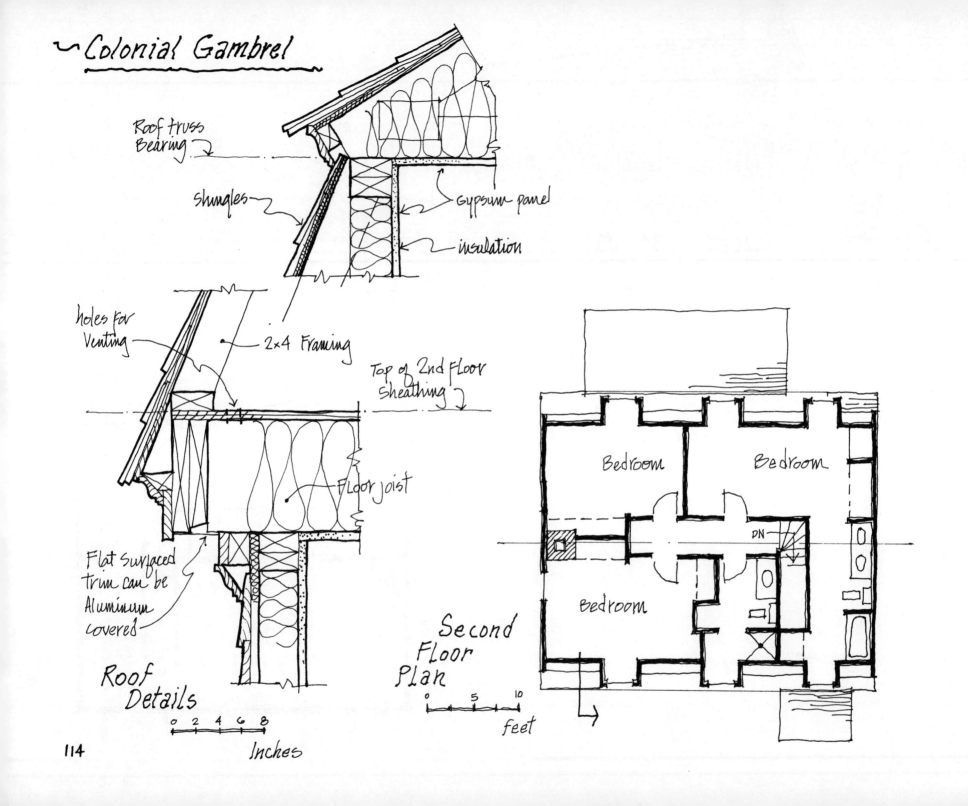

~ Colonial Gambrel

Roof truss Bearing

shingles

Gypsum panel

insulation

holes for Venting

2×4 Framing

Top of 2nd Floor Sheathing

Floor joist

Flat surfaced trim can be Aluminum Covered

Roof Details

0 2 4 6 8

Inches

Bedroom

Bedroom

DN

Bedroom

Second Floor Plan

0   5   10

feet

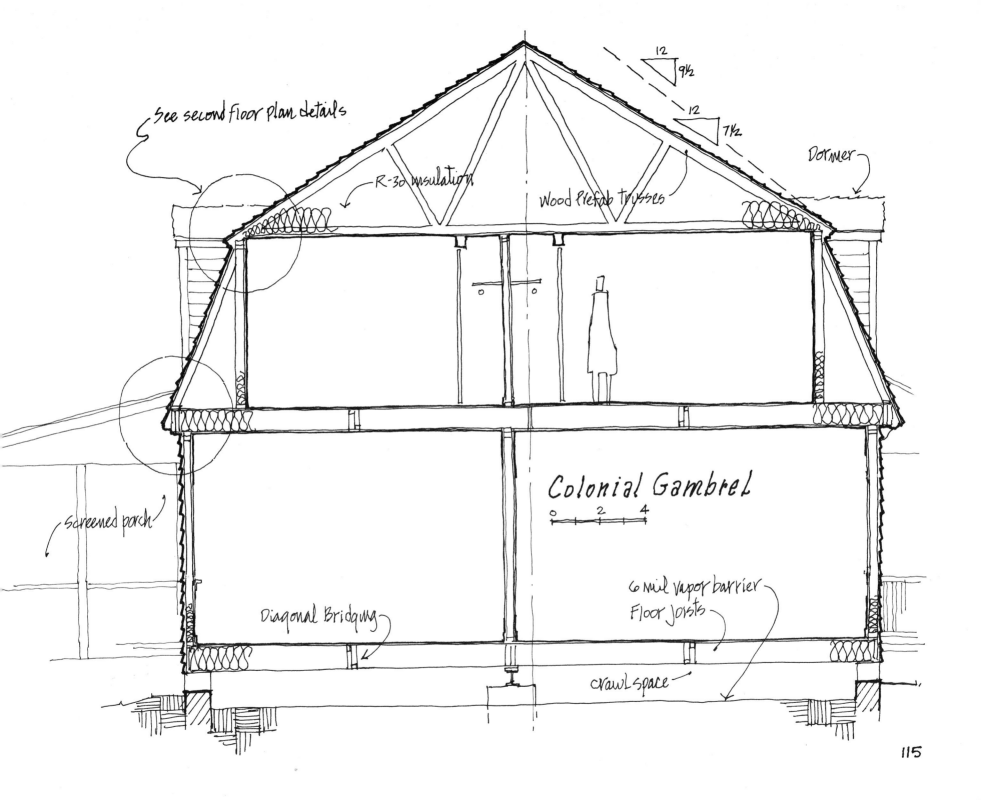

See second floor plan details

R-30 insulation

Wood Prefab trusses

Dormer

12
9½

12
7½

Colonial Gambrel

0   2   4

Screened porch

Diagonal Bridging

6 mil vapor barrier
Floor Joists

crawl space

115

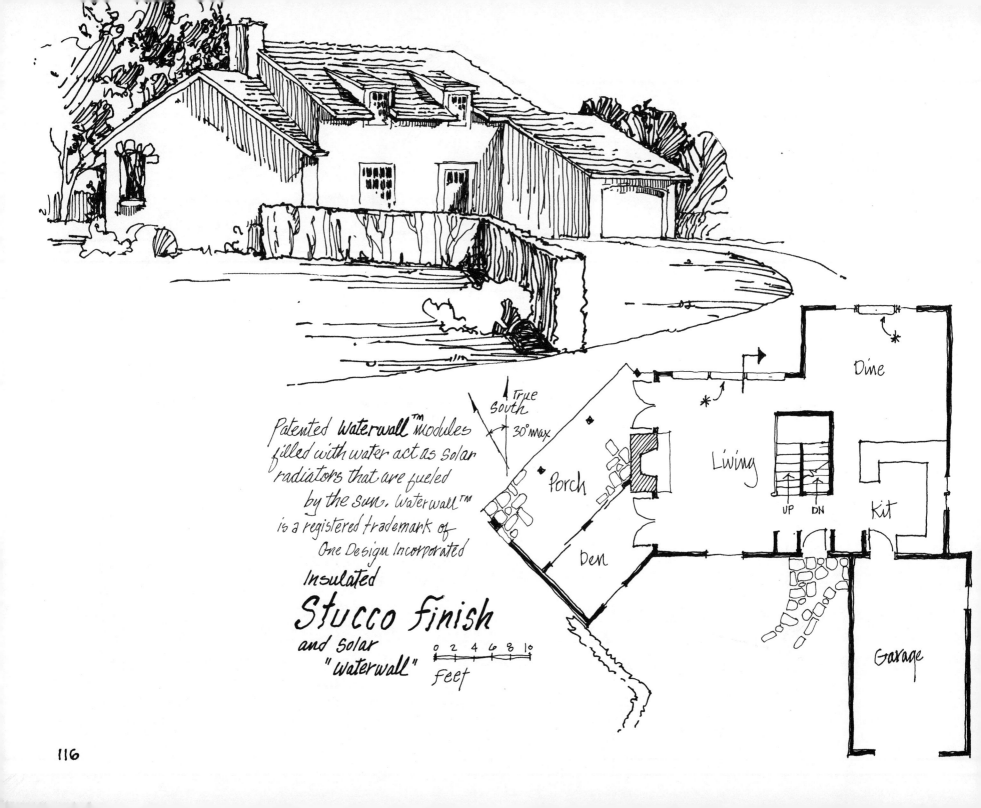

Patented *Waterwall*™ modules
filled with water act as solar
radiators that are fueled
by the sun. Waterwall™
is a registered trademark of
One Design Incorporated

Insulated

Stucco Finish

and solar
"waterwall"

0 2 4 6 8 10
Feet

True
South

30° max

Porch

Den

Living

UP DN

Kit

Dine

Garage

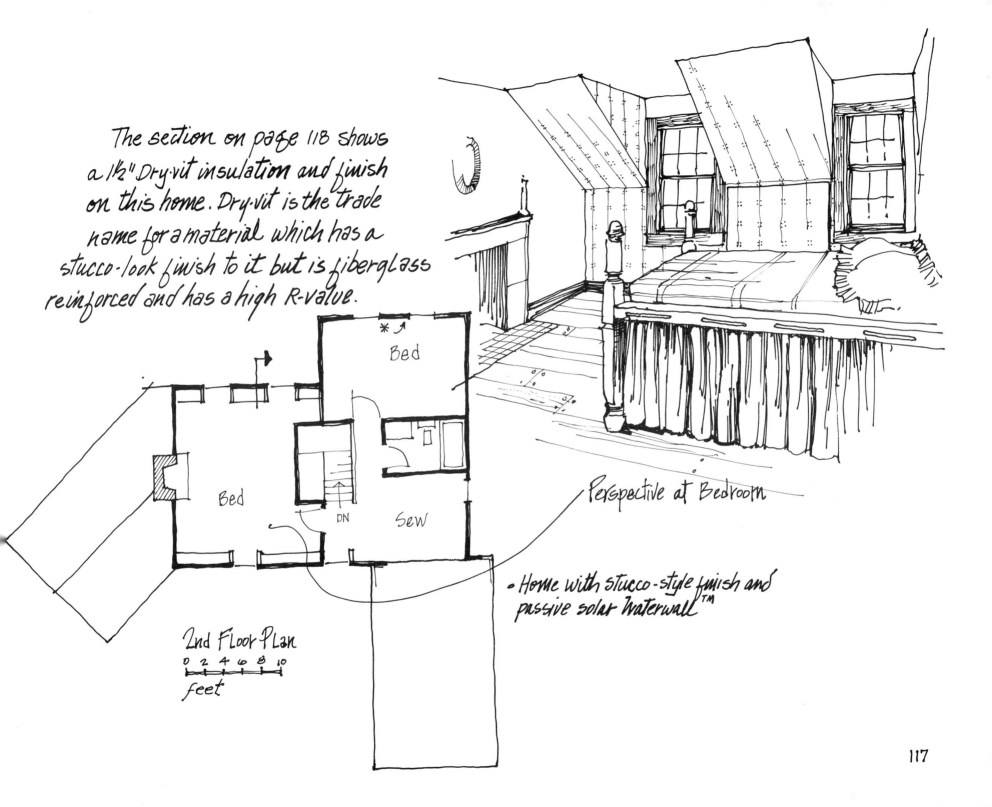

The section on page 118 shows a 1½" Dry-vit insulation and finish on this home. Dry-vit is the trade name for a material which has a stucco-look finish to it but is fiberglass reinforced and has a high R-value.

Bed

Bed

Sew

DN

2nd Floor Plan

0 2 4 6 8 10
feet

Perspective at Bedroom

• Home with stucco-style finish and passive solar Waterwall™

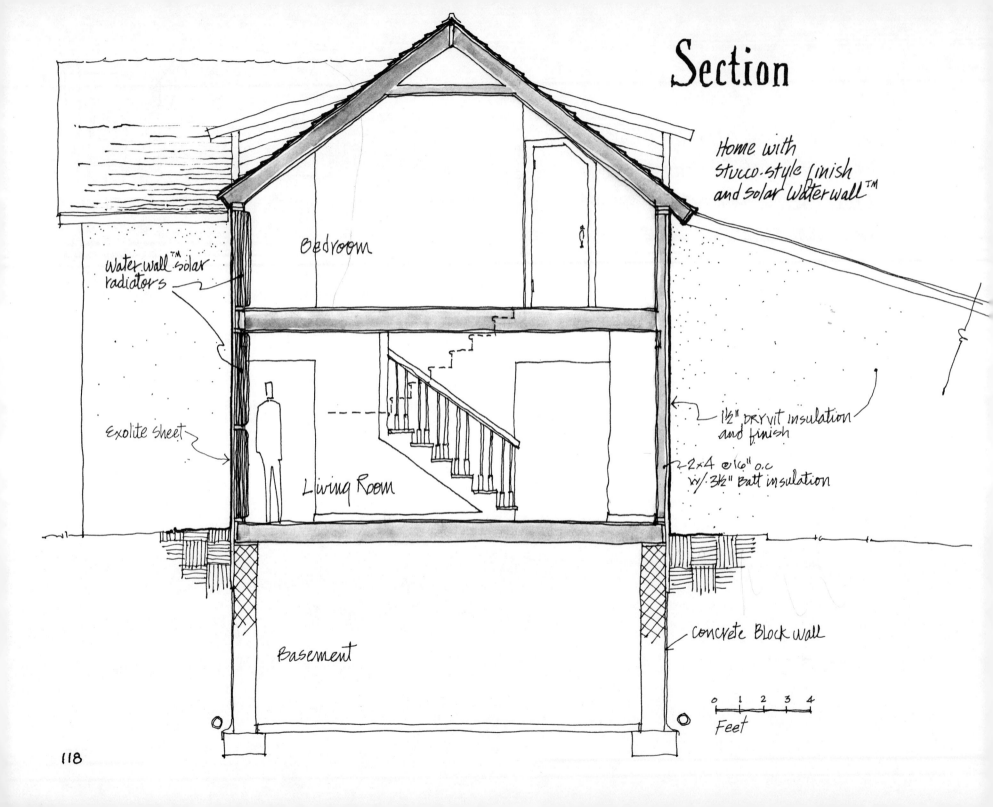

Section

Home with
stucco-style finish
and solar Water wall™

Bedroom

Water wall™ solar
radiators

Exolite sheet

Living Room

1½" DRYVIT insulation
and finish

2×4 @16" o.c
w/ 3½" Batt insulation

concrete Block wall

Basement

0 1 2 3 4
Feet

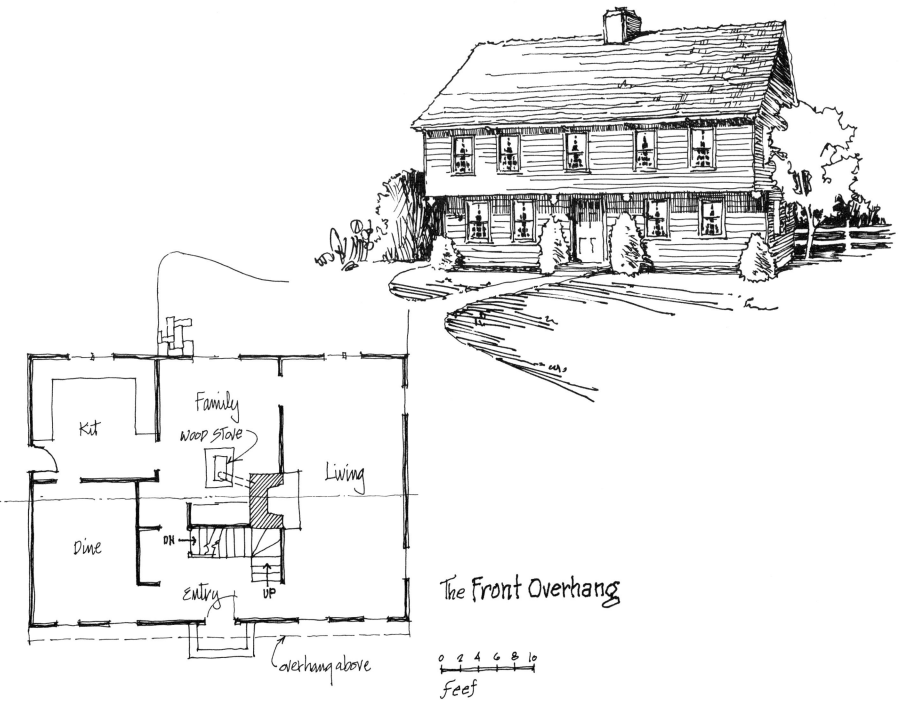

Family

WOOD STOVE

Kit

Living

Dine

DN →

UP

Entry

overhang above

The Front Overhang

0 2 4 6 8 10

Feef

119

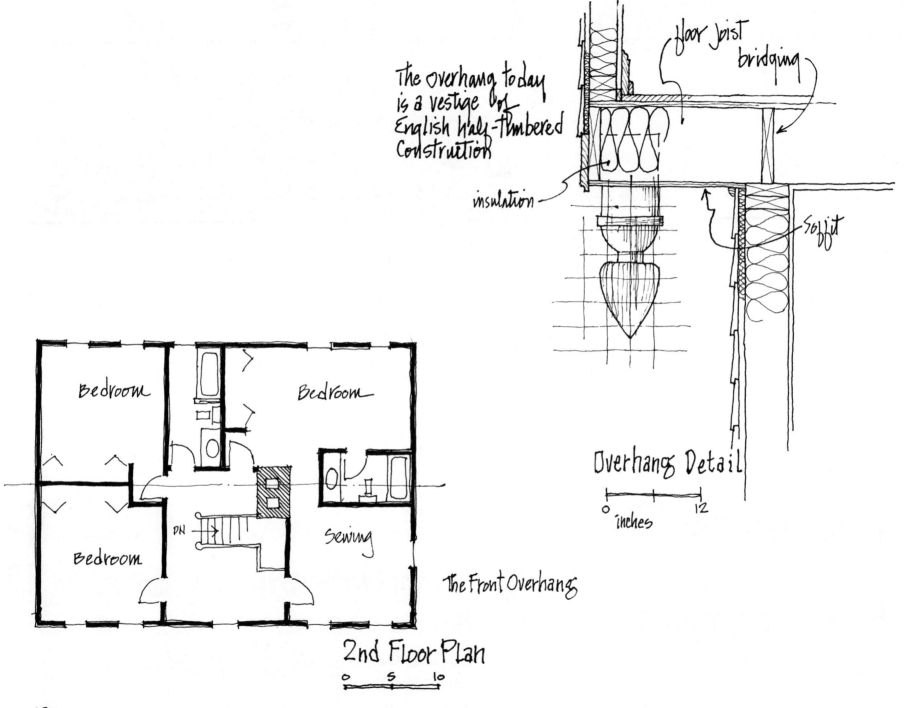

The overhang today
is a vestige of
English half-timbered
Construction

floor joist
bridging

insulation

Soffit

Overhang Detail

0 ————— 12
inches

Bedroom

Bedroom

Bedroom

DN

Sewing

The Front Overhang

2nd Floor Plan

0 ——— 5 ——— 10

Wall Stenciling

In the early 1800s wallpaper was quite expensive. The desire for ornamentation gave rise to the art of wall and floor stenciling. Stenciling was simple and inexpensive.

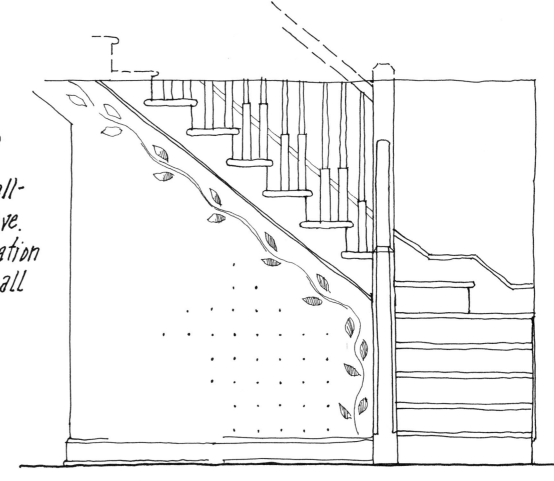

the Front Overhang

Elevation of Front Entry Stair

0   1   2

feet

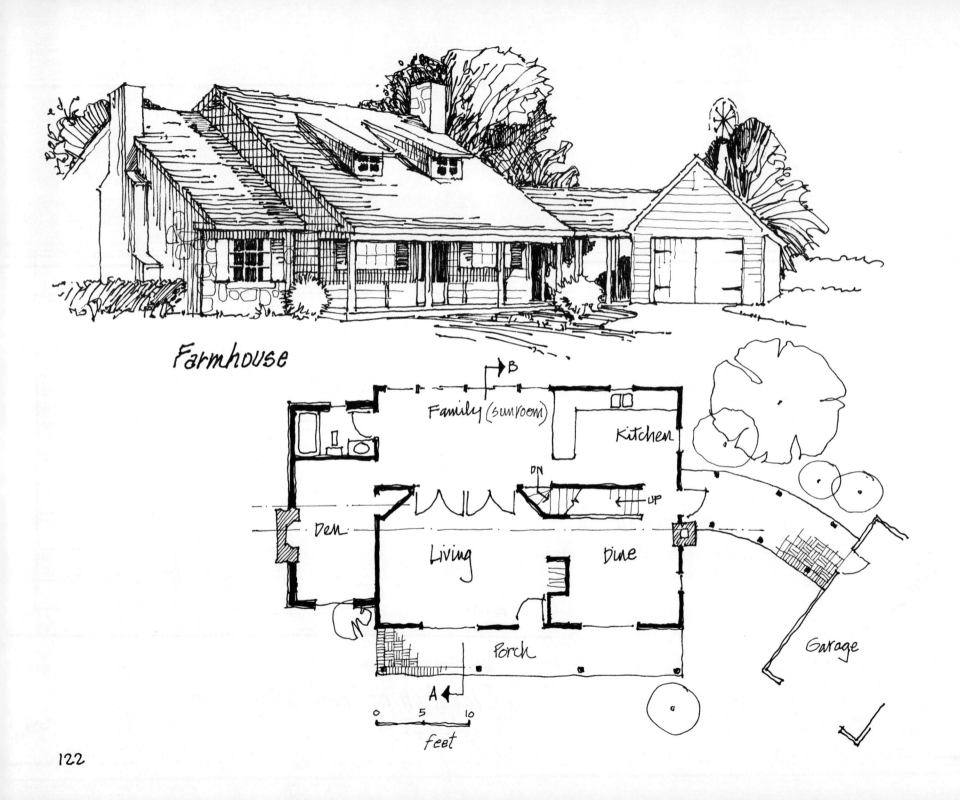

Farmhouse

B

Family (sunroom)

Kitchen

DN

Den

UP

Living

Dine

Porch

A

0   5   10

feet

Garage

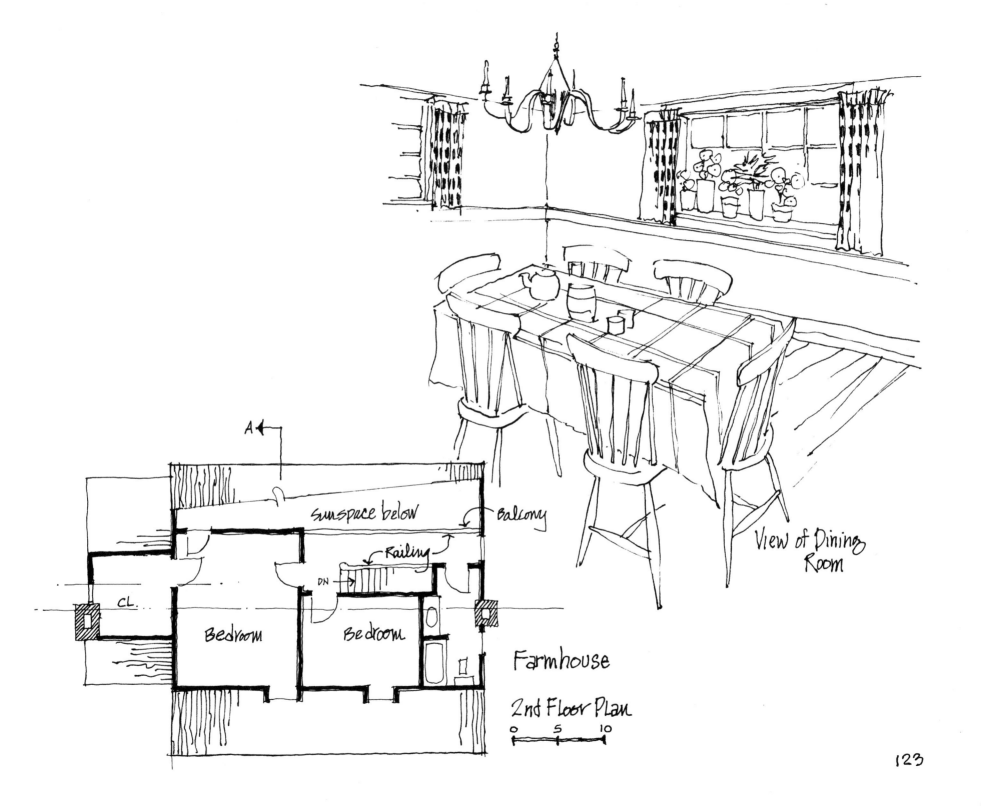

View of Dining Room

A

Sunspace below

Balcony

Railing

DN

CL.

Bedroom

Bedroom

Farmhouse

2nd Floor Plan

0   5   10

123

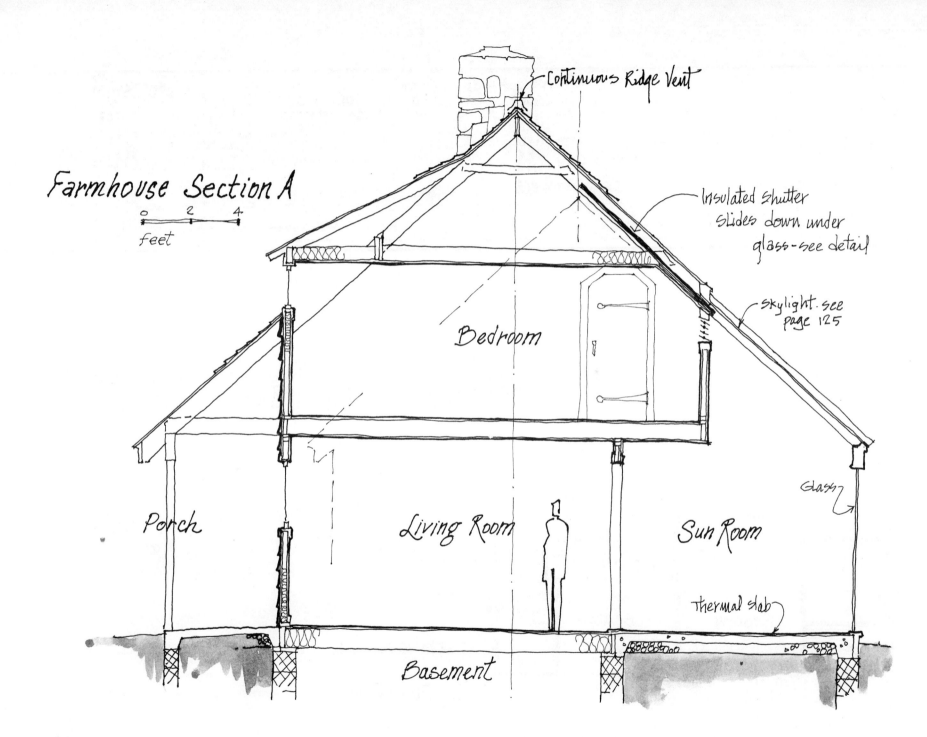

Farmhouse Section A

0   2   4
feet

Continuous Ridge Vent

Insulated Shutter
slides down under
glass - see detail

skylight. see
page 125

Bedroom

Glass

Porch

Living Room

Sun Room

thermal slab

Basement

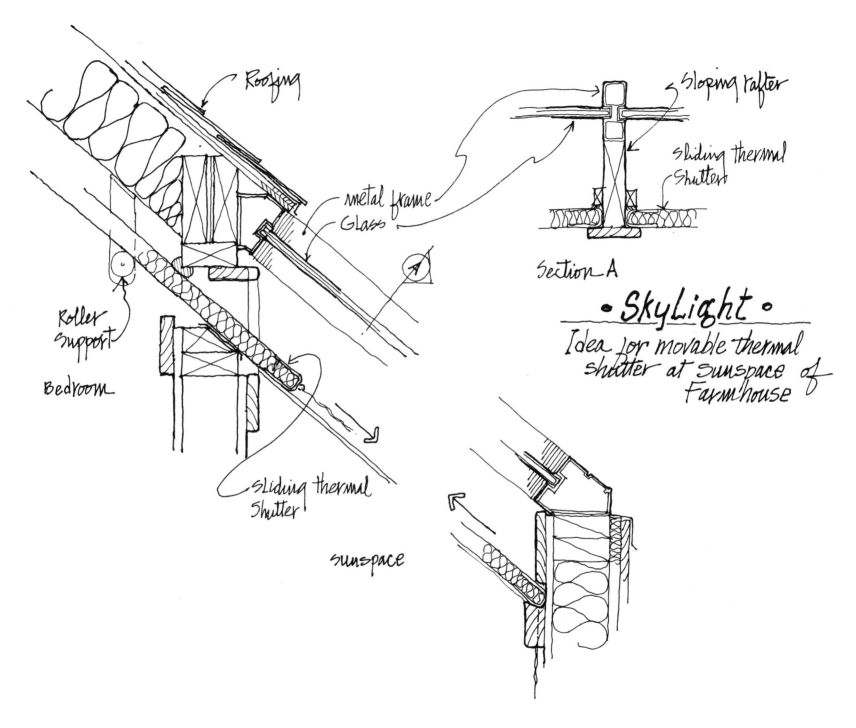

Roofing

metal frame
Glass

Roller
Support

Bedroom

Sliding thermal
Shutter

sunspace

sloping rafter

sliding thermal
Shutter

Section A

• SkyLight •

Idea for movable thermal
shutter at sunspace of
Farmhouse

125

Farmhouse
Sunspace

Skylights

126

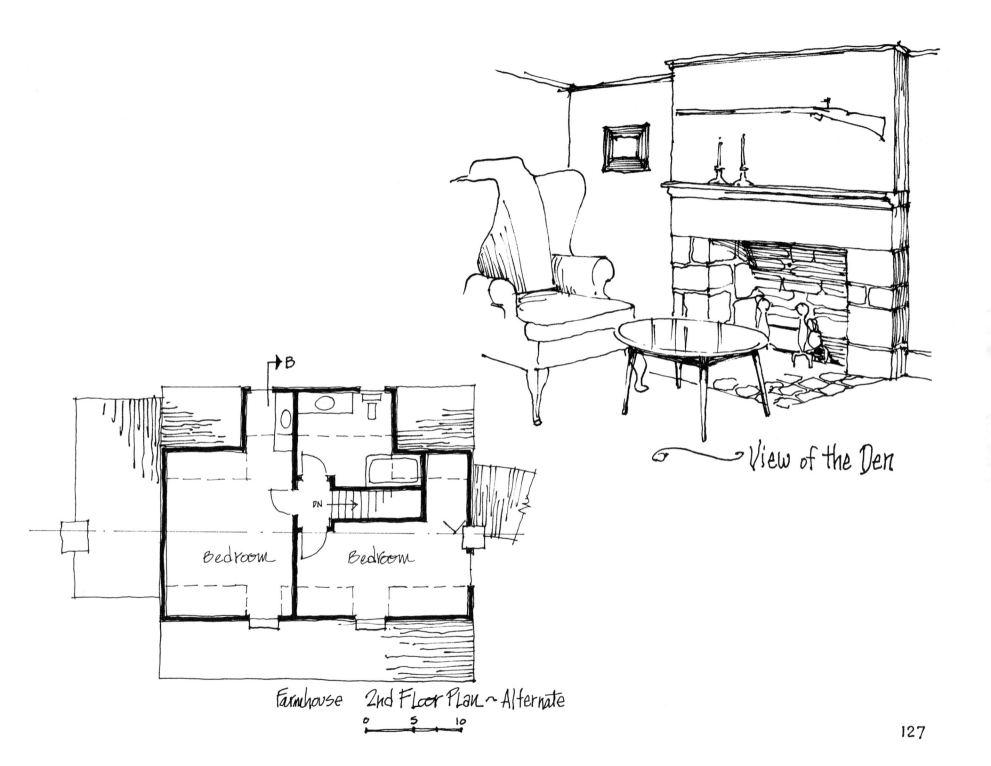

B

DN

Bedroom   Bedroom

View of the Den

Farmhouse   2nd Floor Plan ~ Alternate

0   5   10

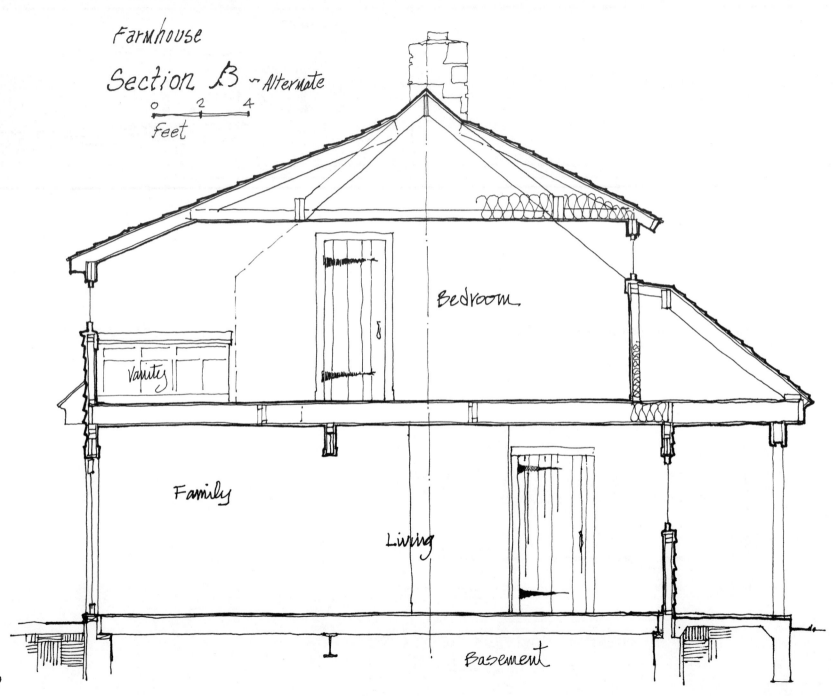

Farmhouse

Section B ~ Alternate

0   2   4
Feet

Bedroom

Vanity

Family

Living

Basement

128

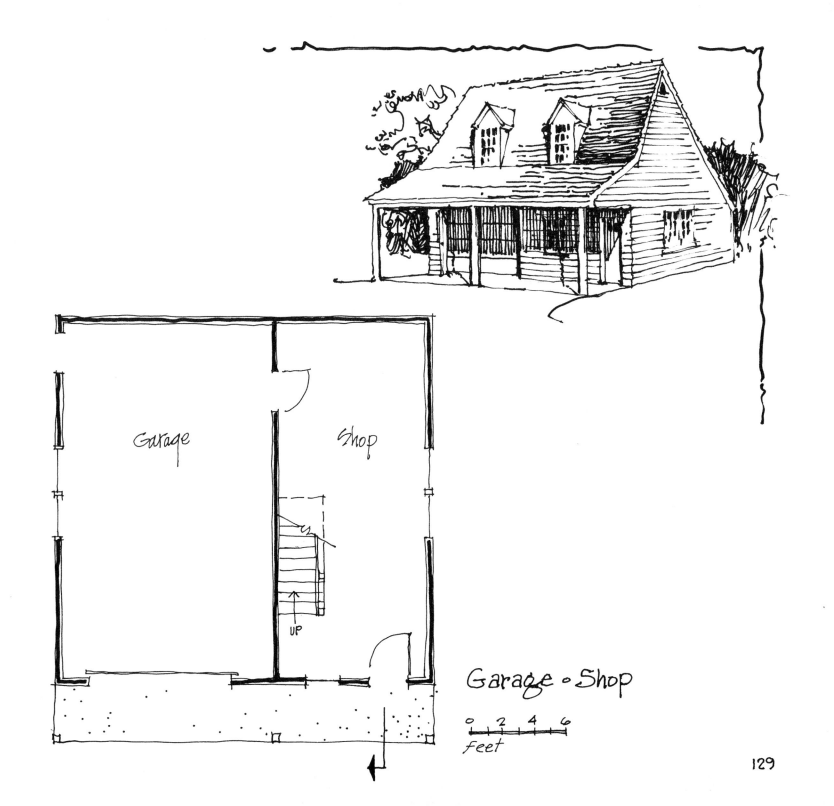

Garage

Shop

UP

Garage ◦ Shop

0 2 4 6
feet

129

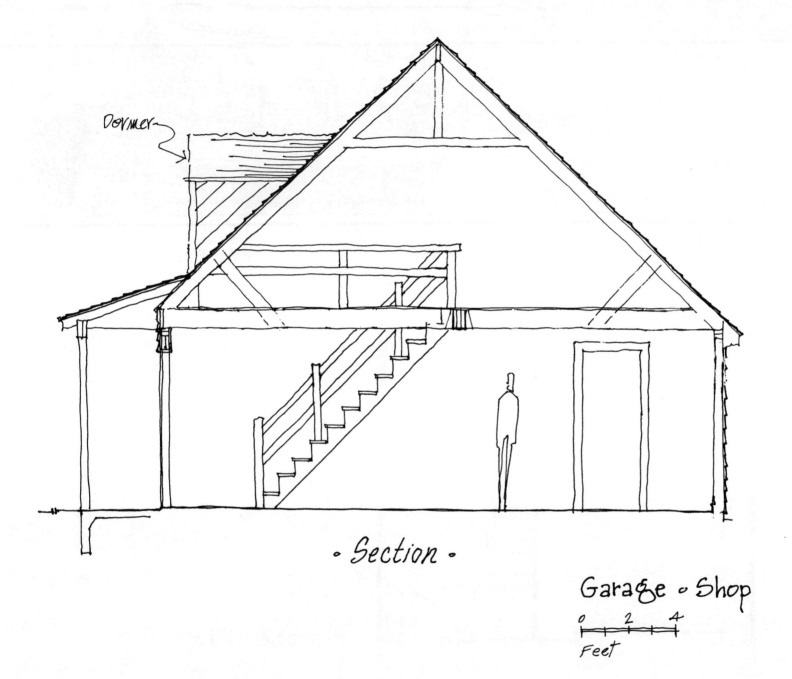

Dormer

· Section ·

Garage · Shop

0   2   4

Feet

130

Miscellaneous
Entrance Details •

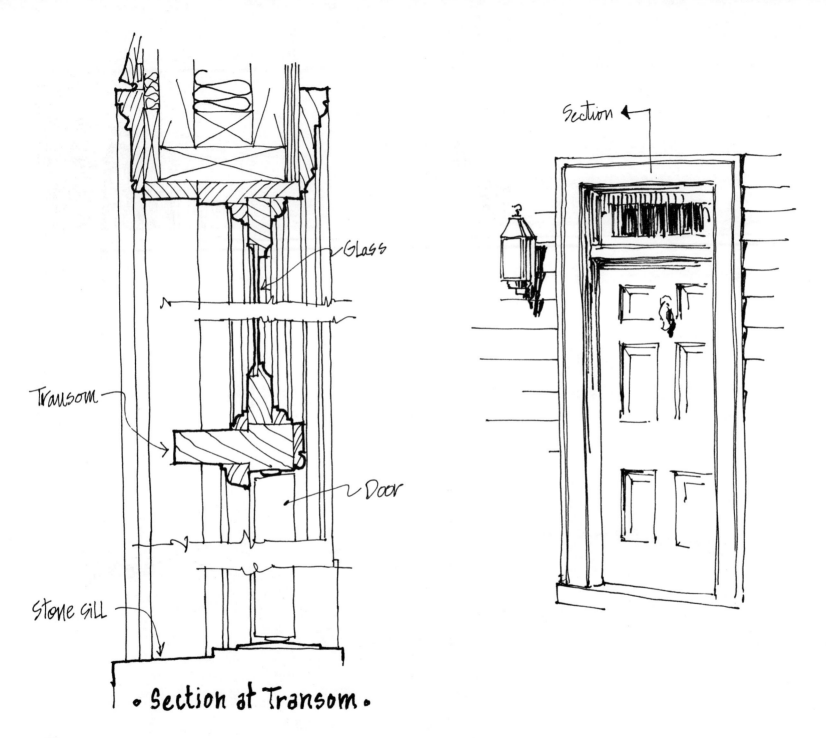

Glass

Transom

Door

Stone Sill

• Section at Transom •

Section

metal foot
scrape

~Entrance
Details~

133

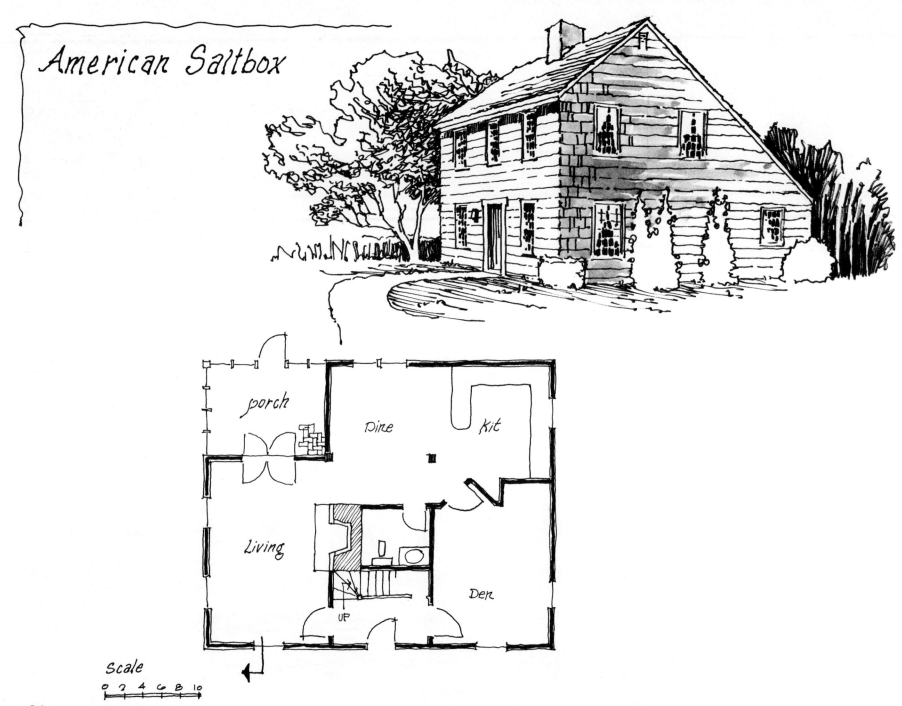

American Saltbox

porch

Dine   Kit

Living

Den

UP

Scale
0 2 4 6 8 10

134

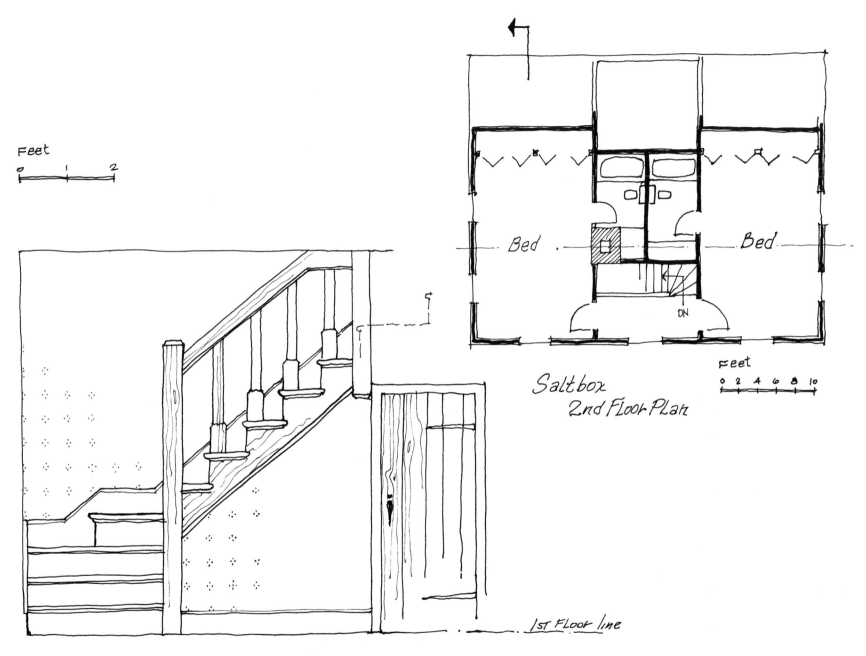

Feet
0   1   2

Saltbox
2nd Floor Plan

Bed   Bed

DN

Feet
0 2 4 6 8 10

1st Floor line

Elevation at Entry Stairs

135

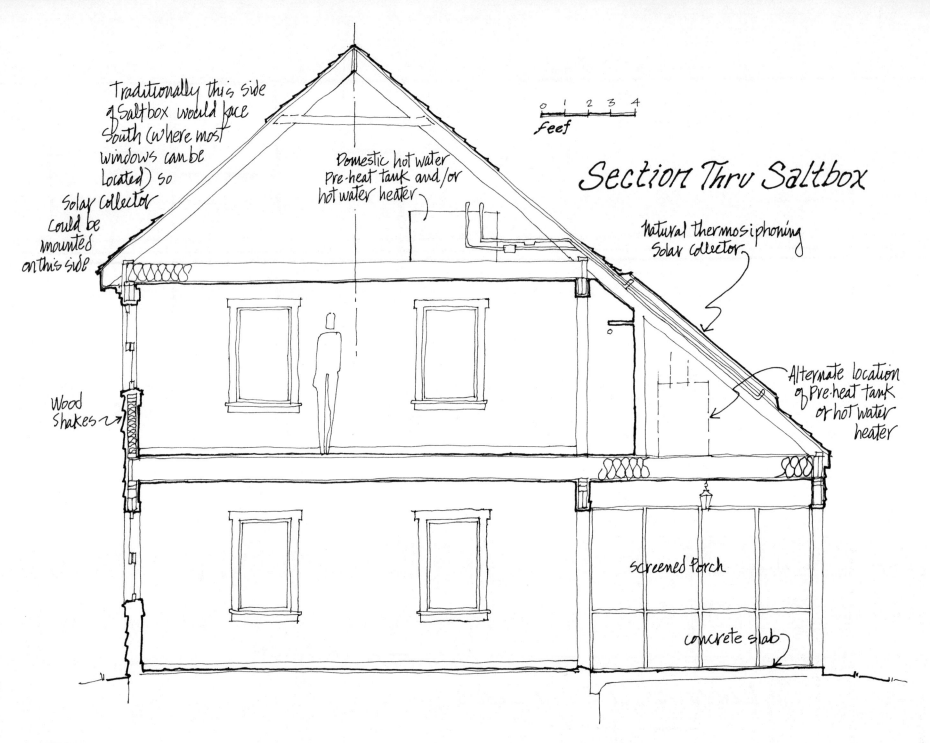

Traditionally this side of Saltbox would face South (where most windows can be located) so Solar collector could be mounted on this side

Domestic hot water Pre-heat tank and/or hot water heater

Section Thru Saltbox

Natural thermosiphoning Solar collector.

Alternate location of Pre-heat tank or hot water heater

Wood Shakes

screened Porch

concrete slab

0 1 2 3 4

feet

136

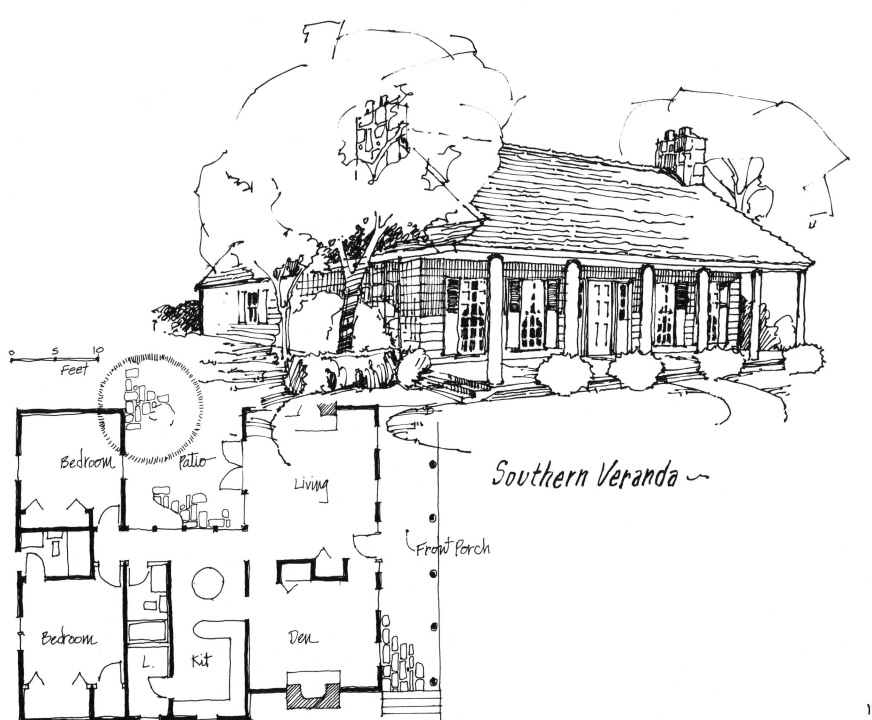

0   5   10
Feet

Southern Veranda

Bedroom

Patio

Living

Front Porch

Bedroom

L.   Kit

Den

137

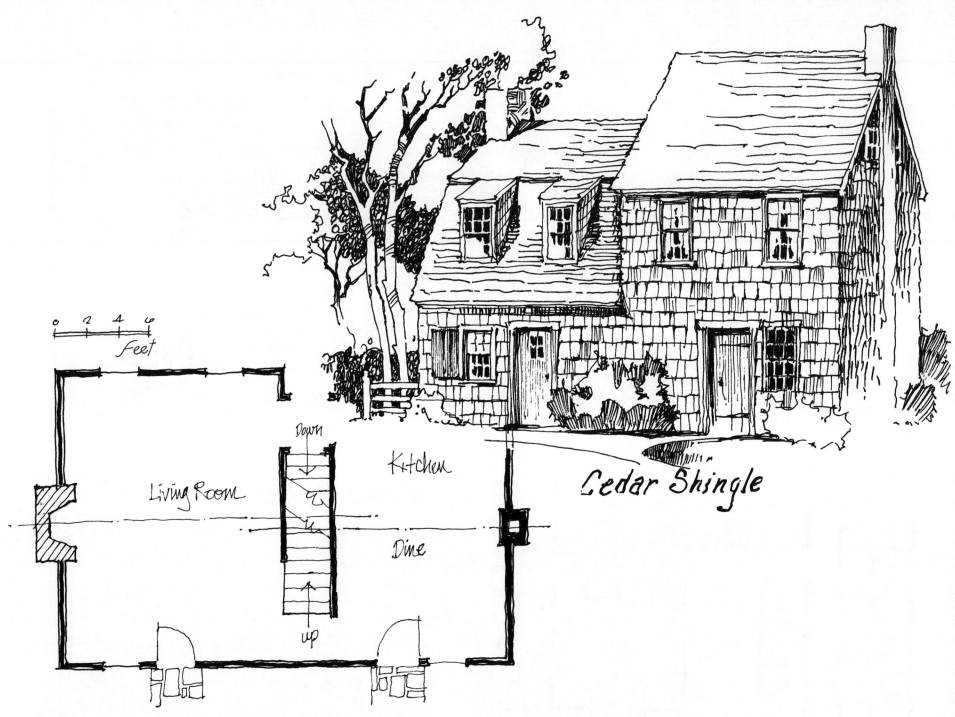

Feet

Living Room

Down

Kitchen

Dine

up

Cedar Shingle

138

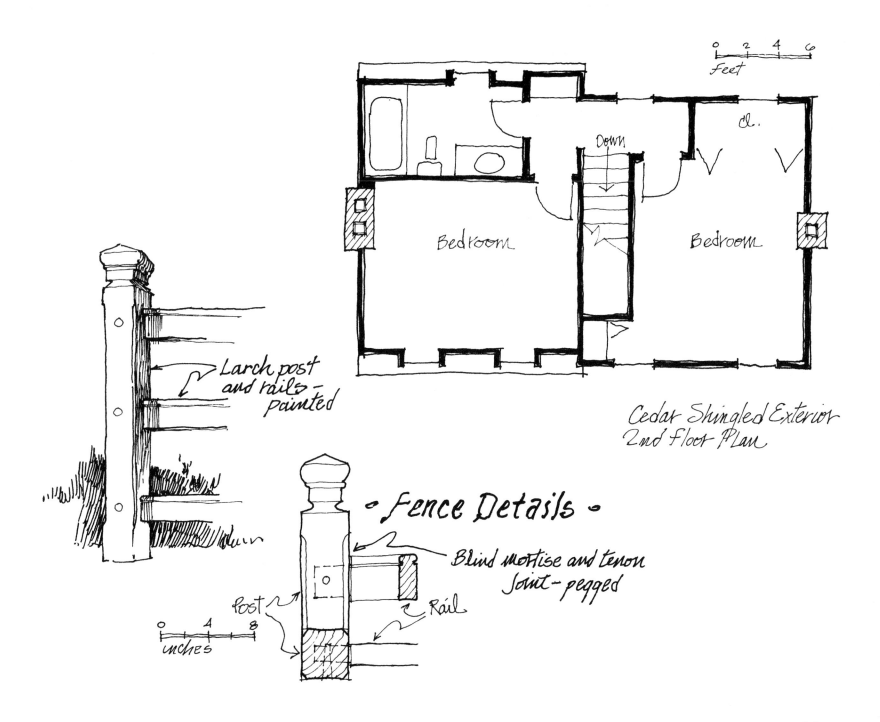

Larch post
and rails –
painted

Cedar Shingled Exterior
2nd floor Plan

Bedroom

Bedroom

Down

Cl.

0 2 4 6
Feet

• Fence Details •

Blind mortise and tenon
Joint – pegged

Post

Rail

0 4 8
inches

139

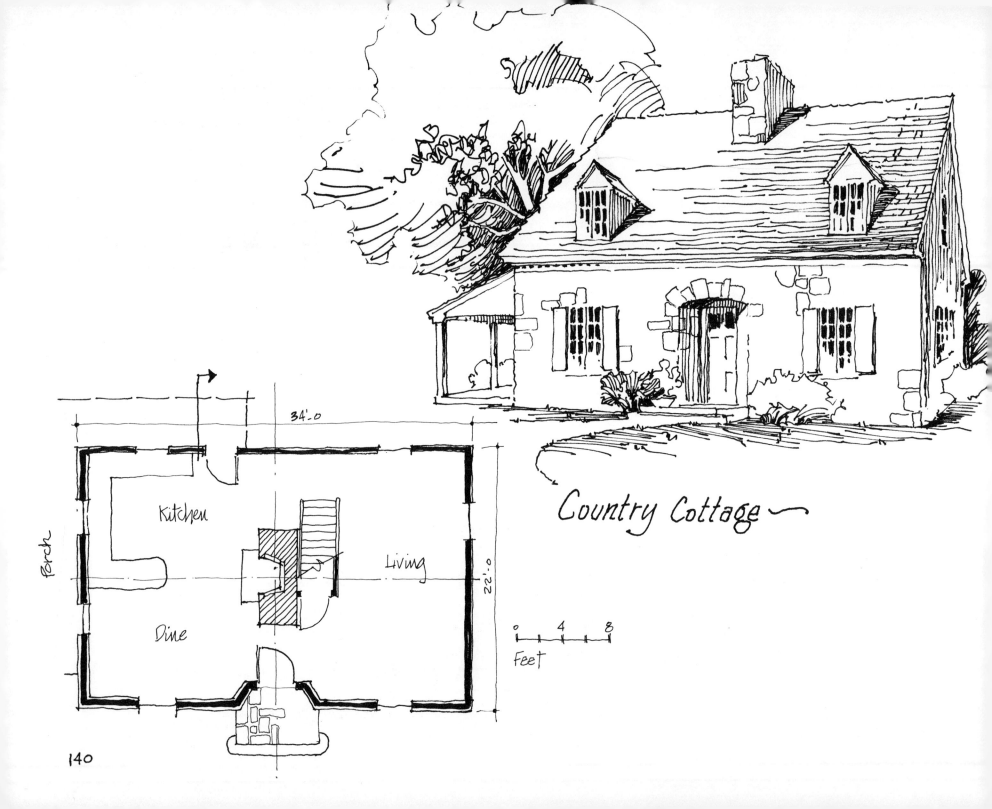

Country Cottage

34'-0

22'-0

Porch

Kitchen

Living

Dine

0   4   8
Feet

140

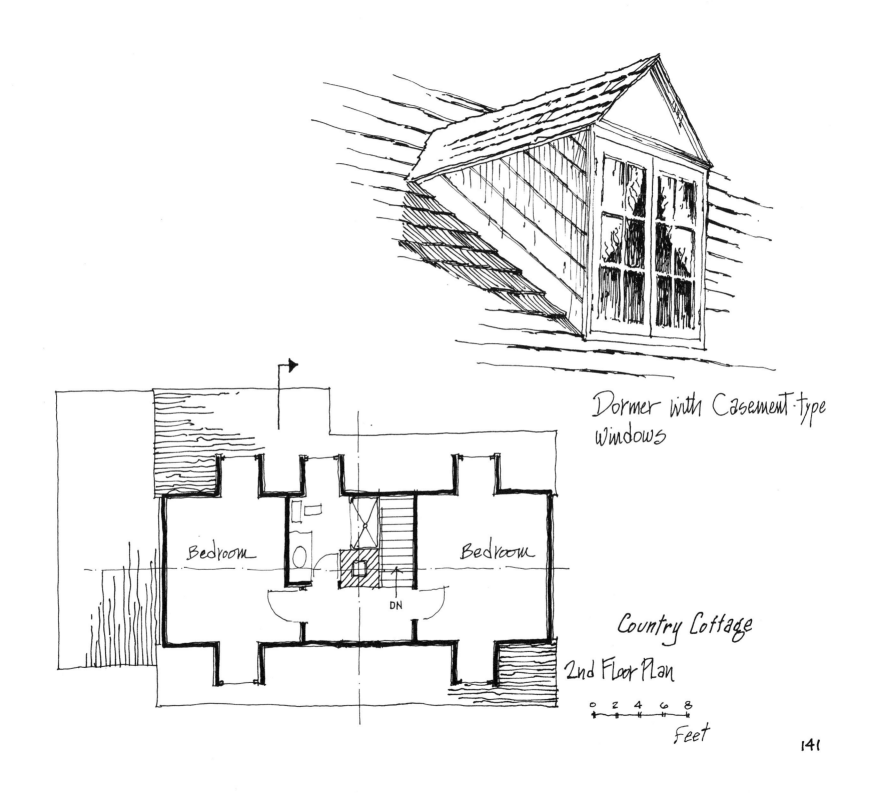

Dormer with Casement-type windows

Country Cottage

2nd Floor Plan

Bedroom

Bedroom

DN

0 2 4 6 8

Feet

141

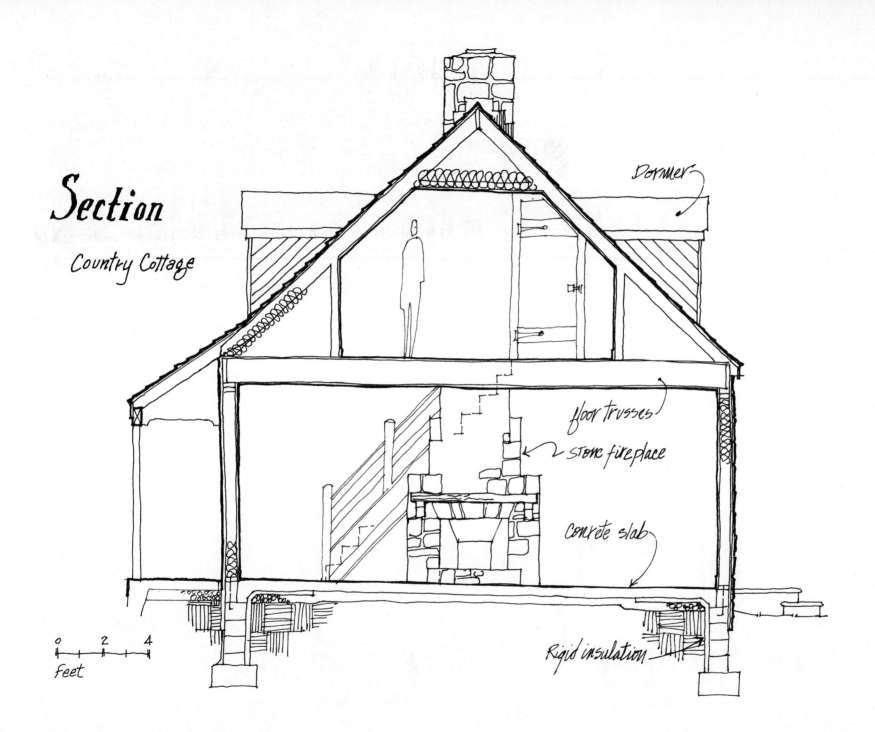

Section

Country Cottage

Dormer

floor trusses

stone fireplace

concrete slab

Rigid insulation

0   2   4
Feet

142

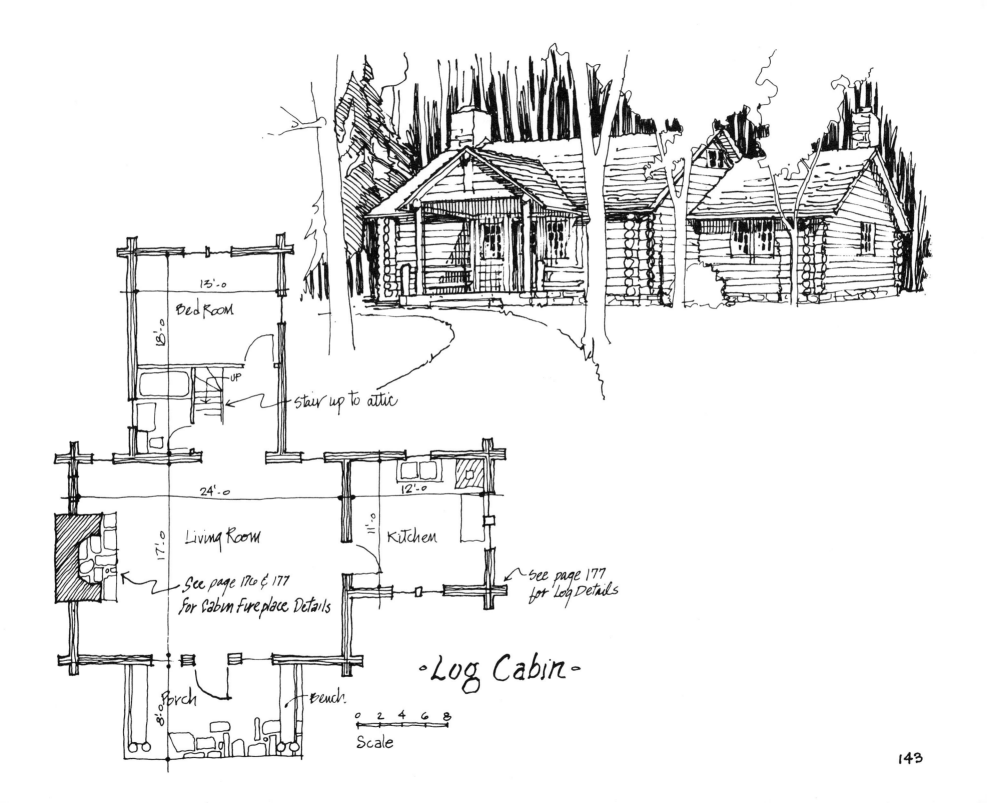

13'-0

BedRoom

18'-0

UP

stair up to attic

24'-0

12'-0

17'-0

11'-0

Living Room

Kitchen

See page 176 & 177
for Cabin Fireplace Details

See page 177
for Log Details

·Log Cabin·

8'-0

Porch

Bench

0 2 4 6 8
Scale

143

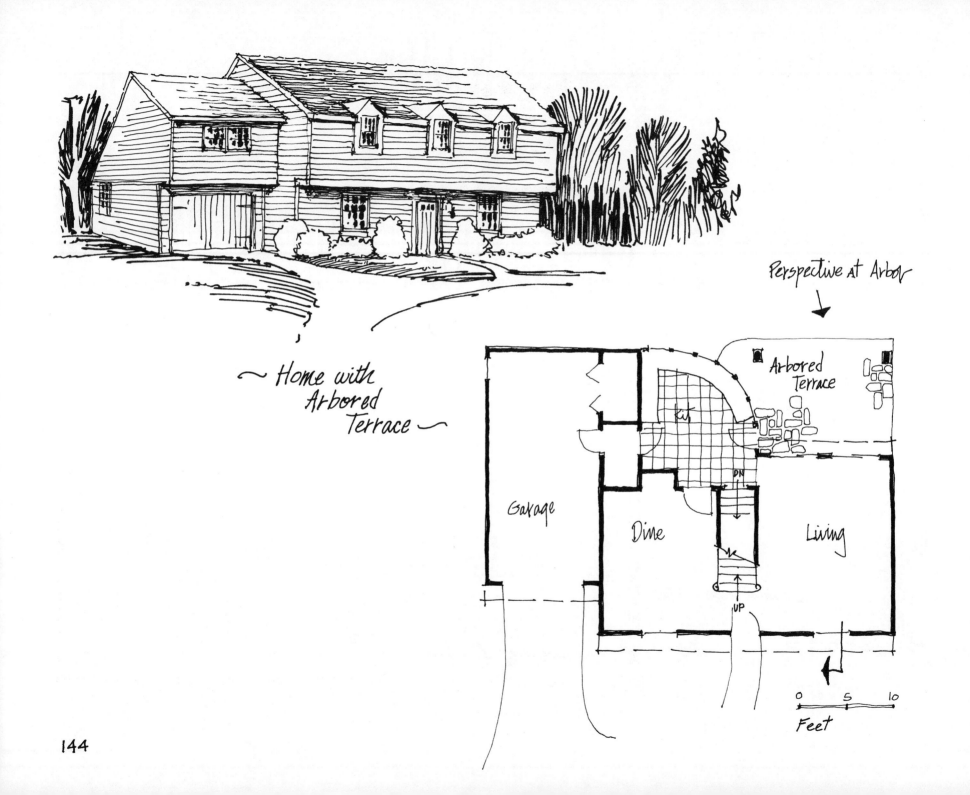

~ Home with
Arbored
Terrace ~

Perspective at Arbor

Arbored
Terrace

Garage

Kit

Dine

DN

UP

Living

0   5   10
Feet

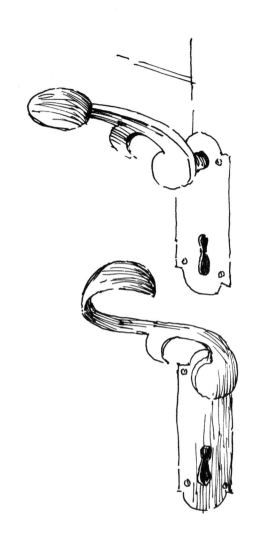

*Two Views of an old
Rim Lock from a
Pennsylvania
Farmhouse*

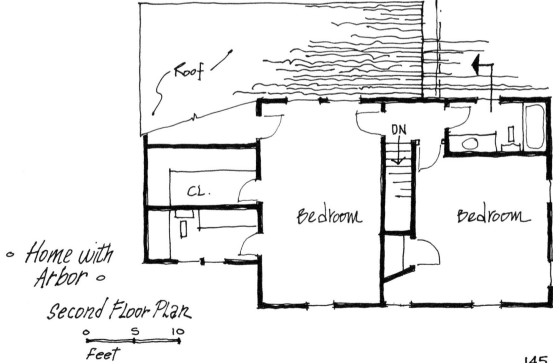

Roof

DN

CL.

Bedroom

Bedroom

∘ *Home with
Arbor* ∘

Second Floor Plan

0   5   10

Feet

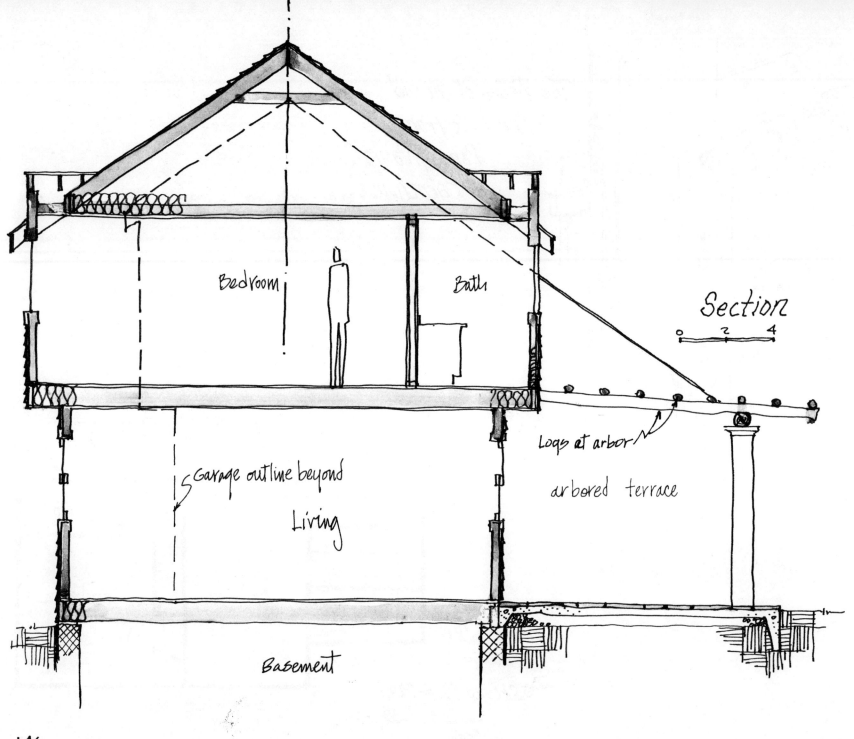

Bedroom

Bath

Section

0   2   4

Logs at arbor

arbored terrace

Garage outline beyond

Living

Basement

146

Arbored Terrace

147

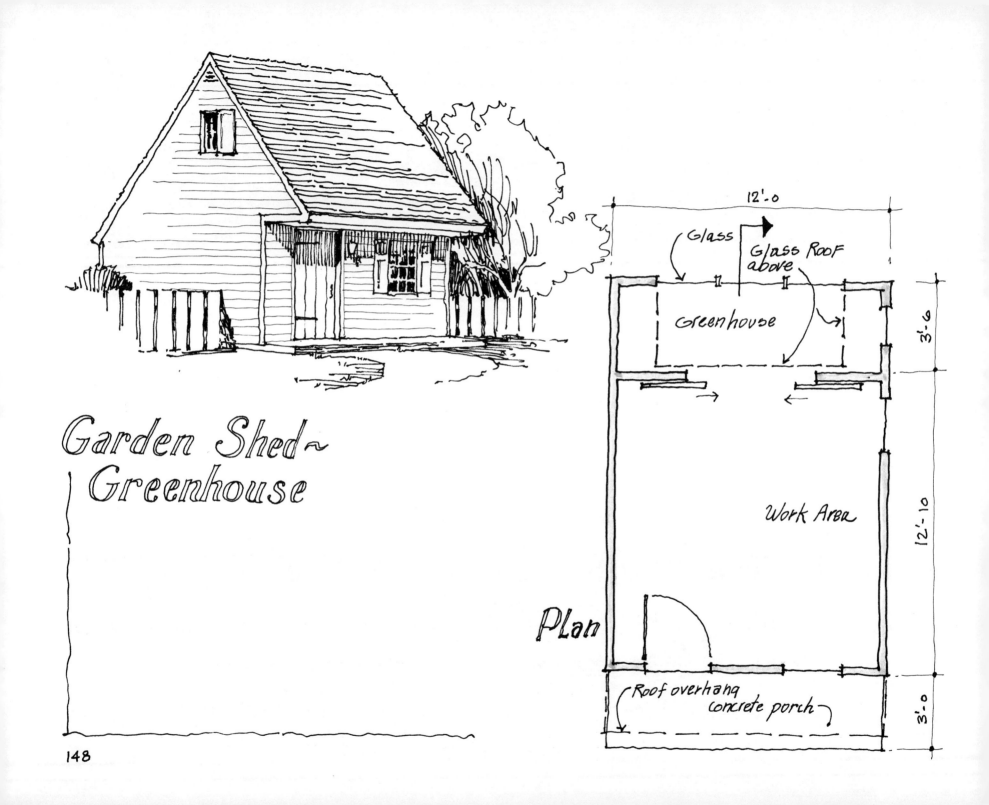

Garden Shed~
Greenhouse

12'-0

Glass

Glass Roof
above

Greenhouse

3'-6

Work Area

12'-10

Plan

Roof overhang

concrete porch

3'-0

148

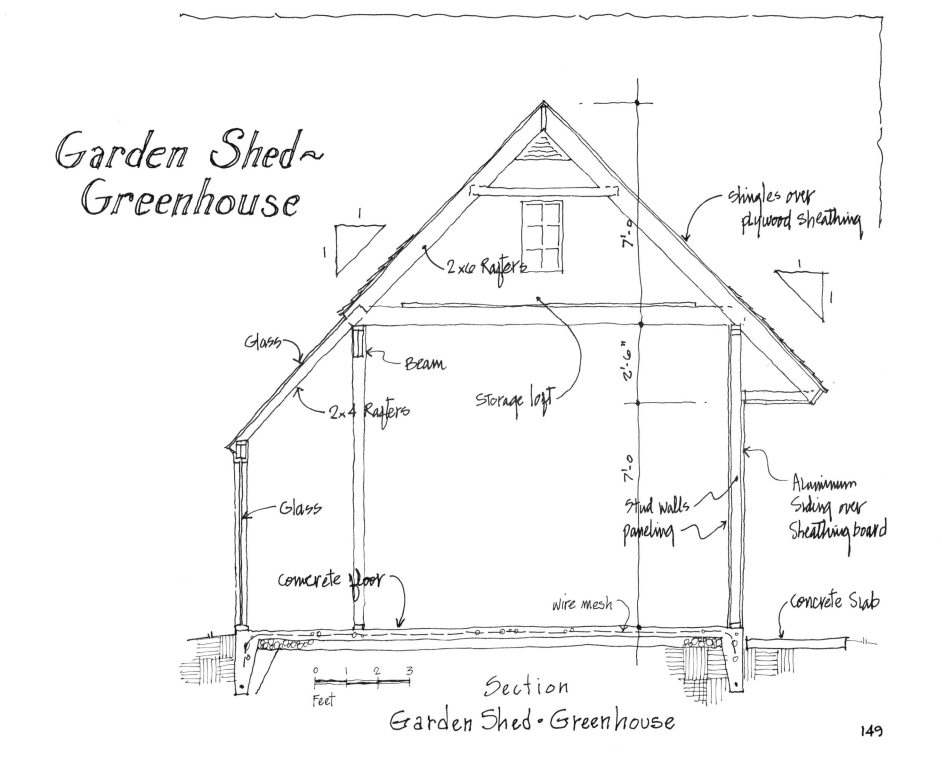

Garden Shed~
Greenhouse

shingles over
plywood sheathing

2×16 Rafters

7'-0

2'-9"

7'-0

Glass

Beam

2×4 Rafters

Storage loft

Stud walls
paneling

Aluminum
Siding over
Sheathing board

Glass

concrete floor

wire mesh

Concrete Slab

0   1   2   3
Feet

Section
Garden Shed • Greenhouse

149

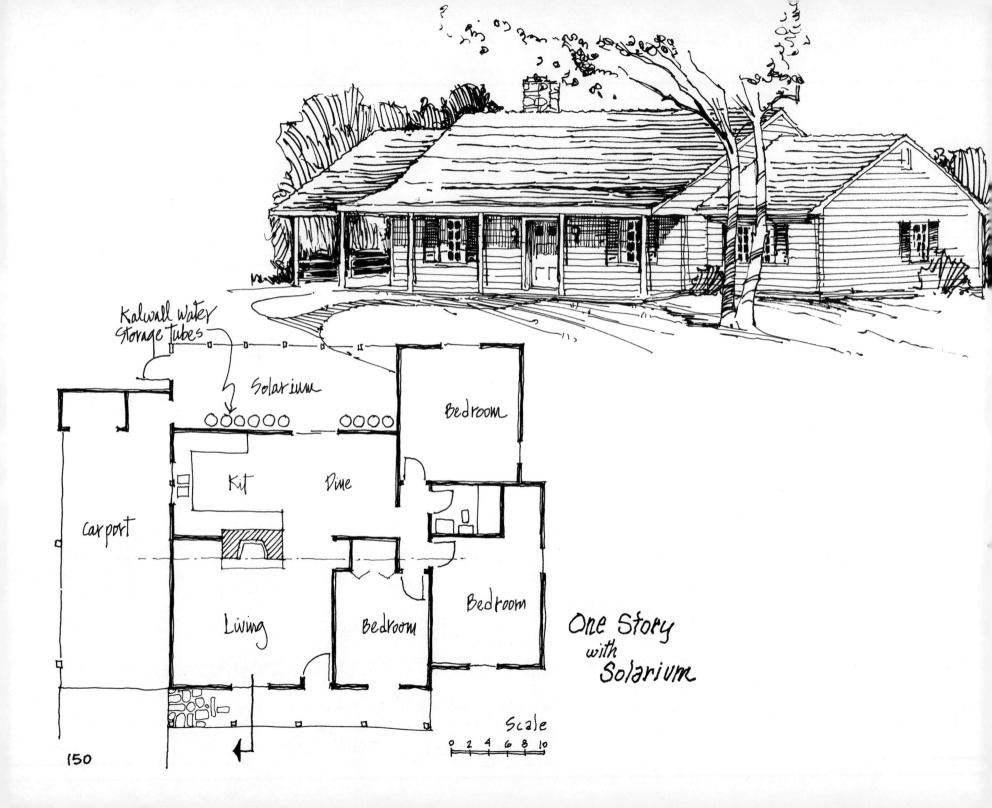

Kalwall water
storage tubes

Solarium

Carport

Kit

Dine

Bedroom

Living

Bedroom

Bedroom

One Story
with
Solarium

Scale
0 2 4 6 8 10

150

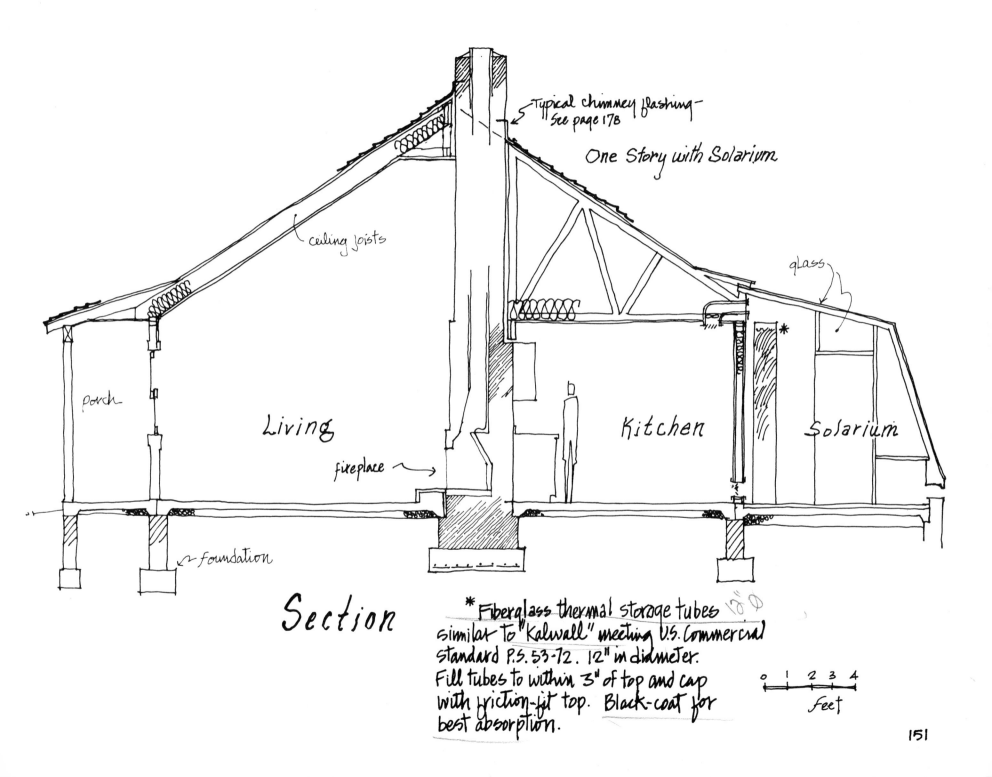

Typical chimney flashing—
See page 178

One Story with Solarium

ceiling joists

glass

porch

Living

Kitchen

Solarium

fireplace →

Section

foundation

* Fiberglass thermal storage tubes 12" Ø
similar to "Kalwall" meeting U.S. Commercial
standard P.S. 53-72. 12" in diameter.
Fill tubes to within 3" of top and cap
with friction-fit top. Black-coat for
best absorption.

0 1 2 3 4
Feet

151

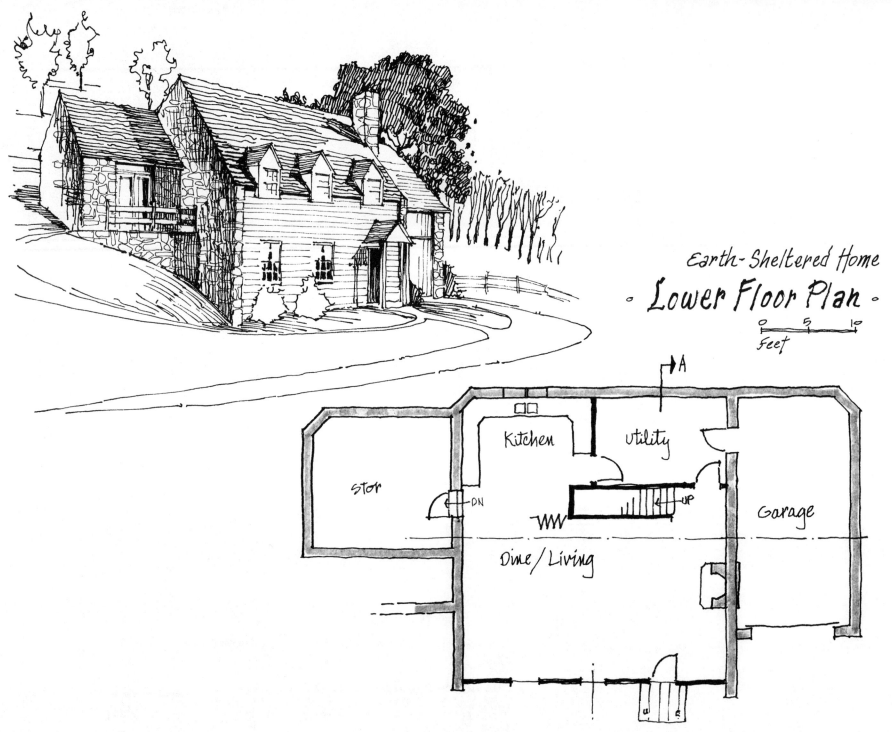

Earth-Sheltered Home
· Lower Floor Plan ·

0 5 10
Feet

A

Kitchen

Utility

Stor

DN

UP

Garage

Dine / Living

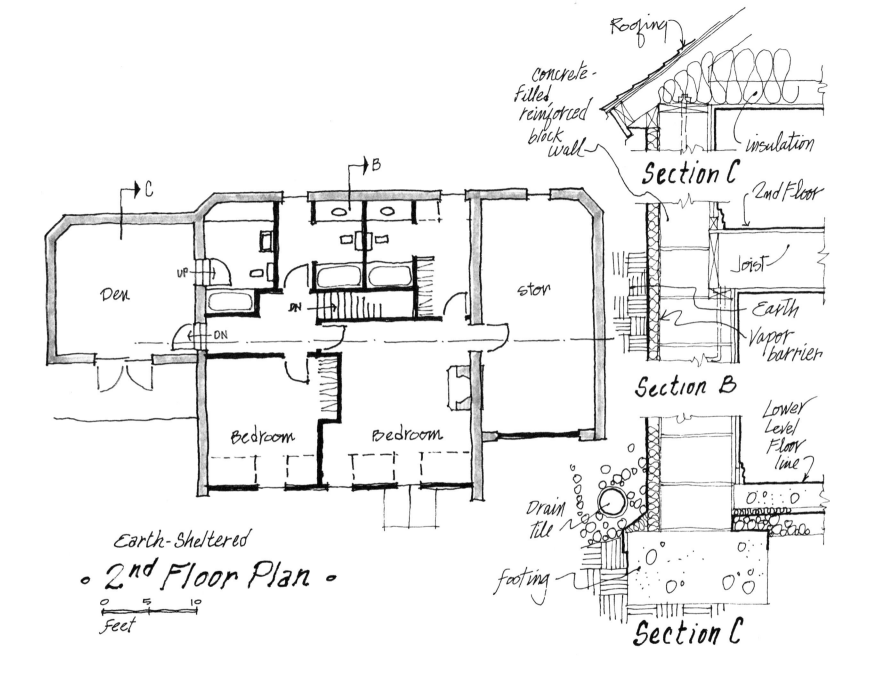

C

B

UP

DN

DN

Den

Bedroom

Bedroom

stor

Earth-Sheltered
· 2ⁿᵈ Floor Plan ·

0   5   10
Feet

Roofing

concrete-
filled
reinforced
block
wall

insulation

Section C

2nd Floor

Joist

Earth

Vapor
barrier

Section B

Lower
Level
Floor
line

Drain
tile

footing

Section C

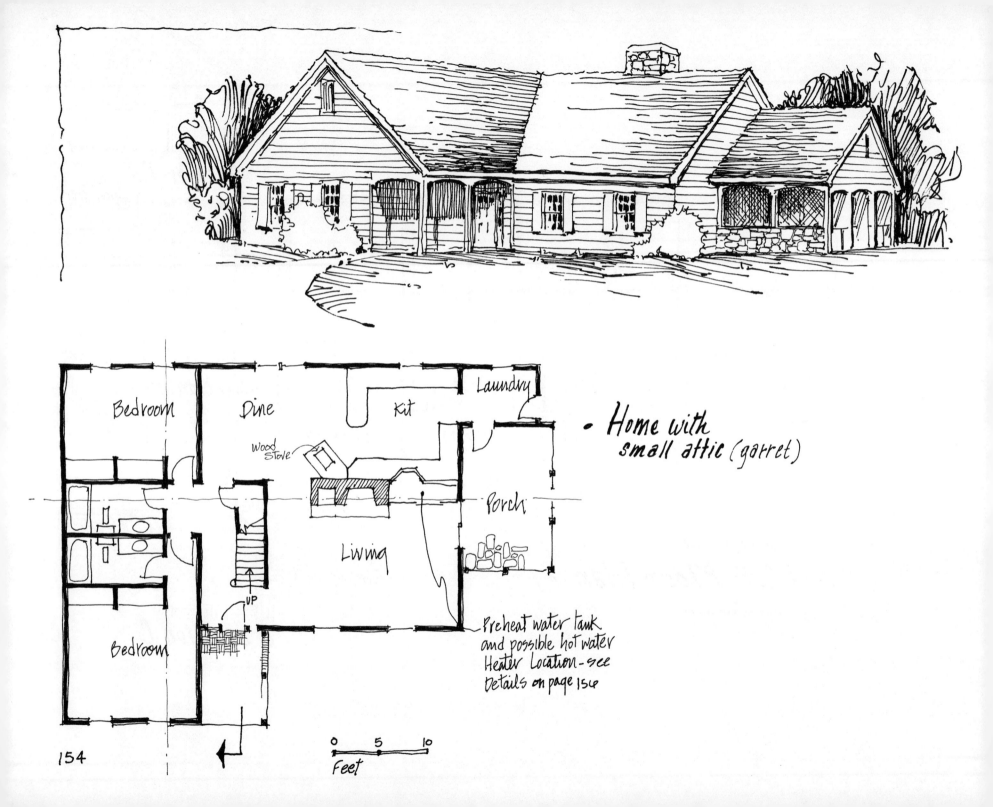

Bedroom

Dine

Kit

Laundry

Wood Stove

• Home with
  small attic (garret)

Porch

Living

UP

Bedroom

Preheat water tank
and possible hot water
Heater location—see
Details on page 156

0   5   10
Feet

154

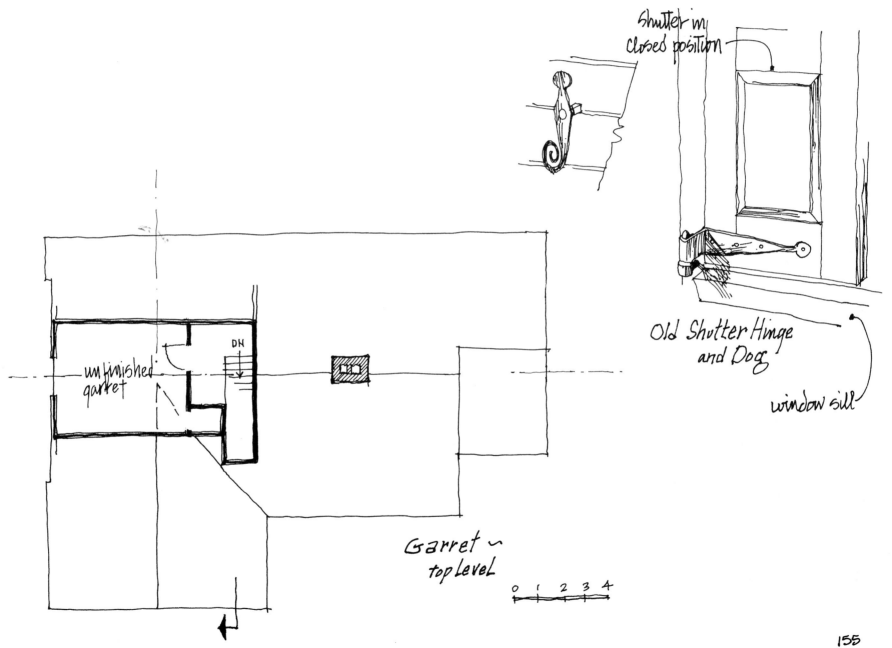

shutter in
closed position

DN

unfinished
garret

Old Shutter Hinge
and Dog

window sill

Garret
top level

0 1 2 3 4

155

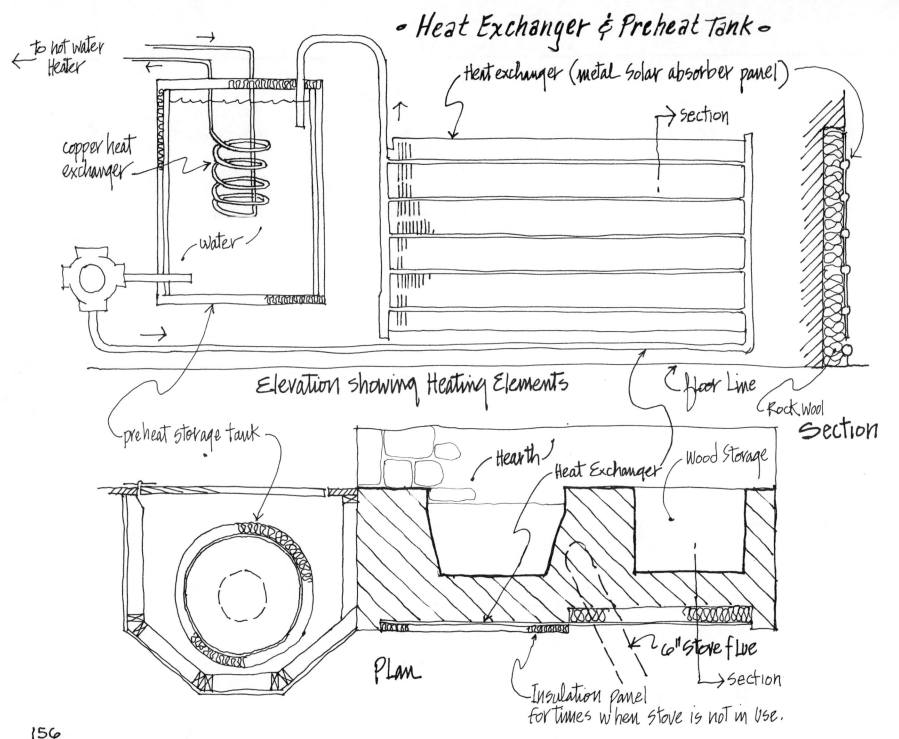

Heat Exchanger & Preheat Tank

to hot water heater

copper heat exchanger

water

Heat exchanger (metal solar absorber panel)

Section

Elevation showing Heating Elements

preheat storage tank

floor line

Rock wool

Section

Hearth

Heat Exchanger

Wood Storage

Plan

6" stove flue

Section

Insulation panel for times when stove is not in use.

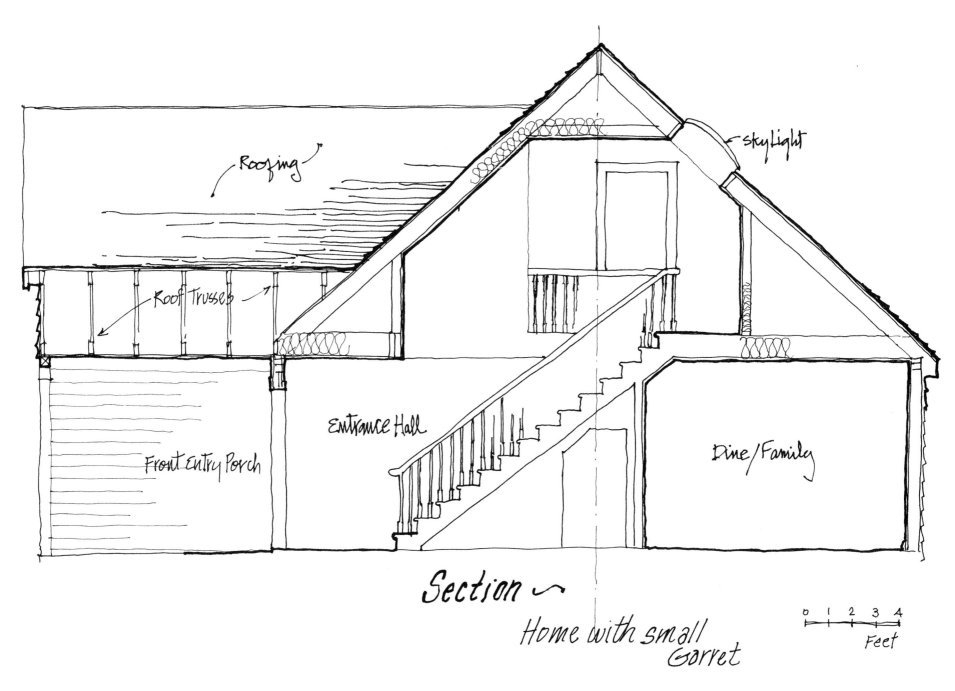

Roofing

Roof Trusses

Skylight

Front Entry Porch

Entrance Hall

Dine/Family

Section

Home with small Garret

0 1 2 3 4
Feet

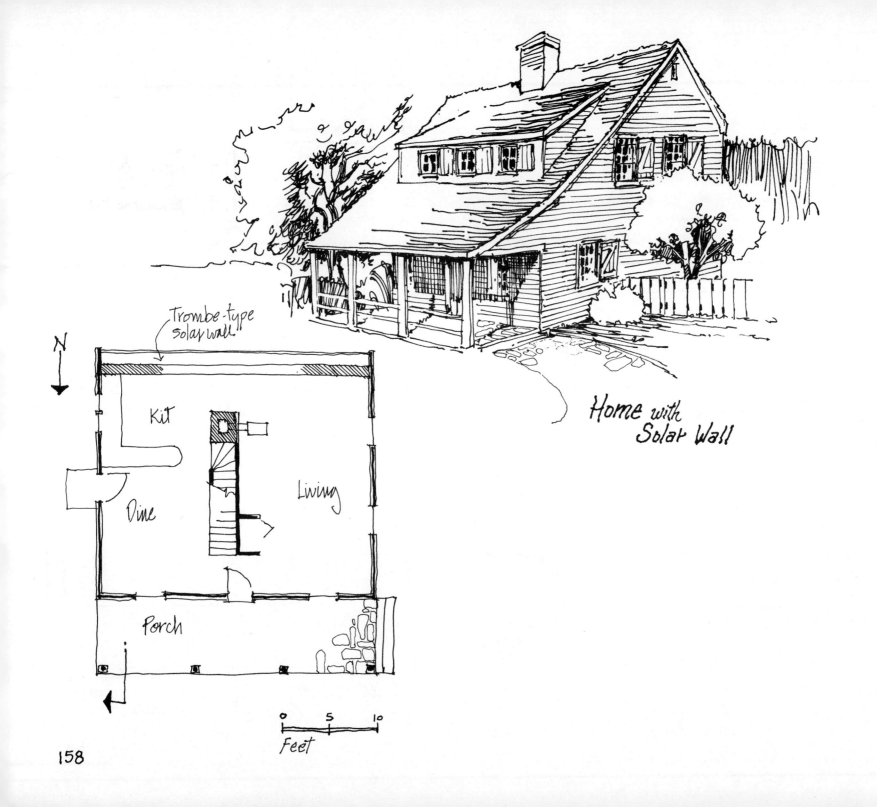

Trombe-type
solar wall

N

Kit

Dine

Living

Porch

Home with
Solar Wall

0   5   10
Feet

158

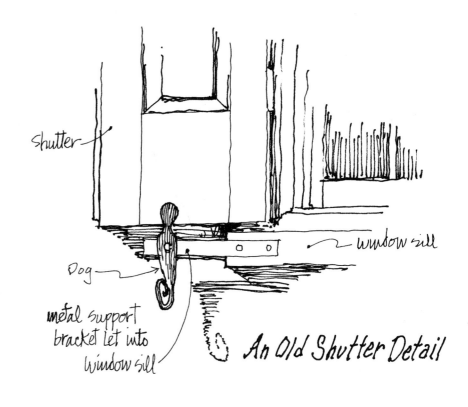

Shutter

window sill

Dog

metal support
bracket let into
window sill

An Old Shutter Detail

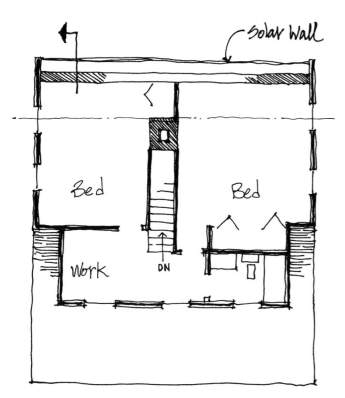

Solar Wall

Bed

Bed

Work

DN

2nd Floor •
Home with Solar Wall

0 2 4 6 8 10

Feet

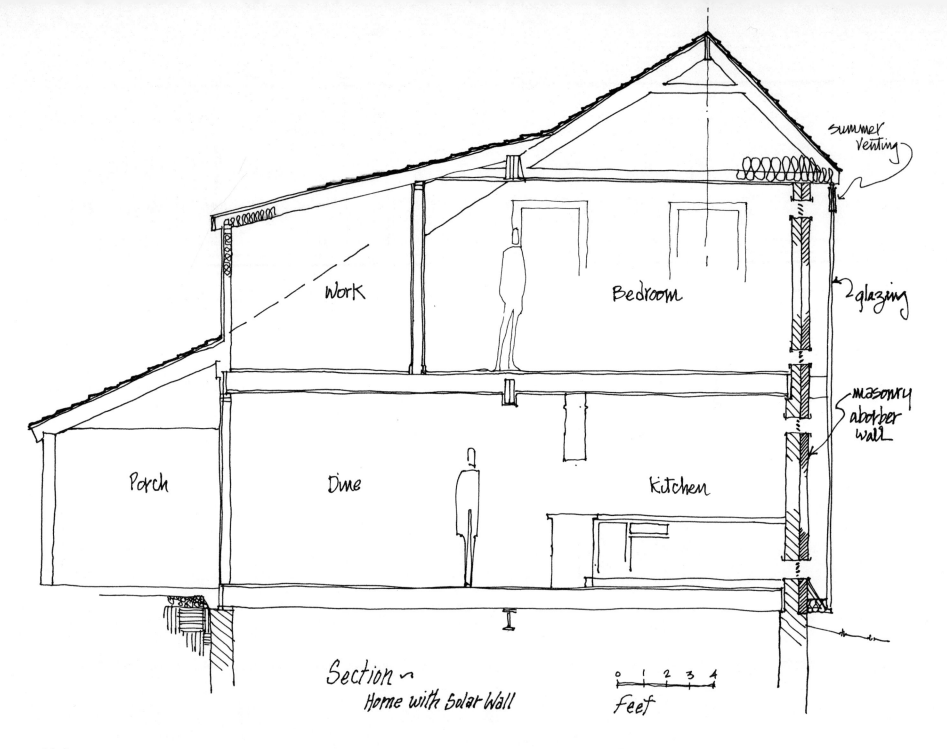

summer
venting

glazing

masonry
aborber
wall

Work

Bedroom

Porch

Dine

Kitchen

Section
Home with Solar Wall

0 1 2 3 4
Feet

160

- Home with
    Solar Heat -

- Ground Floor Plan -

Dine

DN

Living

Family

UP

North

0   5   10

161

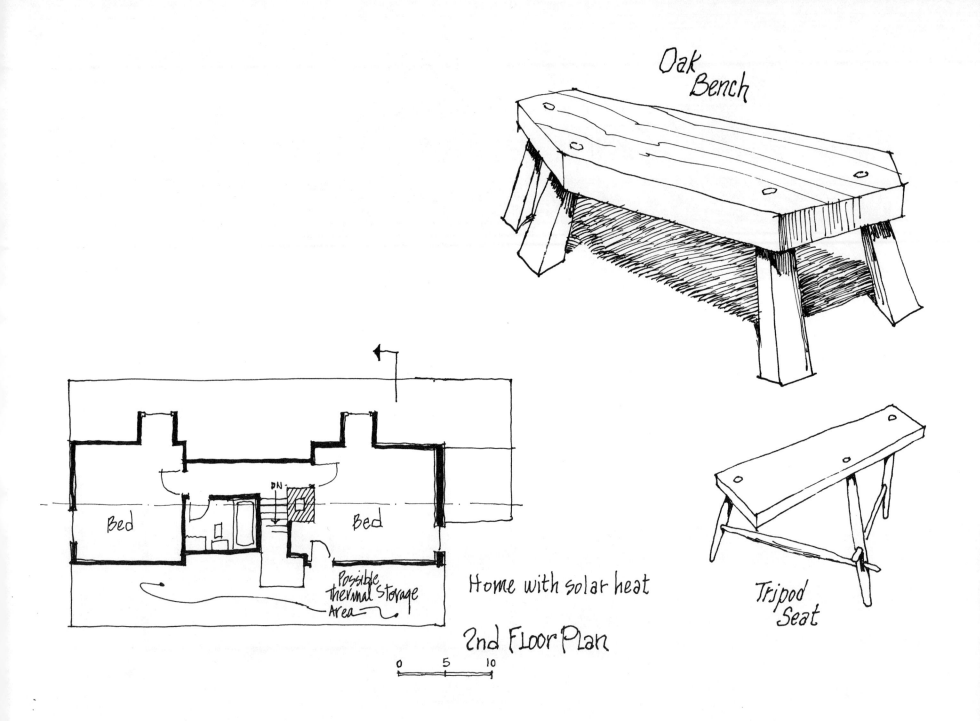

Oak Bench

Bed

DN

Possible thermal Storage Area

Bed

Home with solar heat

2nd Floor Plan

0   5   10

Tripod Seat

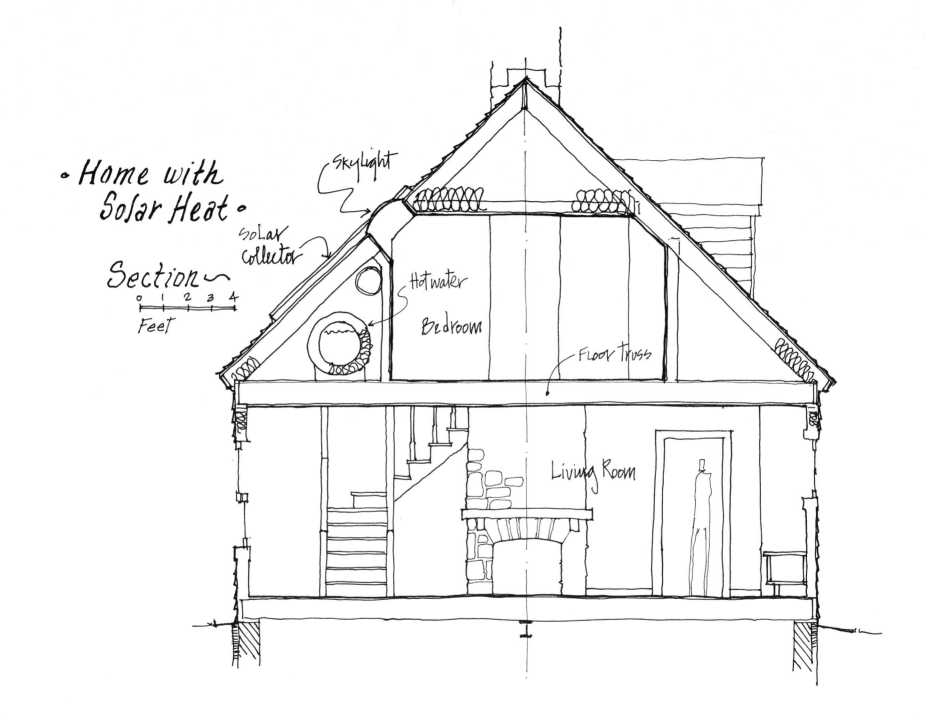

Home with
Solar Heat

Section

0 1 2 3 4
Feet

Skylight

solar
collector

Hot water

Bedroom

Floor Truss

Living Room

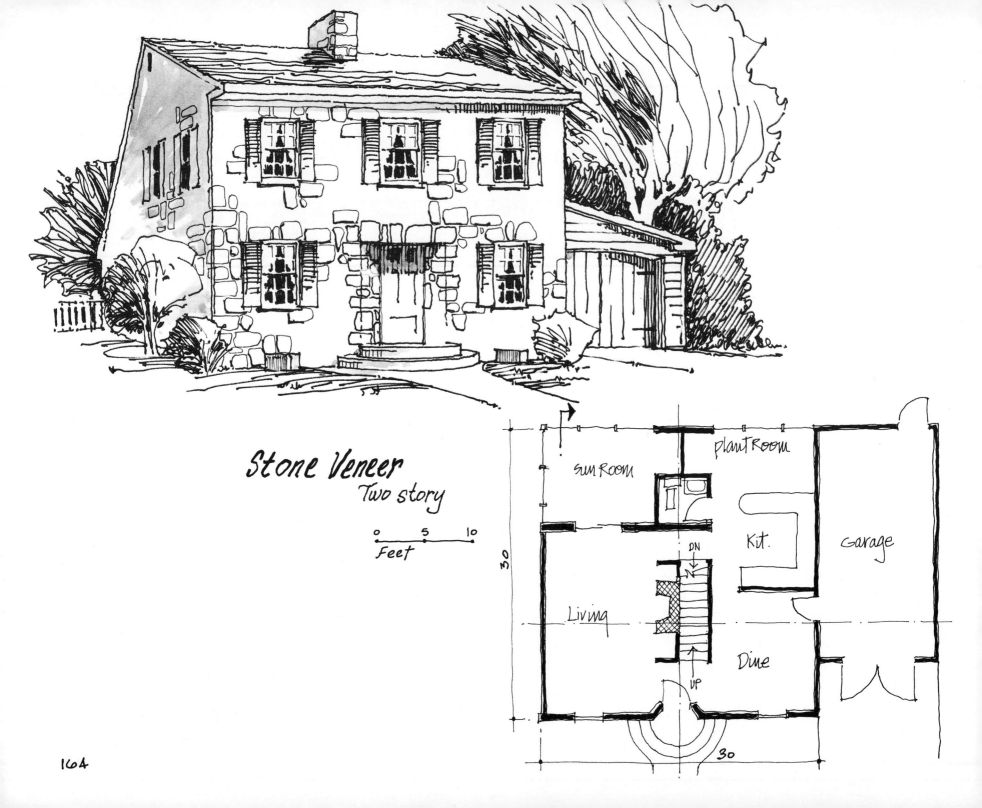

Stone Veneer

Two story

Feet
0   5   10

Sun Room

Plant Room

Kit.

Garage

Living

Dine

DN

UP

30

30

164

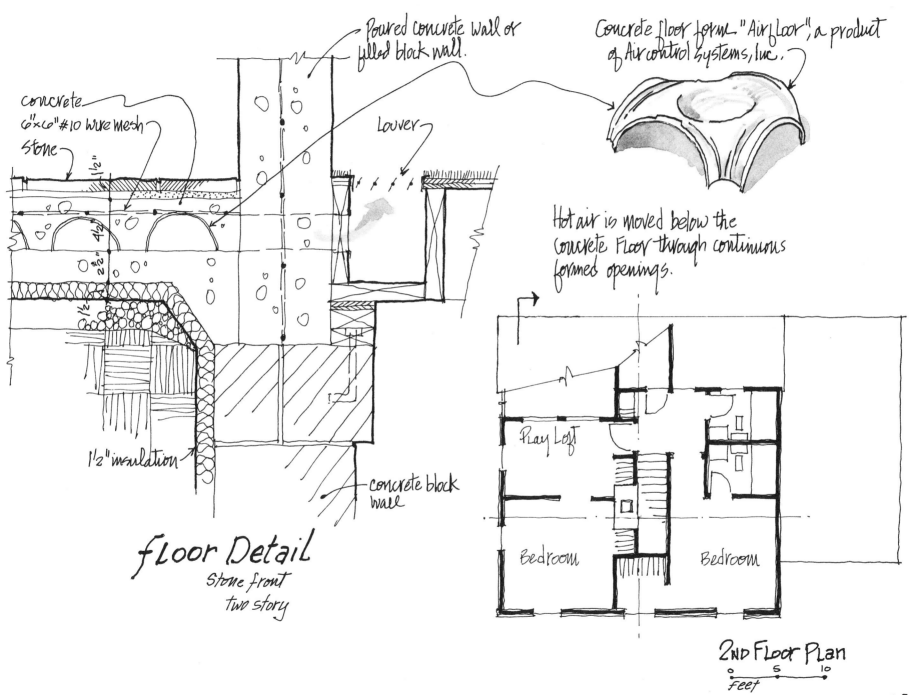

Poured concrete wall or filled block wall.

Concrete floor form "Air floor", a product of Air control Systems, Inc.

concrete
6"x6"#10 wire mesh
stone

Louver

Hot air is moved below the concrete floor through continuous formed openings.

1½"
2½"   4½"
1½"

1½" insulation

concrete block wall

floor Detail
Stone front
two story

Play Loft

Bedroom

Bedroom

2nd Floor Plan

0   5   10
feet

165

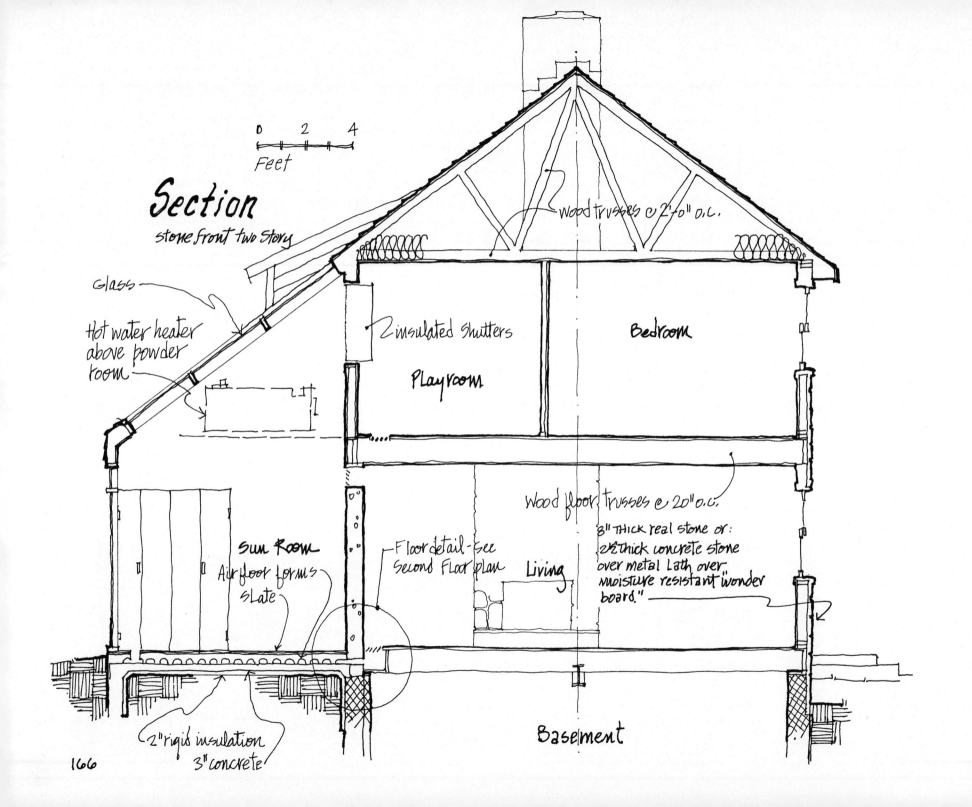

0 2 4

Feet

Section
stone front two story

Wood trusses @ 2'-0" O.C.

Glass

Hot water heater
above powder
room

2 insulated shutters

Playroom

Bedroom

Sun Room
Air floor forms
slate

Floor detail—see
second floor plan

Living

Wood floor trusses @ 20" O.C.

8" thick real stone or:
2½" thick concrete stone
over metal lath over
moisture resistant "wonder
board."

2" rigid insulation
3" concrete

Basement

166

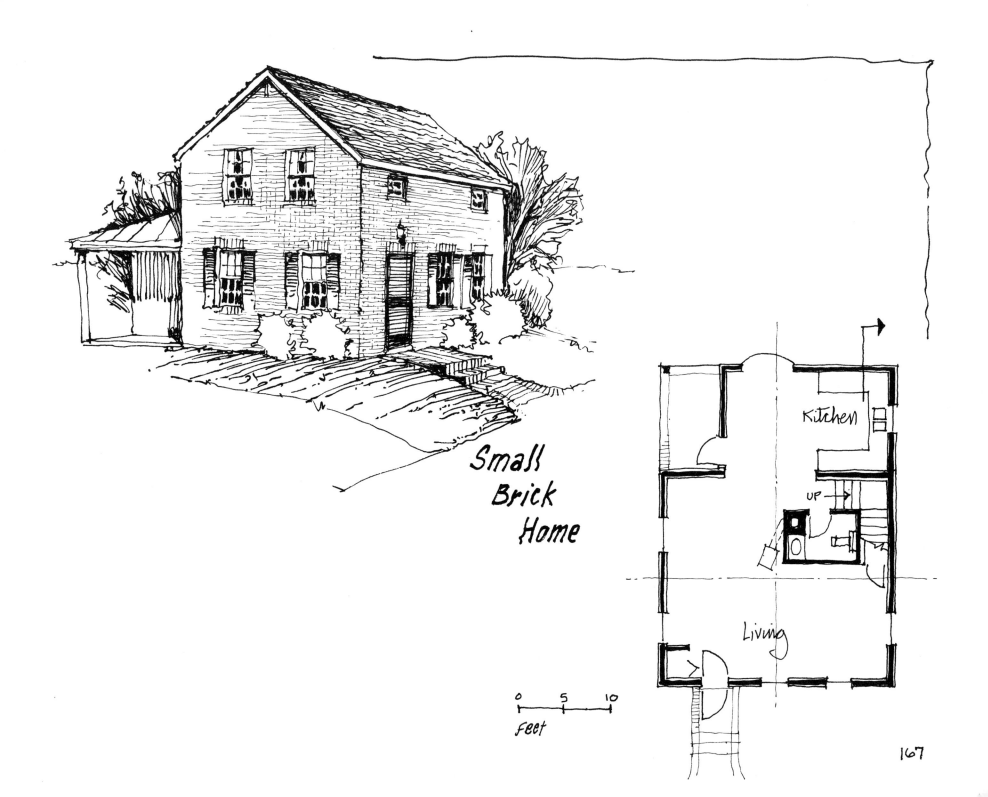

Small
Brick
Home

Kitchen

UP

Living

0   5   10
Feet

167

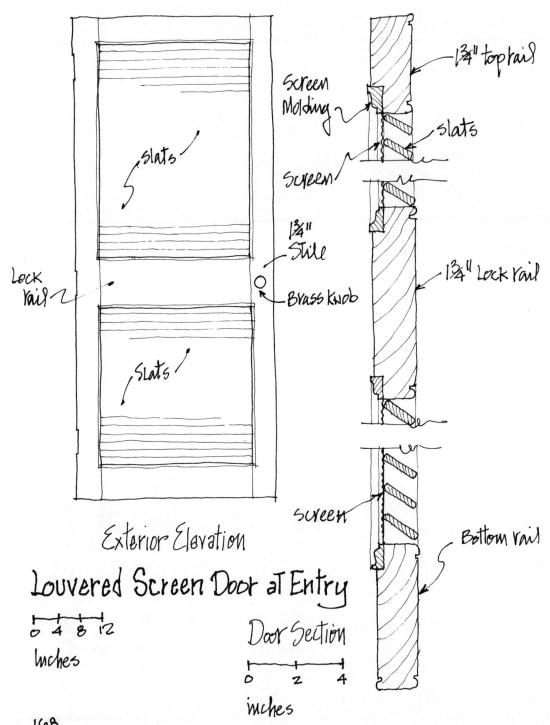

Screen
Molding

slats

Screen

1¾"
Stile

Brass knob

Lock
rail

Slats

slats

1¾" top rail

slats

1¾" Lock rail

screen

Bottom rail

Exterior Elevation

Louvered Screen Door at Entry

0 4 8 12
Inches

Door Section

0   2   4
inches

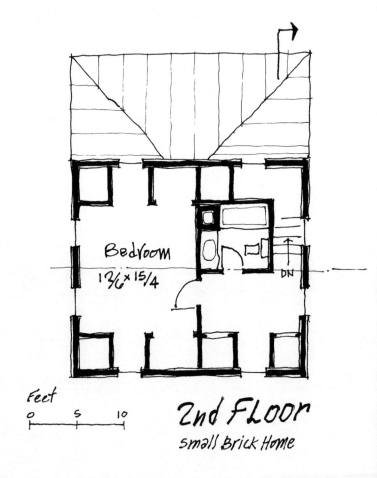

Bedroom
13/6 × 15/4

DN

Feet
0   5   10

2nd Floor
small Brick Home

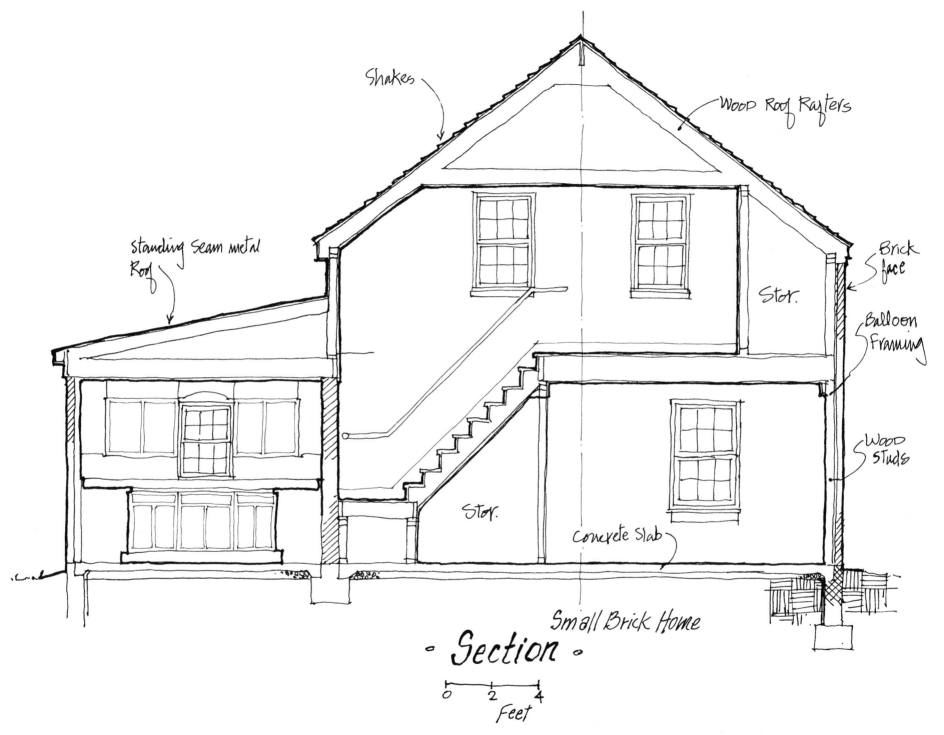

Shakes

Wood Roof Rafters

standing Seam metal Roof

Brick face

Stor.

Balloon Framing

Stor.

Wood Studs

Concrete Slab

Small Brick Home

- Section -

0   2   4

Feet

169

VIII Fireplaces

There is nothing nicer than sitting in front of a masonry fireplace, warming oneself by the bright cozy log fire. But fireplaces take wood - lots of it, and yes, most of the heat goes up the chimney. The fireplace of today should be small - no wider than three feet if economy of wood is important. The Rumford design described herein is an improvement on heating efficiency but may tend to throw more smoke into the house. The traditional fireplace is probably here to stay regardless of its shortcomings so keep in mind that the masonry area immediately adjacent thereto should be utilized as much as possible for heat exchangers, thermal storage and other heating flues.

Some Basic Dimensions

Round flue	Rectangular Flue	Depth A	Width B	height C
8	8½ × 8½	16	24	24
10	8½ × 13	16	28	24
10	8½ × 13	16	30	29
10	8½ × 13	16	32	29
12	13 × 13	16	36	29
12	13 × 13	16	40	29
12	13 × 13	16	42	32
15	13 × 13	18	48	32

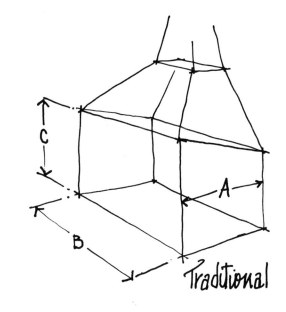

Traditional

Rumford

	Rectangular Flue	Depth A	Width B	height C
	8½ × 8½	8-12	24	24
	8½ × 13	10-12	28	27
	8½ × 13	12	30	29
	8½ × 13	12	32	32
	13 × 13	12-14	36	36
	13 × 13	14-16	40	38
	13 × 13	16	42	38

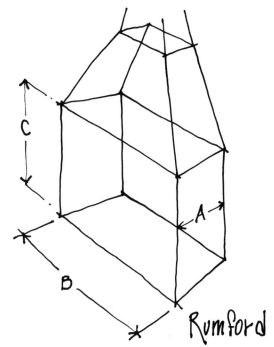

Rumford

171

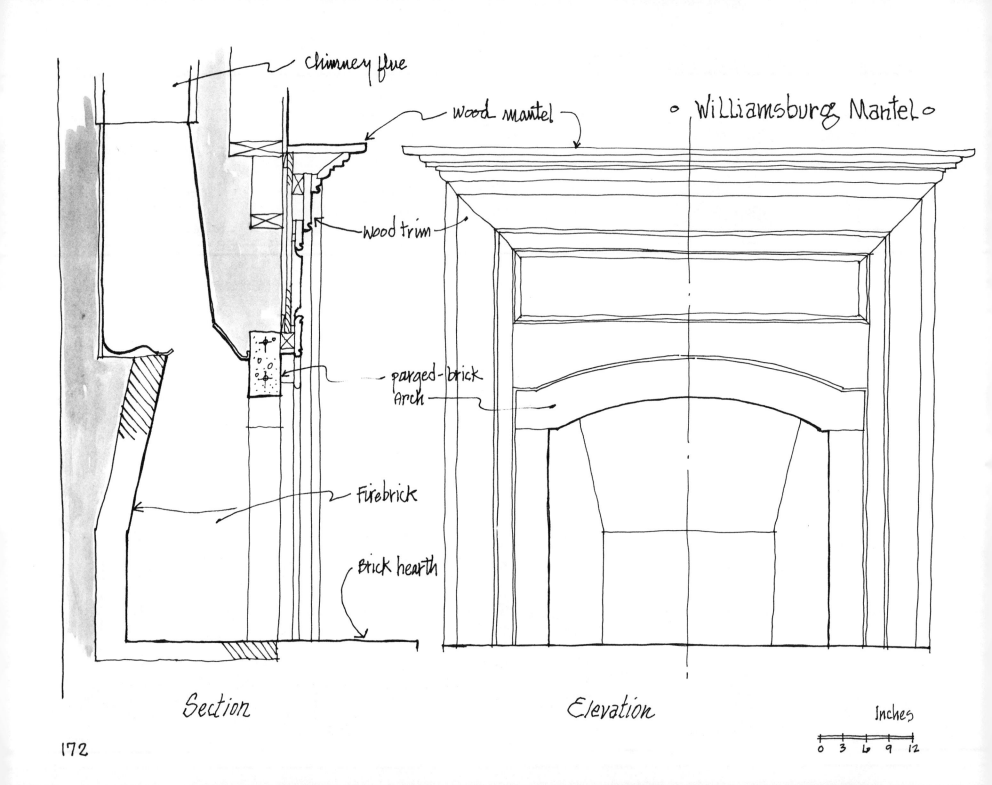

chimney flue

wood mantel

Williamsburg Mantel

wood trim

parged-brick Arch

Firebrick

Brick hearth

Section

Elevation

Inches

0 3 6 9 12

172

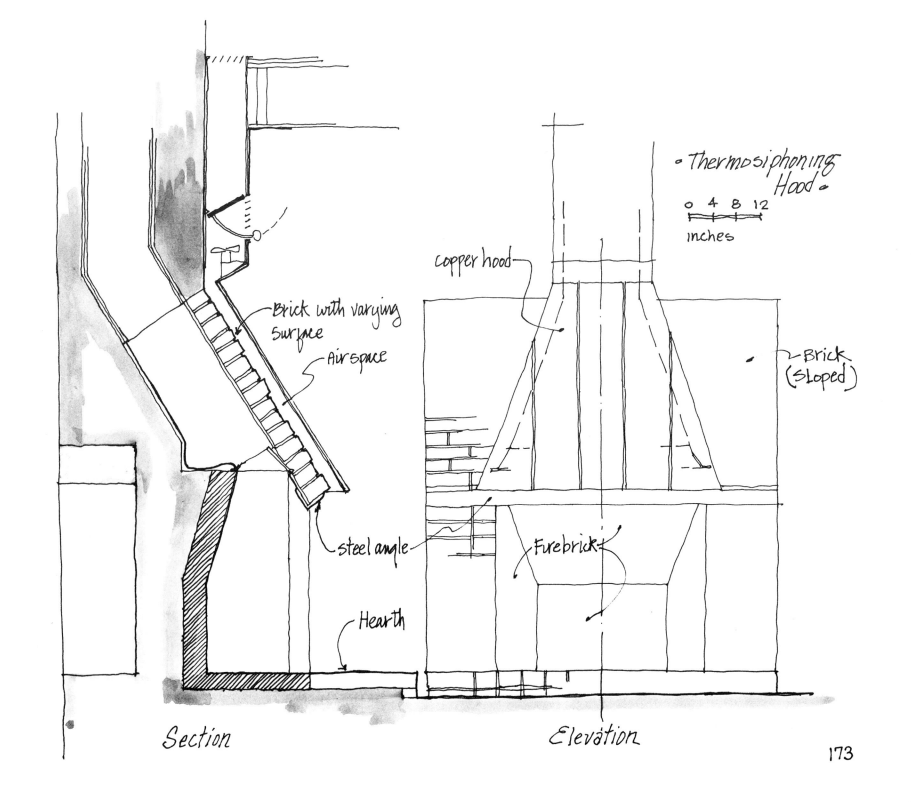

Brick with varying surface

Air space

steel angle

Hearth

Thermosiphoning Hood

0 4 8 12
inches

copper hood

Brick (Sloped)

Firebrick

Section

Elevation

173

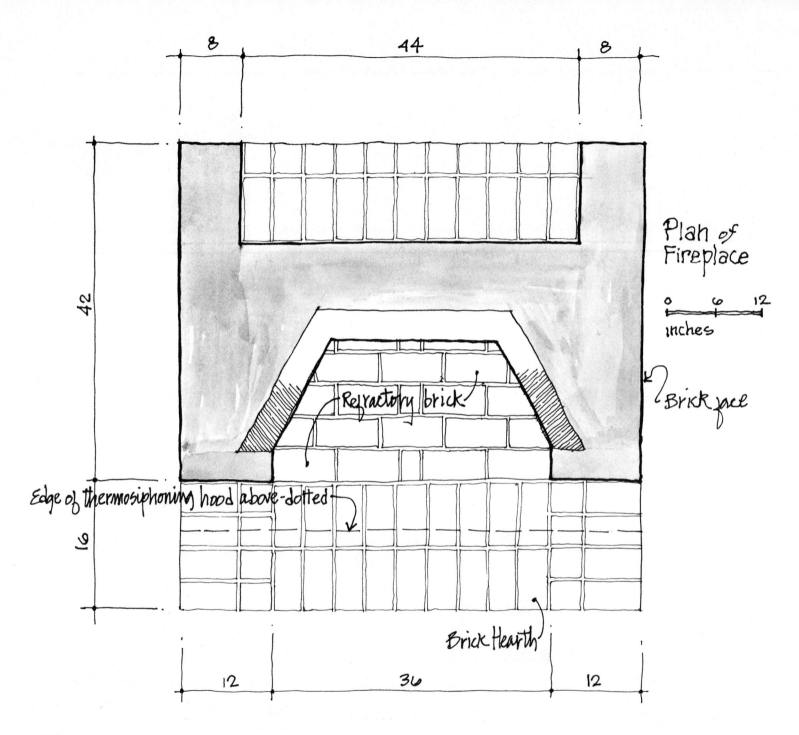

8   44   8

42

Plan of
Fireplace

0   6   12

inches

Refractory brick

Brick face

Edge of thermosiphoning hood above-dotted

16

Brick Hearth

12   36   12

174

° A Paneled Fireplace Wall °

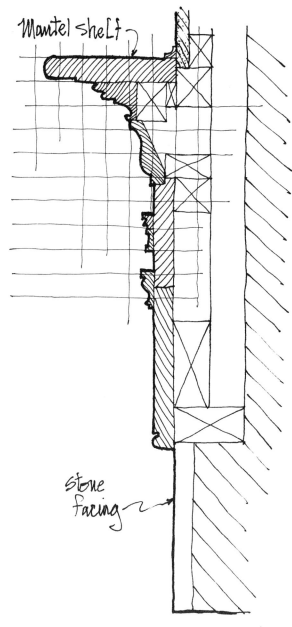

Mantel shelf

stone
facing

Section through Mantel

0   2   4

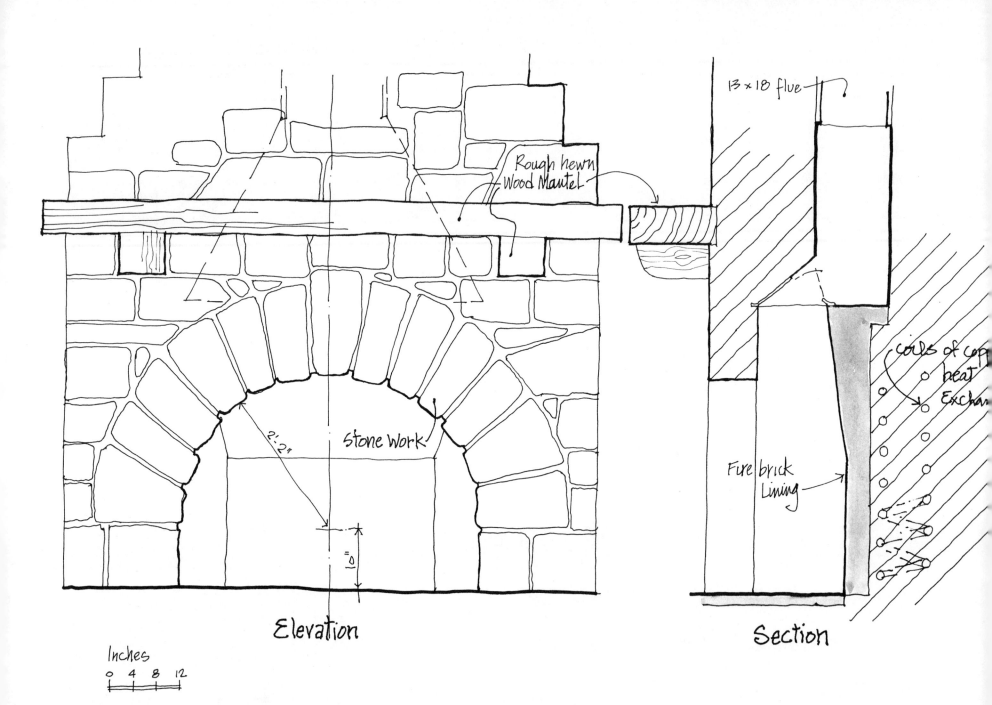

Rough hewn
Wood Mantel

13 × 18 flue

Stone Work

2'-2"

coils of cop
heat
Excha

Fire brick
Lining

Elevation

Section

Inches
0   4   8   12

Fireplace at Log Cabin

176

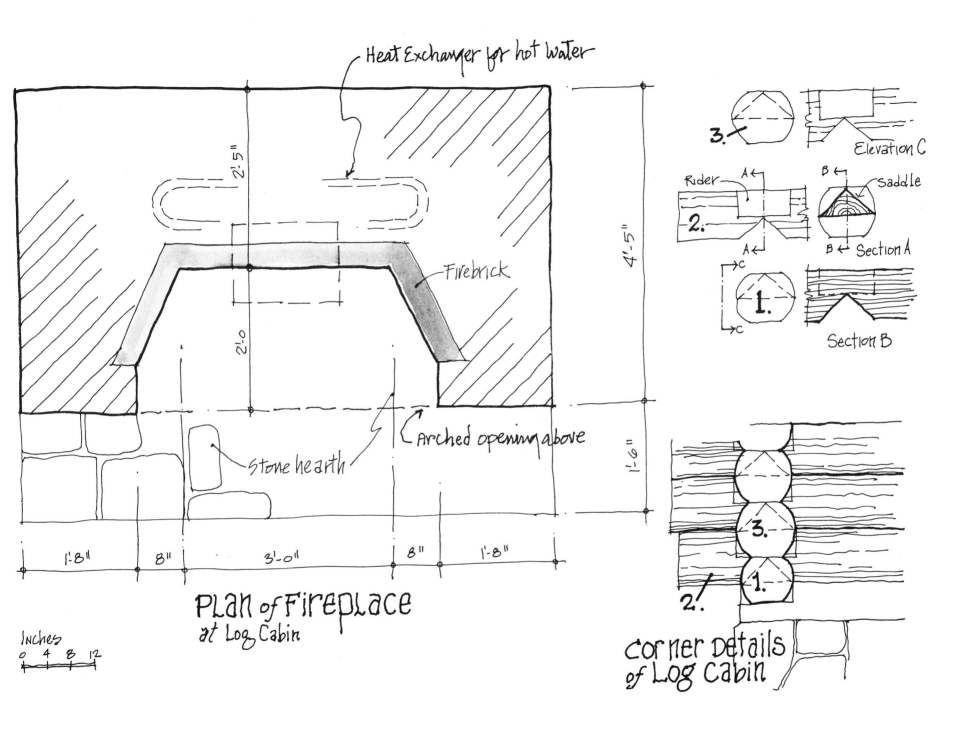

Heat Exchanger for hot water

2'-5"

4'-5"

2'-0"

Firebrick

1'-6"

Arched opening above

Stone hearth

1'-8"   8"   3'-0"   8"   1'-8"

PLAN of FIREPLACE
at Log Cabin

Inches
0 4 8 12

3.

Elevation C

Rider   A

Saddle

2.

B

Section A

C

1.

C

Section B

3.

2.

1.

Corner Details
of Log Cabin

177

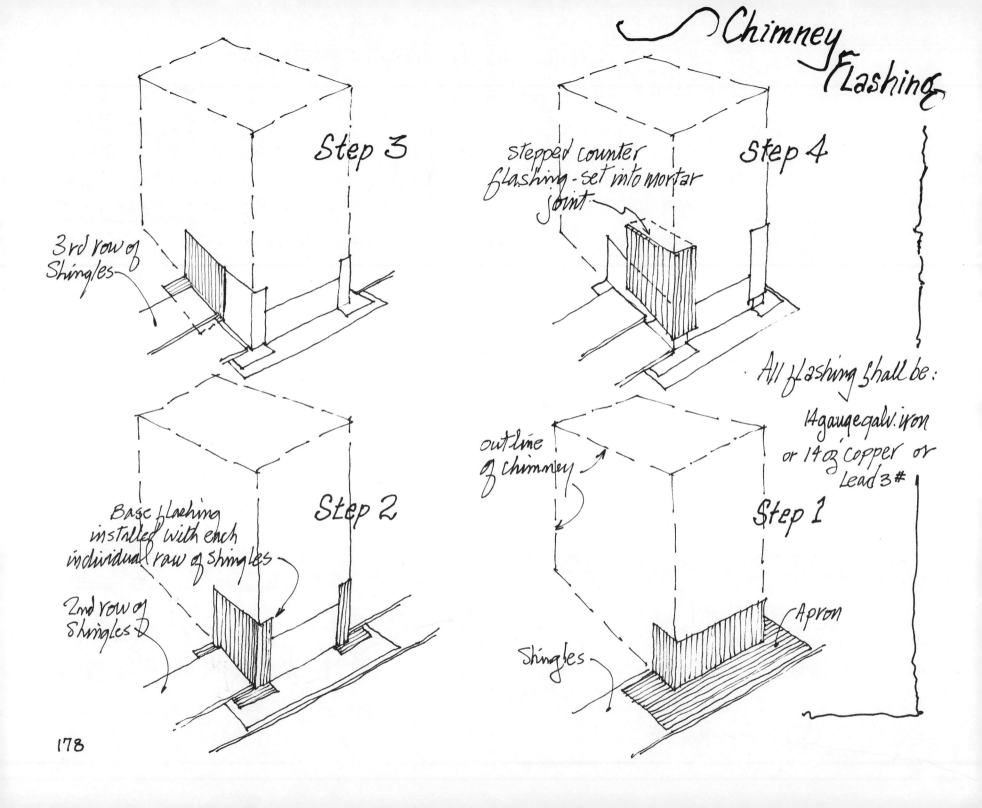

Chimney Flashing

Step 3

3rd row of Shingles

Step 4

stepped counter flashing - set into mortar joint.

All flashing shall be:

14 gauge galv. iron or 14 oz. copper or Lead 3#

Step 2

Base flashing installed with each individual row of shingles

2nd row of Shingles

Step 1

outline of chimney

Shingles

Apron

178

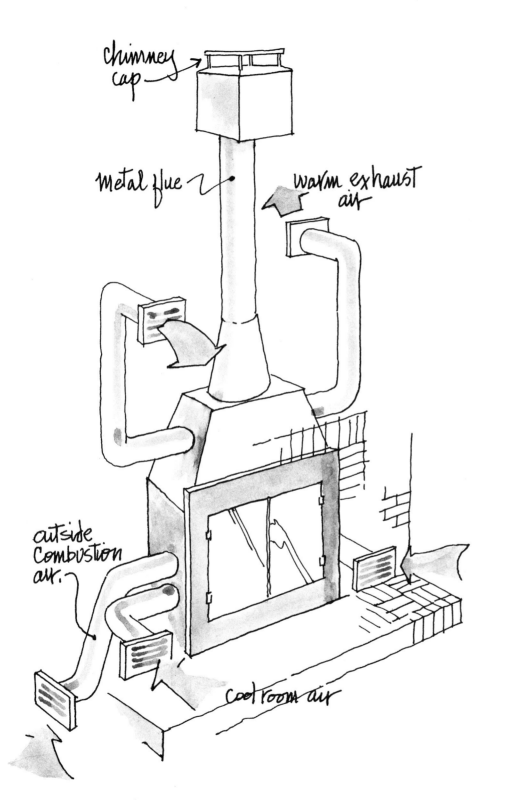

chimney cap

metal flue

warm exhaust air

outside combustion air.

cool room air

Prebuilt Metal Fireplaces

Prebuilt metal fireplaces are sometimes the most practical application for a given home design. The best ones are air circulating. Cool air is drawn in at the bottom, heated and released through grilles at the top of the wall. Some, like the one shown, use outside combustion air saving the warmer room air from being drawn up the flue.

IX Wood Stoves

Americans still cherish the idea of being independent. The Arabs of late, have caused us to reconsider our energy future and turn back to our original fuel source—the tree. Wood is still one of the good fuels that we can produce ourselves. And it's a great feeling to sit next to the stove and get as hot as we want. Electricity, gas, and oil are clean and less troublesome but wood is still the cheapest.

The stoves of today attempt to extract every BTU possible from a log. Some of them are quite good at it. A little understanding of draft control and proper maintenance has made wood heat worth the trouble.

Combustion

There are 3 stages of combustion:

1. The wood is heated to the point where moisture is evaporated and driven off.

2. Volatile matter is vaporized at 500°F. The wood begins to break down chemically. At 1100°F the vapors burn. This high temperature must be maintained in order to obtain an efficient fire.

3. After the volatile gases have been released, the remaining product is charcoal which burns at temperatures above 1100°F.

A supply of oxygen and fuel are necessary for combustion. A fire will rob the room of oxygen. If a home has been built "tightly", additional room or house air will be needed for both the occupants and the fire.

3 Legged Jøtul stove — the door is stored below the stove when a "Franklin" effect is desired. When the door is in the closed position this stove becomes an "airtight."

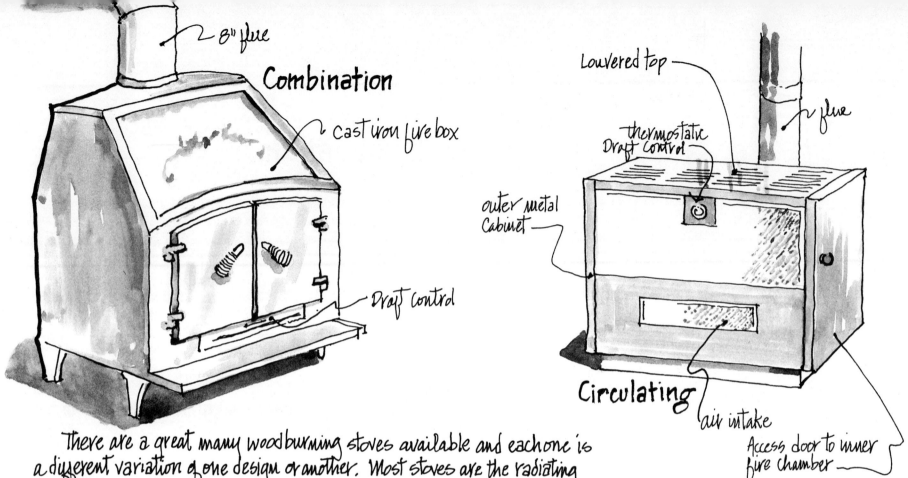

Combination

8" flue

cast iron fire box

Draft Control

Louvered top

thermostatic Draft Control

flue

outer metal Cabinet

Circulating

air intake

Access door to inner fire chamber

There are a great many woodburning stoves available and each one is a different variation of one design or another. Most stoves are the radiating type. Heat is transferred directly to the room by radiant energy. These stoves are single-wall units and are made of sheet metal, steel or cast iron. The old 'pot-belly' stove is an example.

Circulating stoves are another category. These units are double-walled with an inner combustion chamber of cast iron or welded steel and firebrick. The outer covering is made of sheet metal which promotes the flow of air over the inner firebox. The outer covering stays cooler than the inner chamber lessening the chance of skin burns and allowing smaller clearances.

A third category defined by the National Association of Mutual Insurance Companies is the combination stove. These units combine a radiating Franklin stove with the closed airtight design.

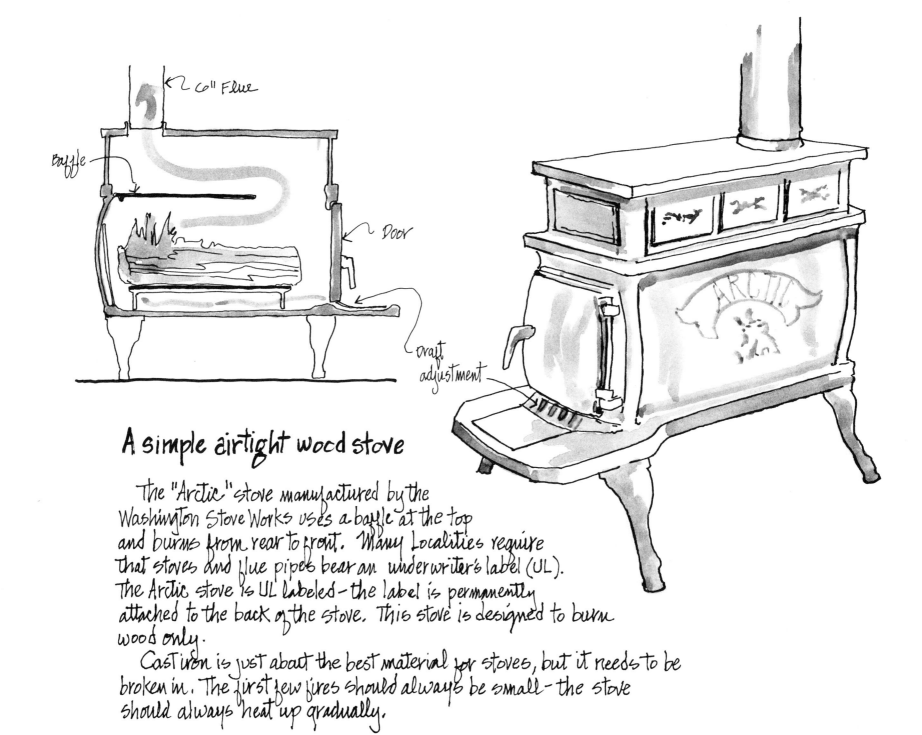

6" Flue

Baffle

Door

Draft adjustment

A simple airtight wood stove

The "Arctic" stove manufactured by the Washington Stove Works uses a baffle at the top and burns from rear to front. Many localities require that stoves and flue pipes bear an underwriter's label (UL). The Arctic stove is UL labeled - the label is permanently attached to the back of the stove. This stove is designed to burn wood only.

Cast iron is just about the best material for stoves, but it needs to be broken in. The first few fires should always be small - the stove should always heat up gradually.

Draft control

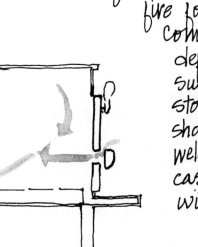

Baffle

Firebrick
Lining

Some Airtight Stoves

The heat is kept in the firebox longer and the unburned wood gases are deflected back over the fire for more complete combustion by deflection devices such as the steel baffle in this stove. The particular models shown are constructed of heavy welded steel bodies with solid cast iron doors and are lined with firebrick.

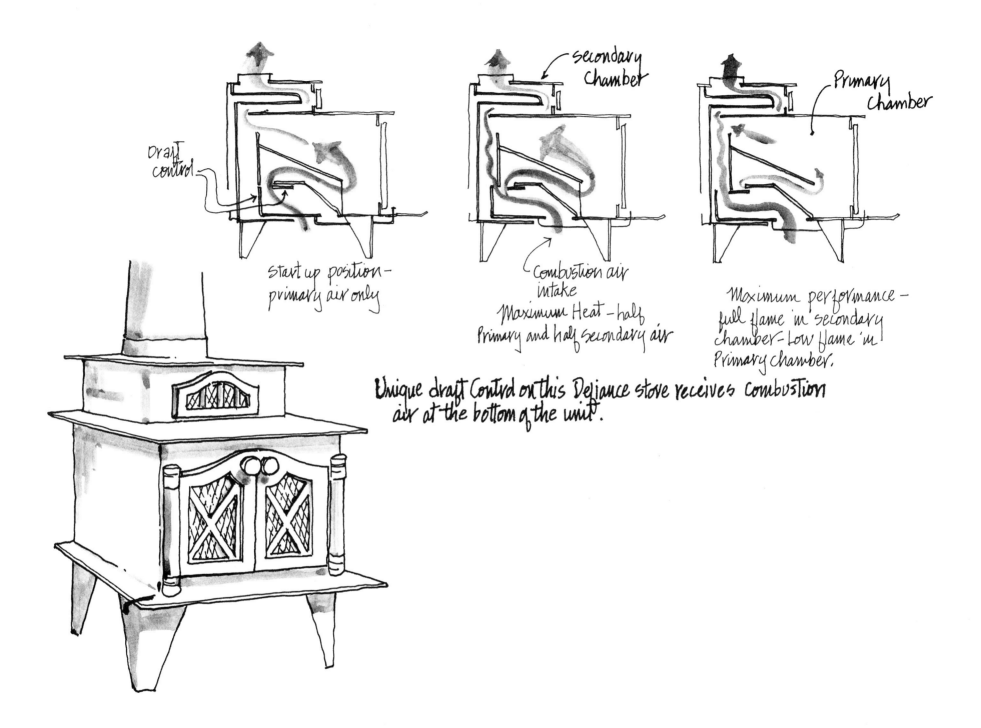

Draft
Control

Start up position—
primary air only

secondary
Chamber

Combustion air
intake
Maximum Heat—half
Primary and half secondary air

Primary
Chamber

Maximum performance—
full flame in secondary
chamber—Low flame in
Primary chamber.

Unique draft Control on this Defiance stove receives Combustion
air at the bottom of the unit.

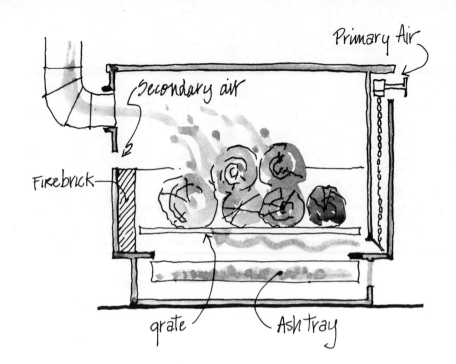

Primary Air

secondary air

Firebrick

grate

Ash Tray

Ashley Airtight Designs

Ashley designs are usually constructed of sheet metal with gasket-lined doors and automatic air inlets. The fire boxes are lined with cast iron panels or fire brick. Primary air is drawn into the Ashley design through an automatic damper controlled by a thermostat.
Air flows downward through a preheating channel on the outside of the fire box, entering the fire box and passing across and upward through the fuel charge. Preheating of the primary air is desirable since it helps maintain a higher fire box temperature, helping to complete the wood combustion cycle.

Most of the Ashley-type designs also provide secondary air inlets for use once the stove is in the charcoal-burning stage. This secondary air generally contributes little to combustion but does help to dilute the water vapor and volatiles so that condensation of acid and creosote is reduced.

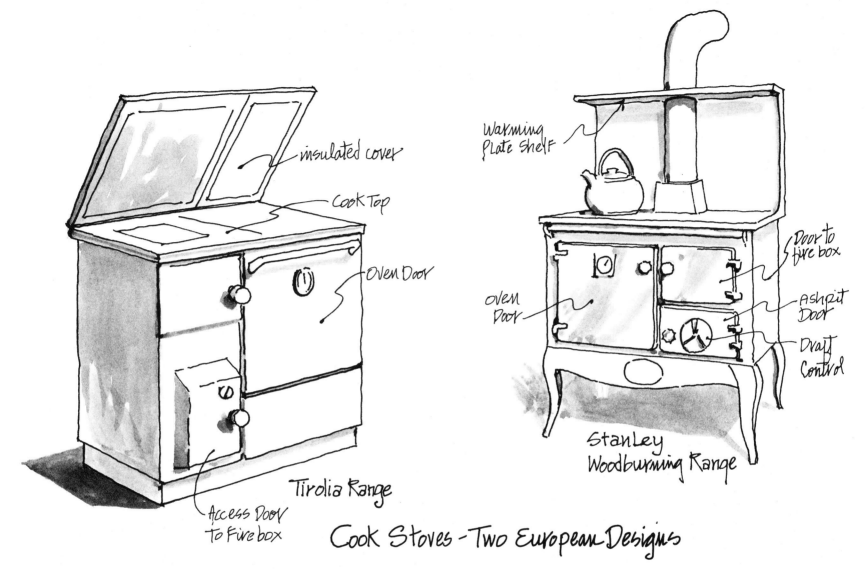

insulated cover

Cook Top

Oven Door

Tirolia Range

Access Door To Fire box

Warming Plate Shelf

Door to fire box

Ash-pit Door

Draft Control

Oven Door

Stanley Woodburning Range

Cook Stoves - Two European Designs

Illustrated above are two examples of woodburning kitchen stoves. The Tirolia range is an interesting contemporary design which features an adjustable scissors jack for height control of the fire grate. The Stanley Range is reminiscent of Grandma's stove. Both stoves can be connected to domestic hot water and heat systems and can be fired-up on most any solid fuel including coal.

187

Standard Clearance Requirements

These dimensions may be altered if the stove has been UL approved at shorter dimensions. Consult local city building codes for variations of these requirements. * the 36" dimensions at sides and rear may be reduced to 12" for circulating stoves. The front dimension may be reduced to 24".

188

Creosote

A fire should burn hot in order to prevent creosote build-up in the flue. Many prefabricated metal flues stay too cool to prevent creosote condensation, especially with lower temperature airtight stoves. The flue must remain above 250°F to do the job. Since it is unlikely that creosote can be prevented, the flue lining should be checked for build-up once a month. Another solution is a rock salt additive made just for the purpose which is thrown onto the fire. This solution is generally not recommended by fire authorities.

The type of wood which is burned is a significant factor in creosote build-up. This does not mean cherry versus oak, but dry versus green. Green wood is fresh-cut, usually sappy. Creosote-forming acids are plentiful in such wood. Dry "seasoned" wood is less risky. Wood logs should be seasoned for six months to a year before burning.

spark screen

the "Vigilant" by Vermont Castings, Inc. This stove can be converted to coal-burning.

Soapstone Stove

The stove depicted here is made primarily of soapstone. It will take a bit longer to radiate heat but will continue to radiate warmth after the fire has died.

The Coal/Wood-burning Stove

The coal or wood-burning stove like the Glacier Bay model shown on page 192 is designed as an insert to fit an existing masonry fireplace. Coal is regaining some of the popularity it once enjoyed. It gives off a steady heat and leaves no creosote deposites. Maximum efficiency of wood-burning occurs after a "seasoning" period. Coal can be used immediately.

Anthracite coal combustion starts at the bottom of the fuel bed. Combustion air must be delivered from below the grate. Consequently the grate design must be such that the ashes can be removed periodically without totally disrupting the oxidation zone. A good coal grate can be shaken in short, gentle strokes so that hot coals aren't lost through the grate into the ash tray.

For maximum efficiency in burning, the coal bed should remain uniform - without large gaps through which primary air can be drawn creating "hot spots." Using a poker can be too disruptive. Coals in the stirred area will meld into clinkers that can't be shaken down - eventually causing the fire to suffocate.

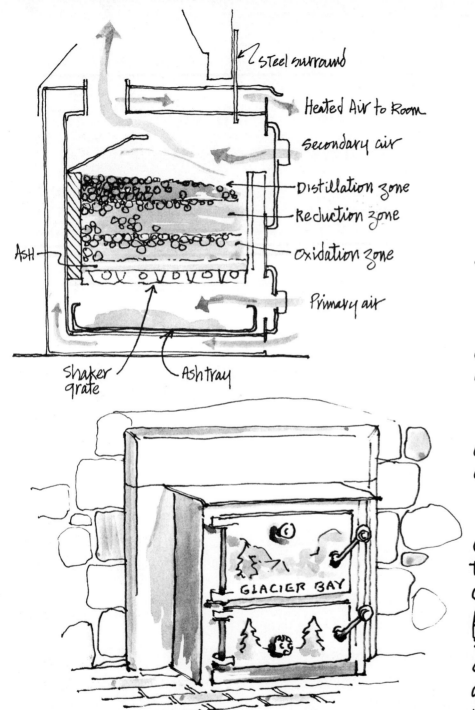

Steel surround

Heated Air to Room

Secondary air

Distillation zone

Reduction zone

oxidation zone

ASH

Primary air

Shaker grate

Ashtray

GLACIER BAY

The Anthracite Combustion Cycle

The hottest layer of the fuel bed is the oxidation zone where most of the combustion occurs and where carbon dioxide gas is produced.

The reduction zone is the layer in which oxygen is removed from the rising gas below and carbon monoxide is produced.

In the distillation zone the firebed is charged with fresh coal. There, the moisture of the fresh coal as well as other volatiles are distilled off and are accumulated below the flue baffle. The Glacier Bay model introduces secondary air above the distillation zone which aids in the combustion of the carbon monoxide gas from the reduction zone and other accumulated volatile matters.

The Furnace

A modern-day phenomenon is the rediscovery of the coal furnace. Depicted on the opposite page is a coal/wood furnace with a schematic diagram of the internal heat flow. This particular furnace (Thermomax) is manufactured by Hunter Energy Inc. of Canton, Ohio. It employs an electric damper and can supply hot air by natural conduction (gravity heat) or by the use of a blower system. It can supply up to 225,000 BTU's per hour.

Coal or Wood?

Under ideal conditions a gallon of fuel oil produces 140,000 BTU's per hour; a pound of dry wood produces 8,600 BTU's per hour; and a pound of anthracite (hard) coal produces 13,000 BTU's per hour. A cord of wood is approximately equal in heat value to 2300 lb of coal, 200 gallons of oil, 305 gallons of propane; 23,000 cubic feet of natural gas or 884 kw of electricity.

Creosote deposites build up in the flues of wood-burning fireplaces and stoves whereas ash dust build-up may result from coal fires. Wood should be seasoned for at least a year or until it reaches the normal air-dryed level of 23% moisture content. Coal can be burned immediately. Also, a wood fire can be started immediately whereas coal might take 10 to 20 minutes.

There are many more pros and cons including availability and price — reasons enough for the development of stoves and furnaces which burn both coal or wood.

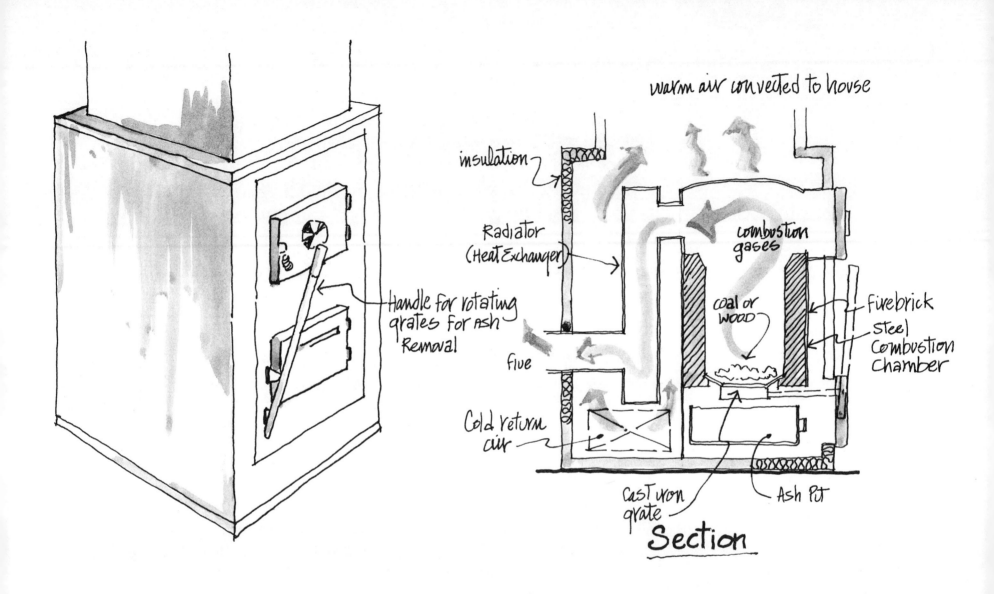

warm air convected to house

insulation

Radiator
(Heat Exchanger)

flue

Cold return
air

combustion
gases

coal or
wood

firebrick

steel
Combustion
Chamber

Cast iron
grate

Ash Pit

Section

Handle for rotating
grates for ash
Removal

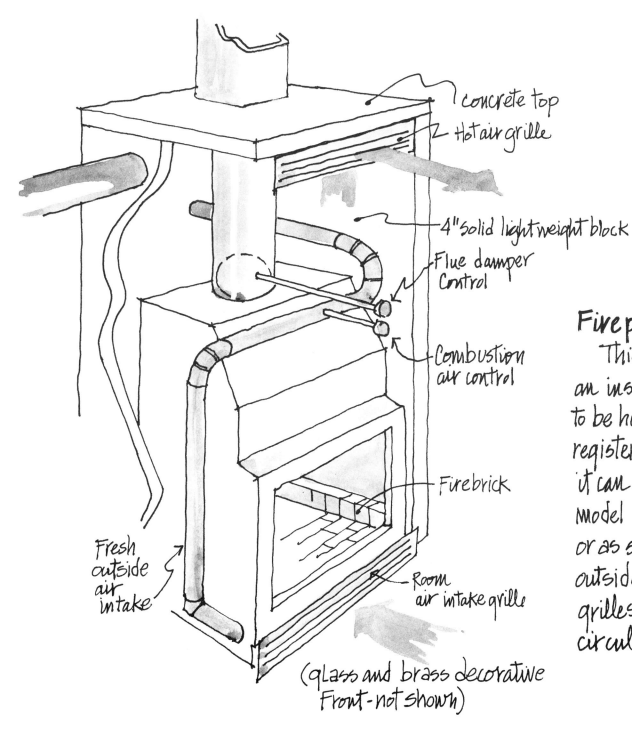

concrete top

Hot air grille

4" solid light weight block

Flue damper control

Combustion air control

Firebrick

Fresh outside air intake

Room air intake grille

(glass and brass decorative front - not shown)

Fireplace Furnace

This prefabricated fireplace is not an insert. It is a steel fireplace designed to be housed in a masonry enclosure. The registered trade name is Timberland and it can be purchased as a see-through model with doors on two opposite sides or as shown. Note that it takes in outside combustion air and has grilles top and bottom for the circulation of room air.

Prefabricated Insulated Metal Flue

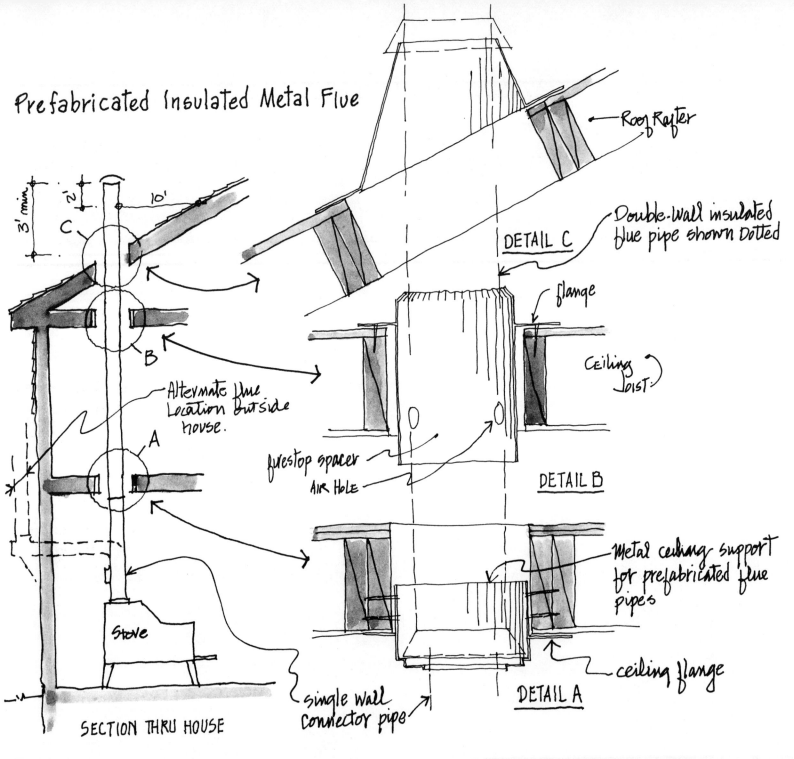

Roof Rafter

Double-Wall insulated flue pipe shown Dotted

DETAIL C

flange

Ceiling Joist

3' min

2'

10'

C

B

Alternate flue Location outside house.

firestop spacer

Air Hole

DETAIL B

A

Metal ceiling support for prefabricated flue pipes

Stove

ceiling flange

SECTION THRU HOUSE

single wall Connector pipe

DETAIL A

Prefabricated Insulated Metal Flue

In the example sketch the pipe flue is taken up through the inside of the house. Single wall 24 gauge stove pipe is used to connect the stove to the insulated flue pipe. The flue assembly is supported at the first floor by a special flue support which is nailed to the sides of the floor opening. At the ceiling of the second floor a "fire stop spacer" section is placed over the ceiling opening. The flue runs up through this spacer. The spacer has a flange on it (the firestop) and a guide on the underside to indicate the smallest safe ceiling opening.

Prefabricated insulated flue pipe is made of a stainless steel inner wall separated by about an inch of non combustible insulation from an outer stainless steel casing. Each flue section should be stamped with a UL label and marked "all-fuel flue." Pipe sections fit together mechanically so that no tools or bolts are required.

Not shown in the illustration is a wall around the flue which is recommended so that nothing accidentally falls against the pipe. The flue should be braced to the wall at intervals of eight feet. The UL label will usually give the minimal clearance between the flue and combustible material.

X Wood

It is remarkable what a value is still put upon wood even in this age and in this new country, a value more permanent and universal than that of gold.

—Henry D. Thoreau, *Walden*

Three materials were the most common to Early American builders: brick, stone and wood. Brick was used primarily for structural walls and as an exterior finish. Stone likewise was used on the exterior and in many cases exposed on a chimney face. Brick and stone have always had a condensation or moisture related problem. Our ancestors never understood the flow of water vapor so they were never able to resolve its effects. The most interesting and versatile material was the wood. It, of course was and still is used for furniture as well as for building. Wood has always been valued for its finished appearance as well as for weather-proofing in such forms as paneling, trim, siding and roofing.

Types of Wood

Ash, white   Ash is a hardwood. Used in making handles of striking tools like sledge hammers. Hard and strong.

Beech   White color. Strong and hard. Good for curved parts like rocking chair runners. A hardwood.   Good for bowls - no taste or smell.

Basswood   Creamy white color. Softwood. Good for moldings.

Birch   A hardwood. Good for trim and paneling. Great in natural finish. Stains well. Good veneer. Little shrinkage.

Cedar   Softwood. Closed grain. Decay Resistant. Rough texture. Holds paint. Red cedar repels moths. Used for cedar roof shakes, Exterior siding, interior paneling.

Cherry   Hardwood. A beautiful wood. Great for Early American furniture. Carves well.

Chestnut - wormy   Fabulous Paneling. Try and find it. Used for paneling in the park headquarters building of the Shenandoah National Park.

Cypress   Weathers silver gray. Great for siding.

Douglas Fir   Used for structural framing. Does not hold paint well. Will check.

Mahogany   Great for Early American furniture. Beautiful natural finish. Carves well.

Types of Wood

Maple
Black/sugar

Very hard. Used for miter boxes. Hardwood floors. Originally used in Early American furniture. Durable.

Oak
various varieties

Very popular for floors, paneling and furniture.

Pine
various varieties

Closed grain. Great for Early American furniture. Will decay in contact with earth or the elements. Used for paneling and window frames.

Hickory

Very strong. Good for basement columns. Ladder rungs. Tool handles.

poplar

Soft and weak. Good for picture frames. Trim. Takes paint and stain. Trees grow fast. By absorbing water from clay soil, can cause building foundation movement.

Redwood

Reddish brown color. Exterior walls, siding, furniture. Resists decay. Splinters.

Rosewood

Great for Early American furniture. Hard, durable, beautiful. Limited supply.

Spruce
many varieties

A softwood. Lightweight. Used for trim. Takes paint fair.

Teak

Great for carved furniture. Durable. open grain. Takes stain well.

Walnut

Finishes beautifully. Great for furniture. Durable. Little shrinkage.

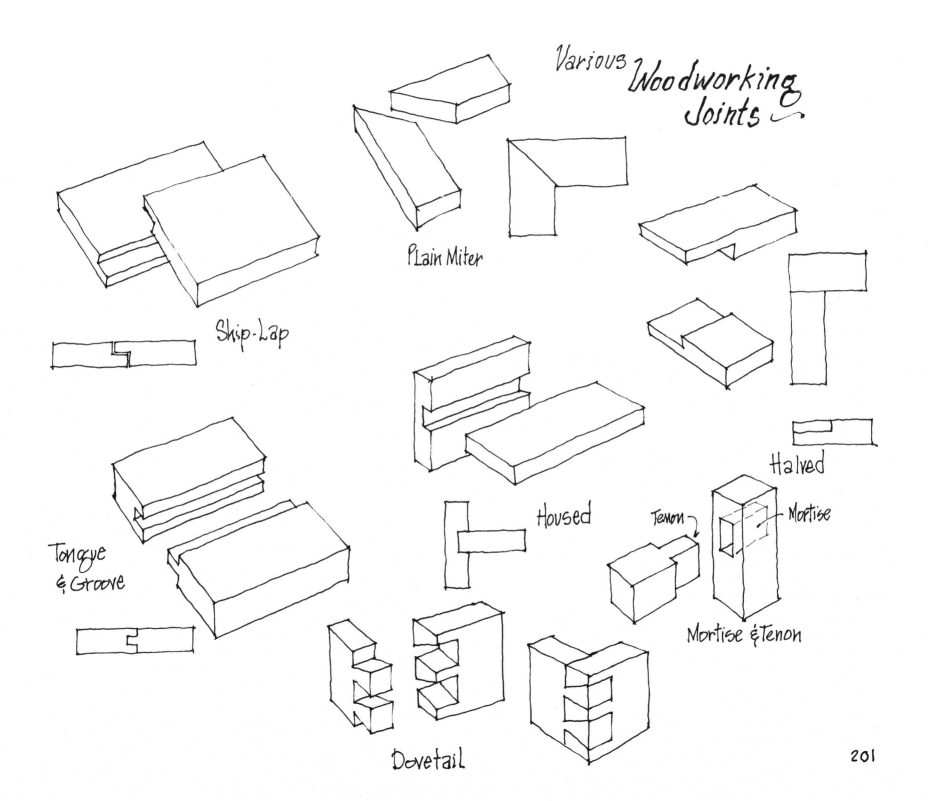

Various **Woodworking Joints**

Ship-Lap

Plain Miter

Tongue & Groove

Housed

Halved

Tenon · Mortise

Mortise & Tenon

Dovetail

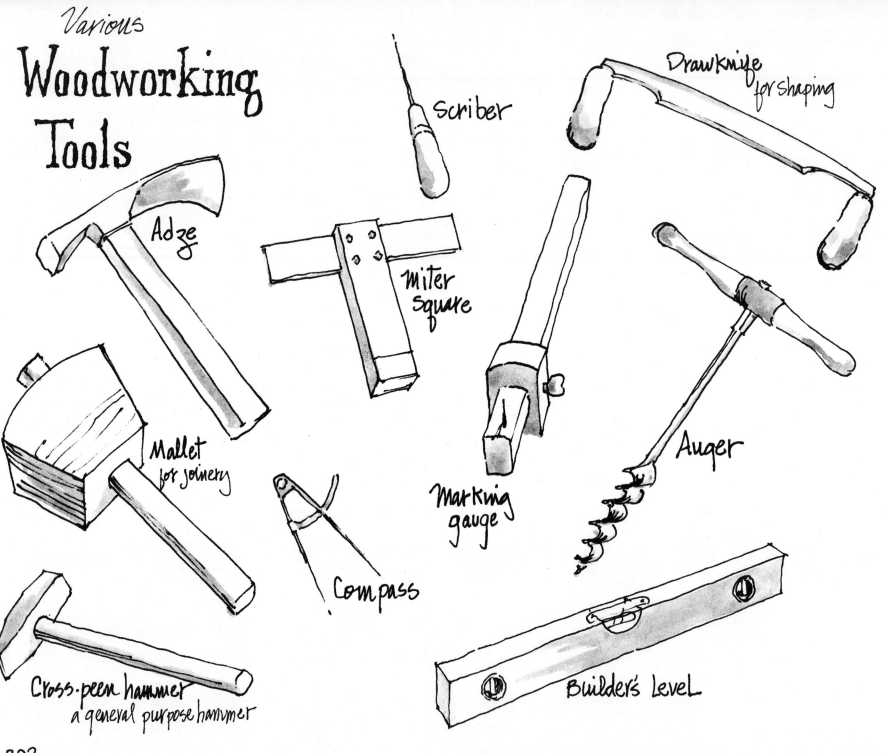

Various

Woodworking Tools

Adze

Scriber

Drawknife
for shaping

Miter
Square

Mallet
for joinery

Compass

Marking
gauge

Auger

Cross-peen hammer
a general purpose hammer

Builder's level

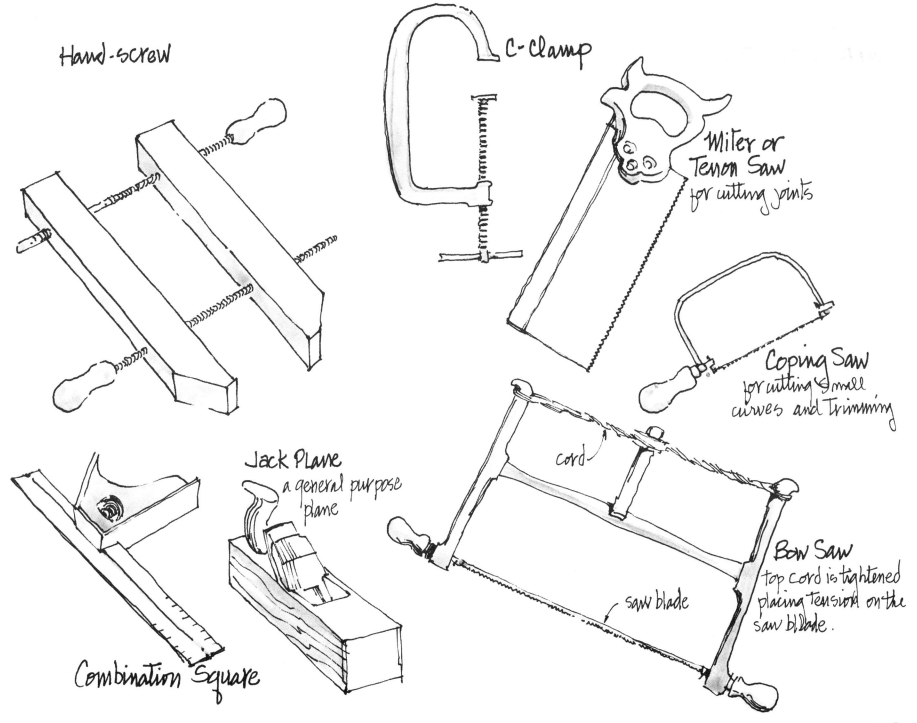

Hand-screw

C-Clamp

Miter or Tenon Saw
for cutting joints

Coping Saw
for cutting small
curves and Trimming

Jack Plane
a general purpose
plane

cord

Combination Square

saw blade

Bow Saw
top cord is tightened
placing tension on the
saw blade.

The use of wood moldings is a fascinating aspect of Early American construction. Early hand-hewn post and beam construction displays primitive attempts to decorate exposed woodwork.

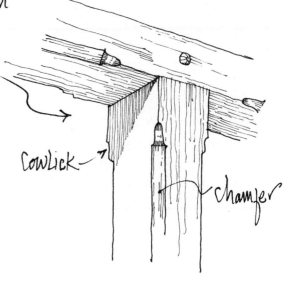

Cowlick

Chamfer

As the art of woodworking in this country progressed, so did the artistic refinements in molding shapes used. Such shapes were originally developed in one fashion or another by the Romans and Greeks.

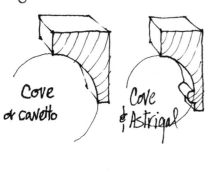

Cove or canetto

Cove & Astrigal

Ovolo

Ogee (cimareversa)

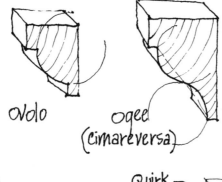

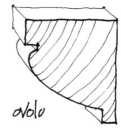

Some Greek Shapes

Ovolo

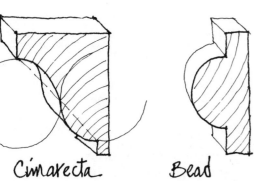

Cimarecta

Bead

Scotia

Quirk

Quirk Ogee

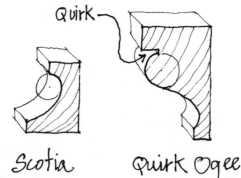

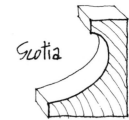

Scotia

Later refinements of moldings in this country led to the use of Greek shapes based on the ellipsis, parabola, and hyperbole.

Roman Moldings

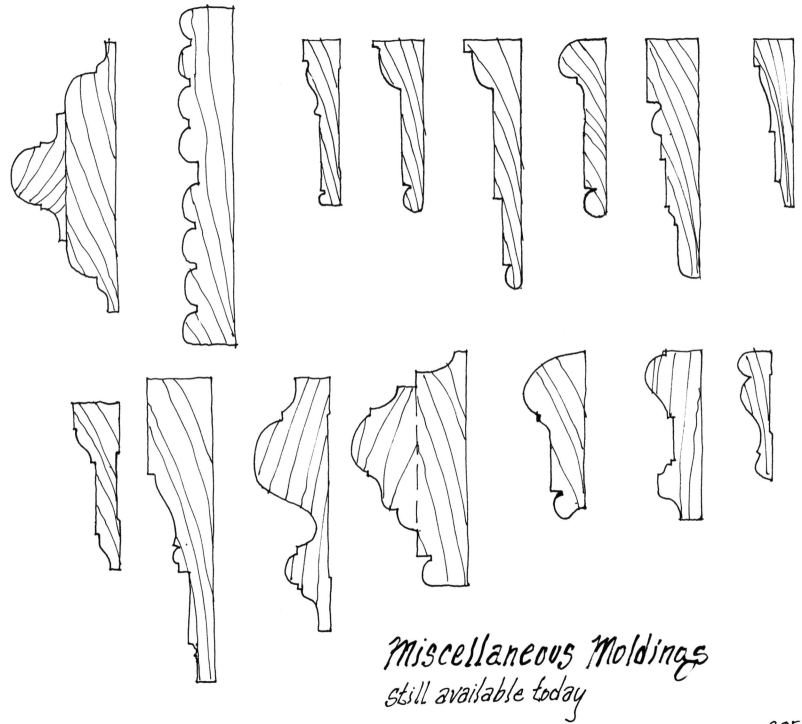

Miscellaneous Moldings
still available today

Wood Screws

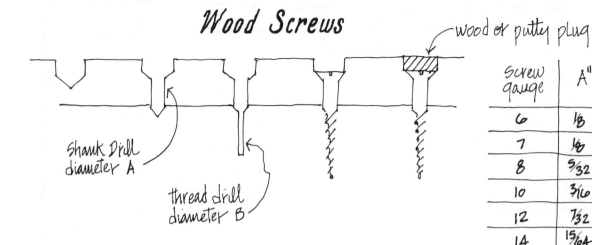

wood or putty plug

Shank Drill diameter A

thread drill diameter B

Screw gauge	A"	B"
6	1/8	1/16
7	1/8	1/16
8	5/32	1/16
10	3/16	3/32
12	7/32	1/8
14	15/64	5/32
16	9/32	3/16
18	5/16	3/16

Length	1/2	3/4	1	1¼	1½	1¾	2	2¼	2½	2¾	3	3½	4	4½	5
usual gages	6	6 8	8	8 10 12	8 10 12	10 12	10 12	10 12	12	12 14	12 14	14 16	14 16	14 16 18	16 18

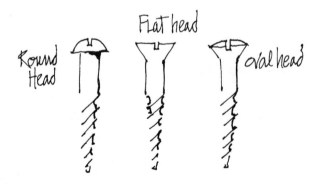

Round Head

Flat head

oval head

Wooden Stool

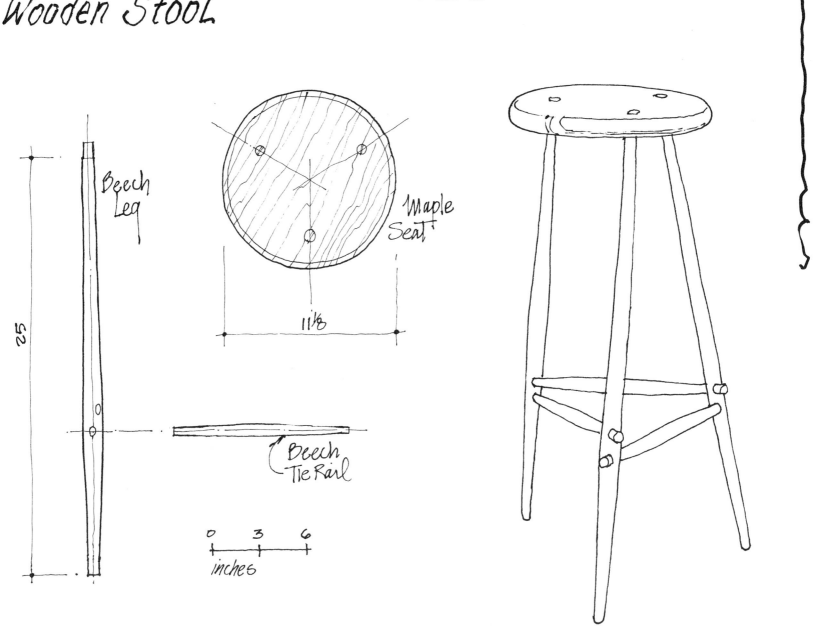

Beech Leg

Maple Seat

52

11⅛

Beech Tie Rail

0   3   6

inches

Footstool

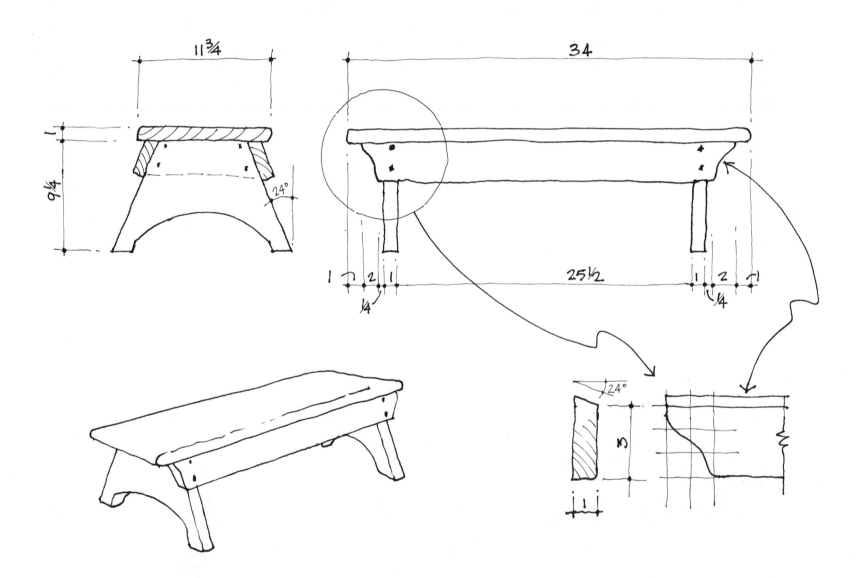

11¾

9¼

1

24°

34

1 2 1

¼

25½

1 2 1

¼

24°

5

1

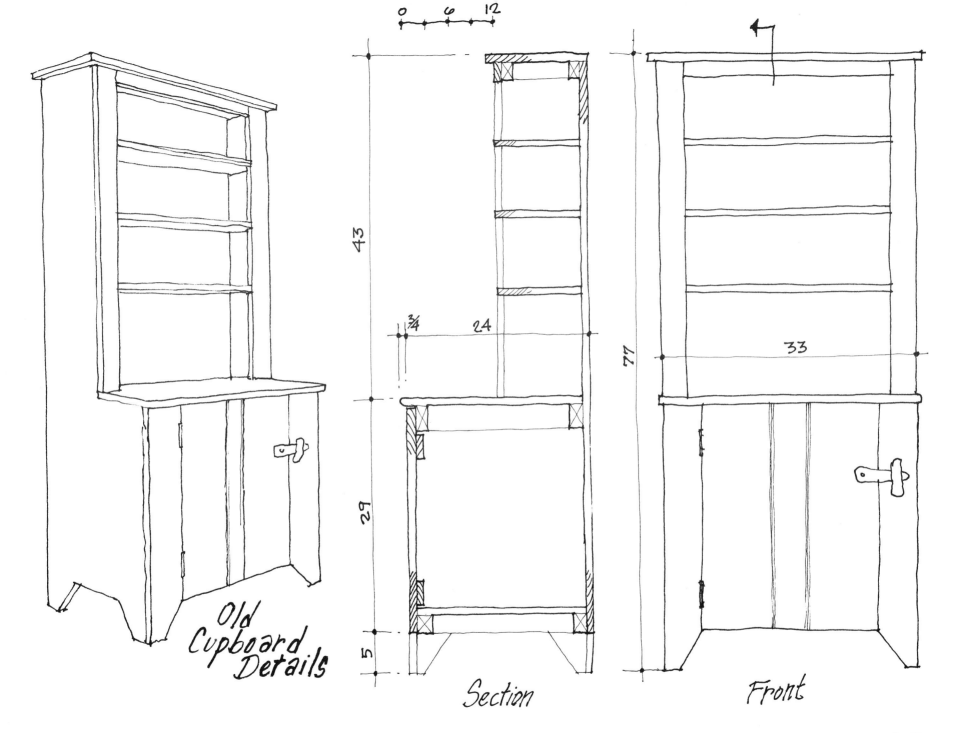

0   6   12

43

3/4   24

77

29

5

Old
Cupboard
Details

Section

Front

209

Pine Cupboard

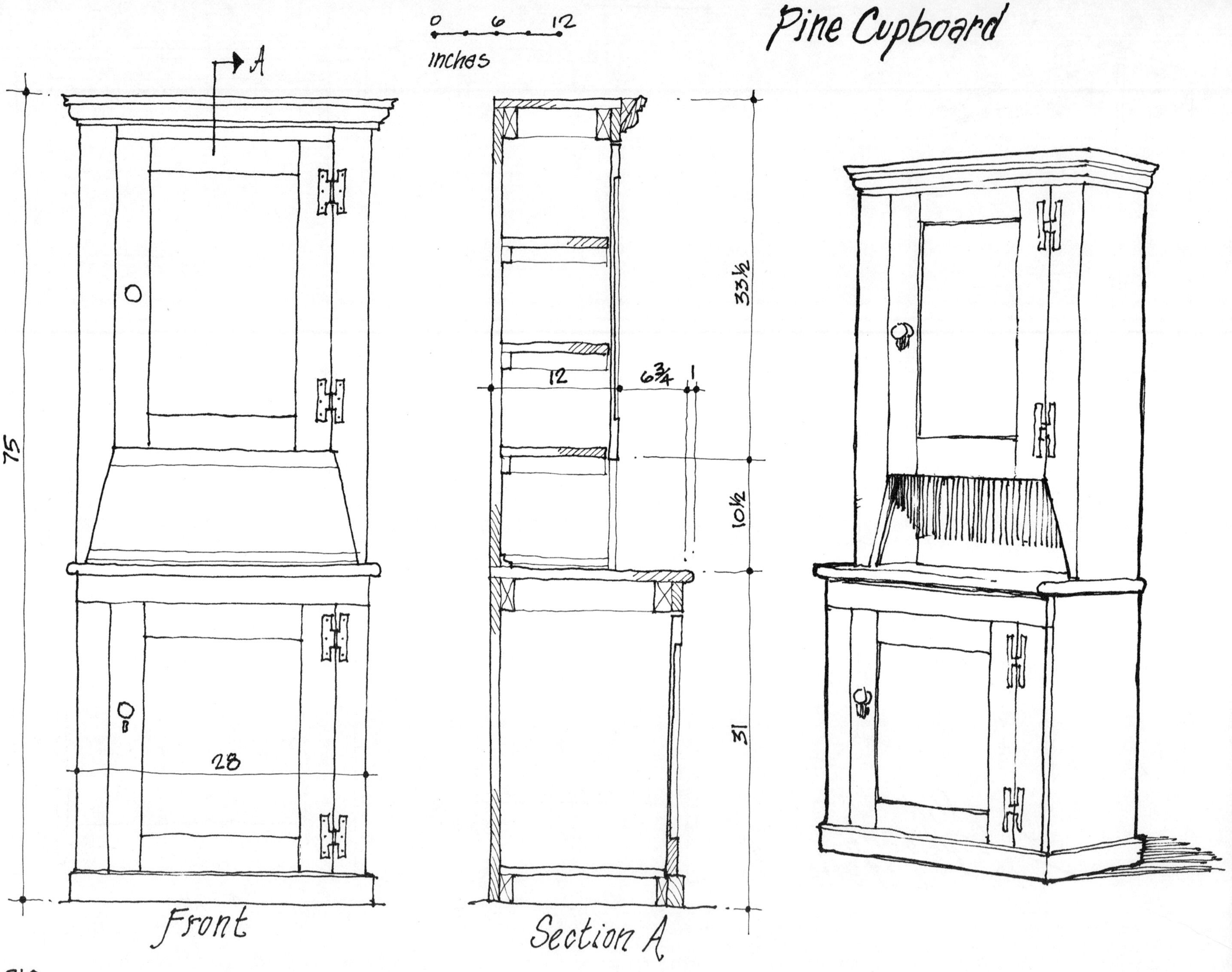

0 · · 6 · · 12
inches

A

75

28

Front

33½

12   6¾ 1

10½

31

Section A

210

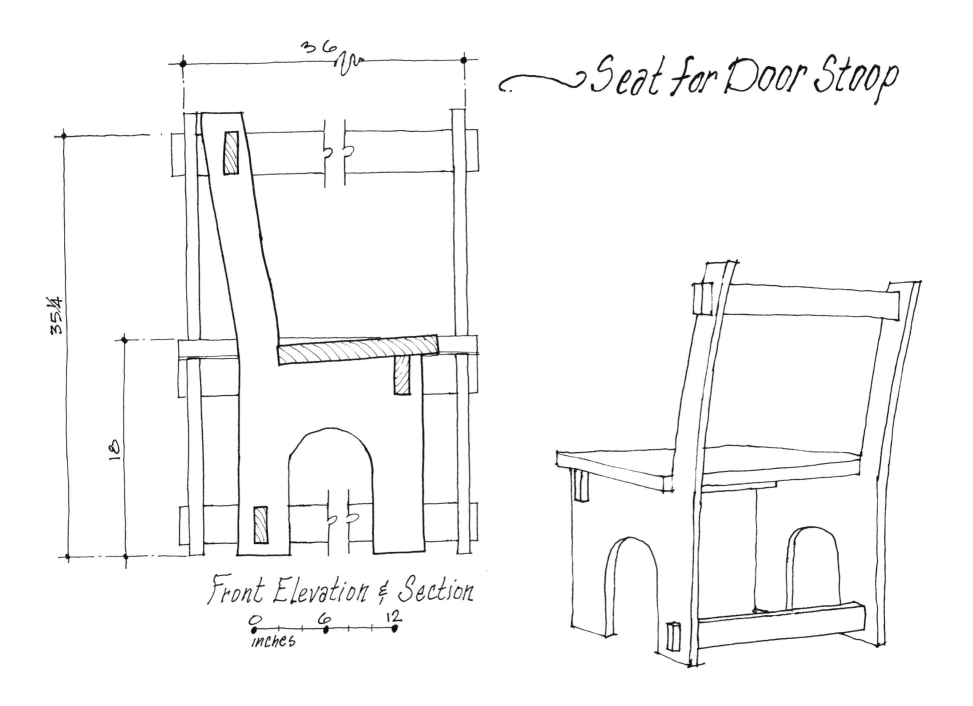

~Seat for Door Stoop

36"

35¼

18

Front Elevation & Section

0   6   12
inches

211

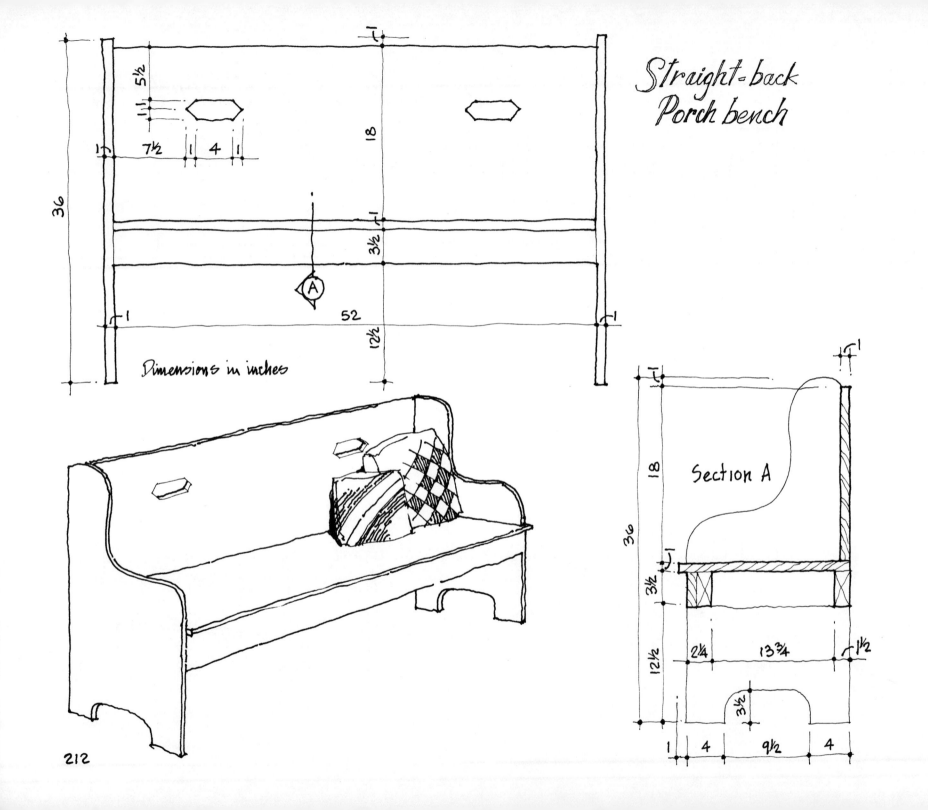

Straight-back Porch bench

5½

11

7½ 1 4 1

36

18

1

52

3½

A

12½

Dimensions in inches

Section A

18

36

3½

12½

2¼ 13¾ 1½

3½

1 4 9½ 4

212

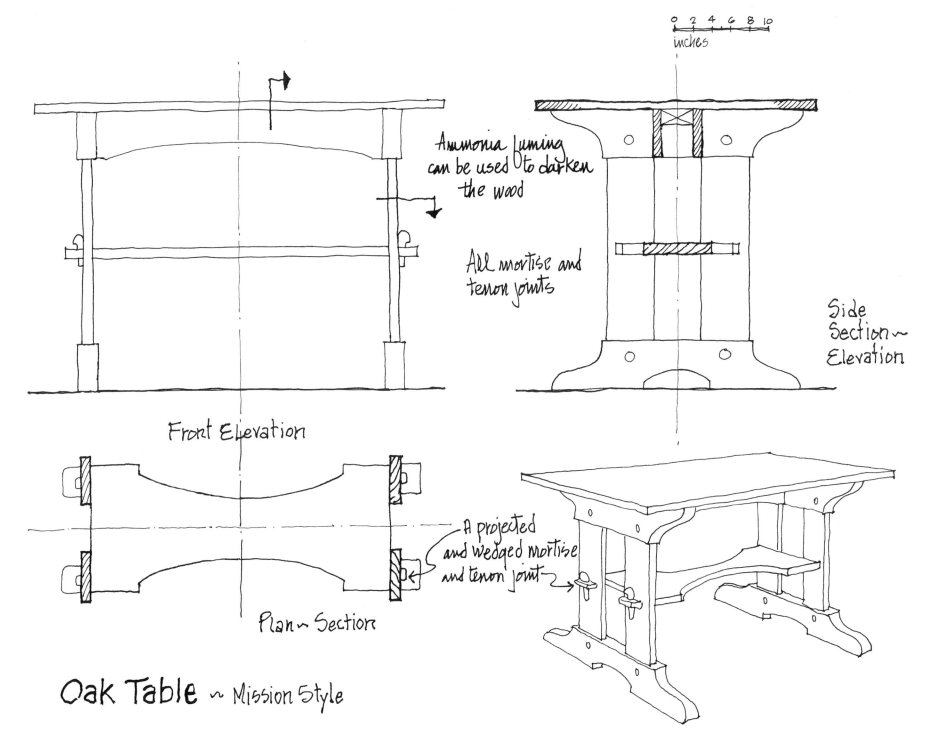

inches
0 2 4 6 8 10

Ammonia fuming
can be used to darken
the wood

All mortise and
tenon joints

Side
Section ~
Elevation

Front Elevation

Plan ~ Section

A projected
and wedged mortise
and tenon joint ~

Oak Table ~ Mission Style

213

Writing Desk

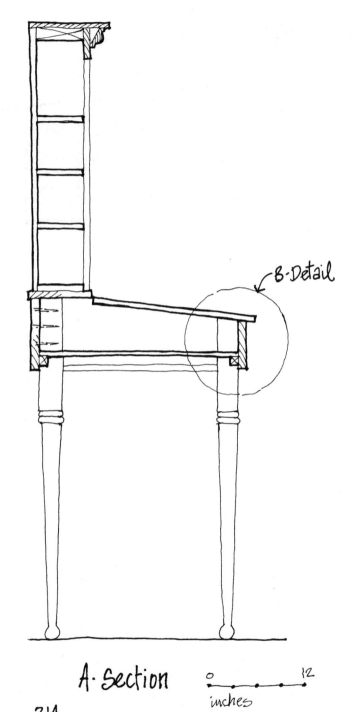

A·Section

B·Detail

0 12
inches

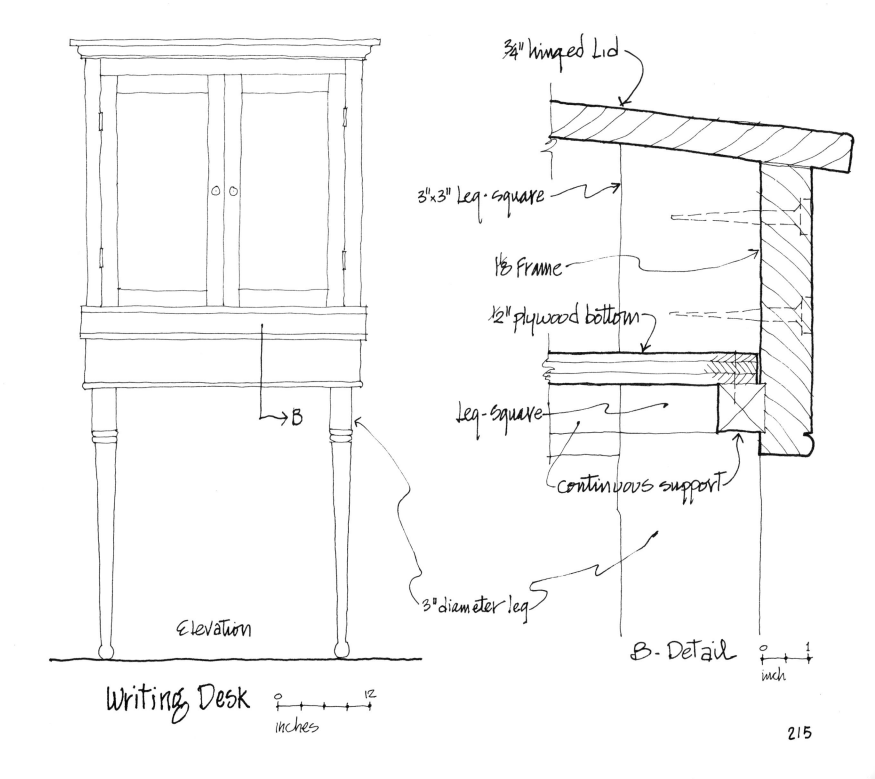

¾" hinged Lid

3"x3" Leg·square

1⅛ Frame

½" plywood bottom

Leg·square

continuous support

3" diameter leg

Elevation

B·Detail

0 —— 1
inch

Writing Desk   0 — — — — 12
inches

215

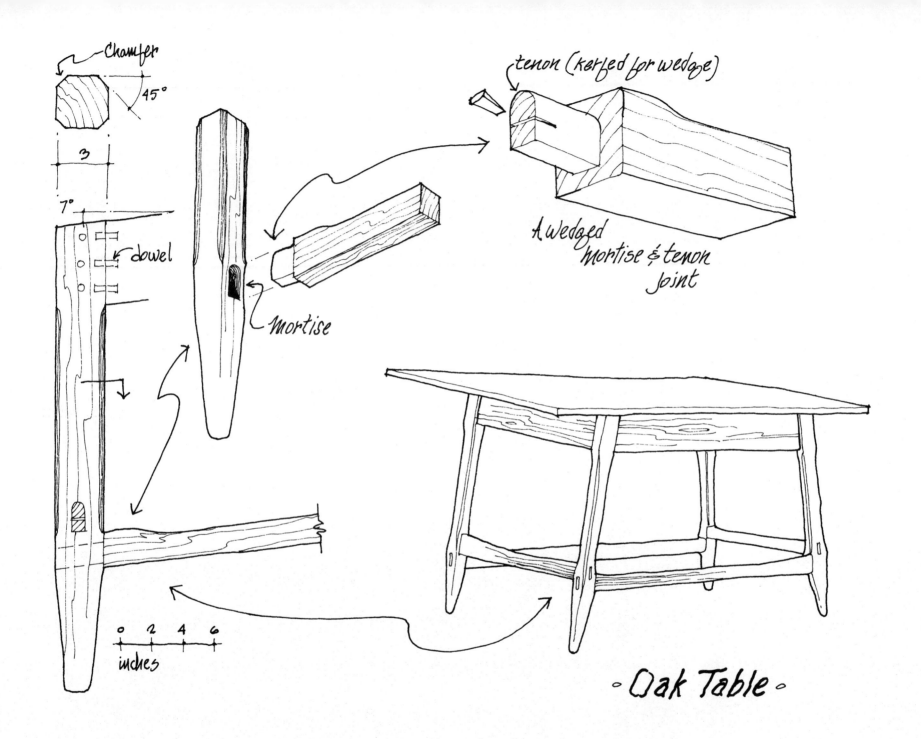

Chamfer

45°

3

7°

dowel

Mortise

tenon (kerfed for wedge)

A Wedged
Mortise & tenon
Joint

0 2 4 6
inches

- Oak Table -

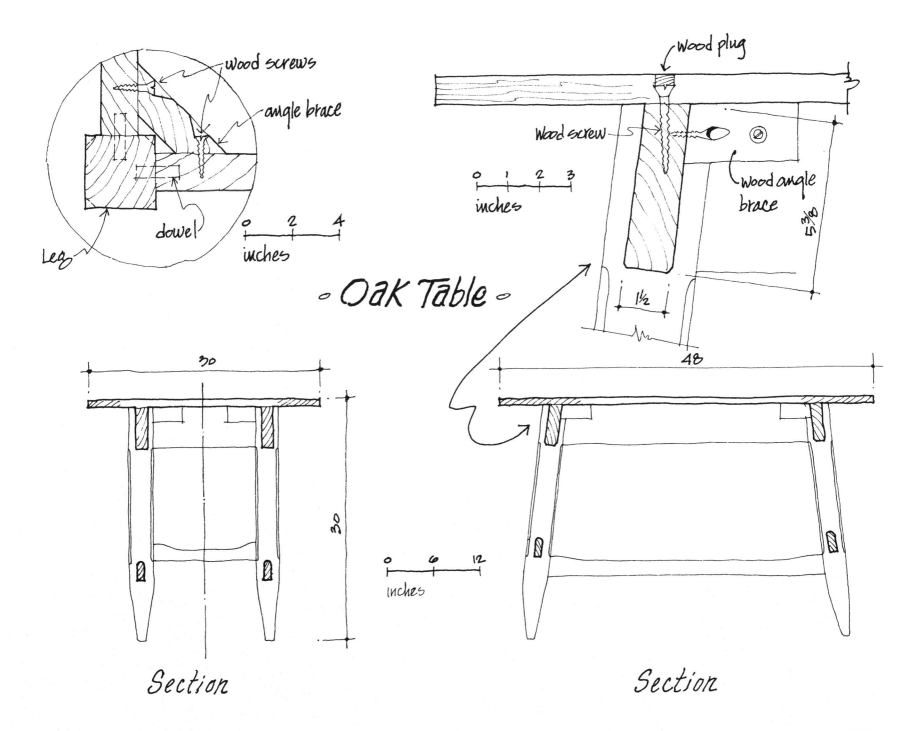

wood screws

angle brace

dowel

Leg

0 2 4
inches

Oak Table

Wood plug

Wood screw

wood angle brace

0 1 2 3
inches

5⅜

1½

48

30

30

Section

0 6 12
inches

Section

217

Corner Cupboard

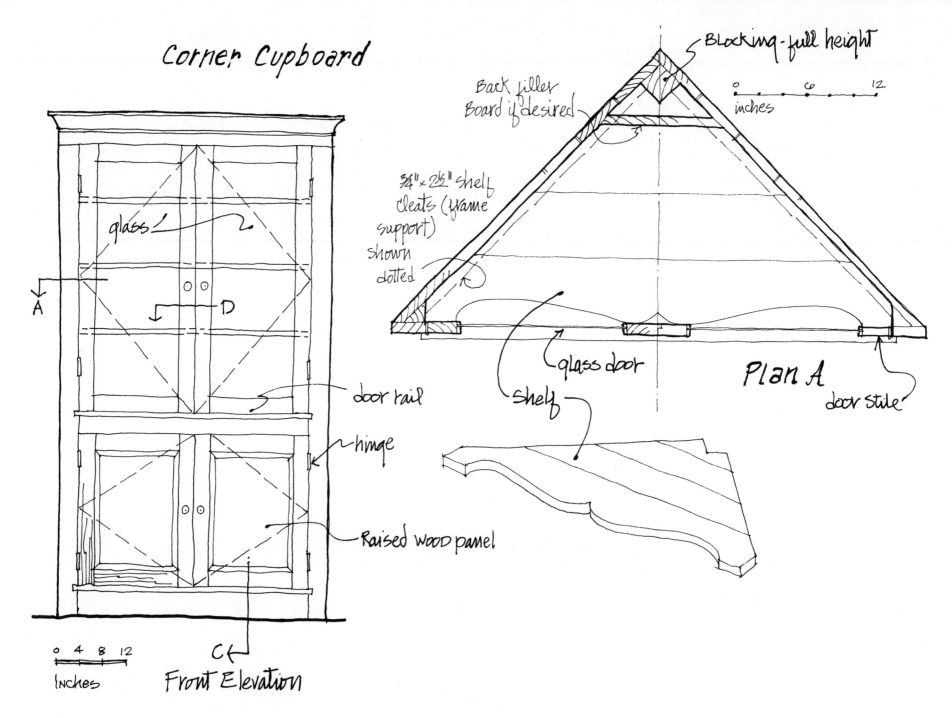

glass

A

D

door rail

hinge

Raised wood panel

0 4 8 12
Inches

Front Elevation

C

Blocking - full height

Back filler
Board if desired

0 . . . 6 . . . 12
inches

3/4" x 2½" shelf
Cleats (frame
support)
shown
dotted

glass door

Shelf

Plan A

door stile

218

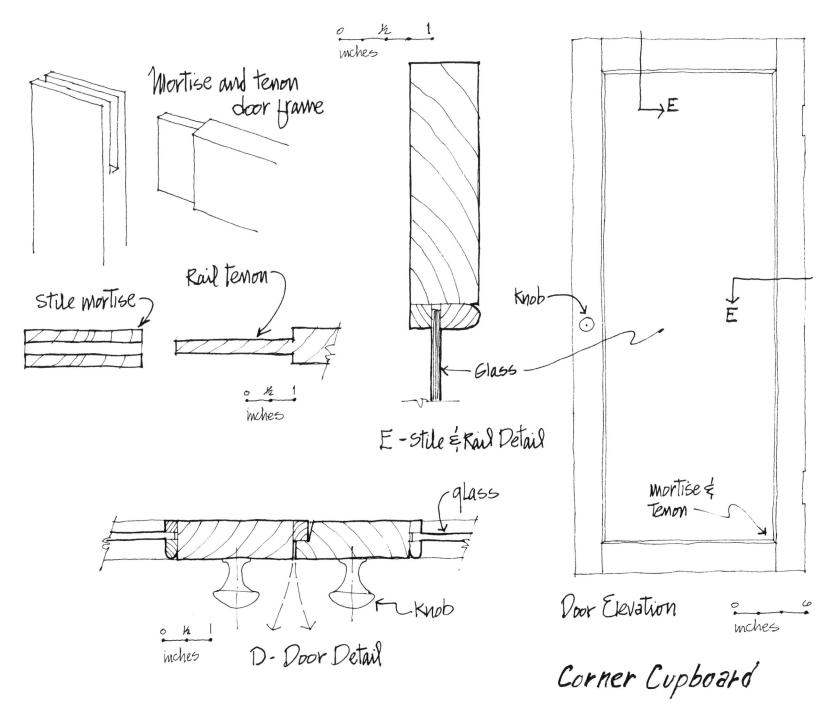

Mortise and tenon
door frame

stile mortise

Rail tenon

0   ½   1
inches

0   ½   1
inches

Knob

Glass

E - Stile & Rail Detail

Glass

Knob

0   ½   1
inches

D - Door Detail

E

E

Mortise &
Tenon

Door Elevation

0   6
inches

Corner Cupboard

219

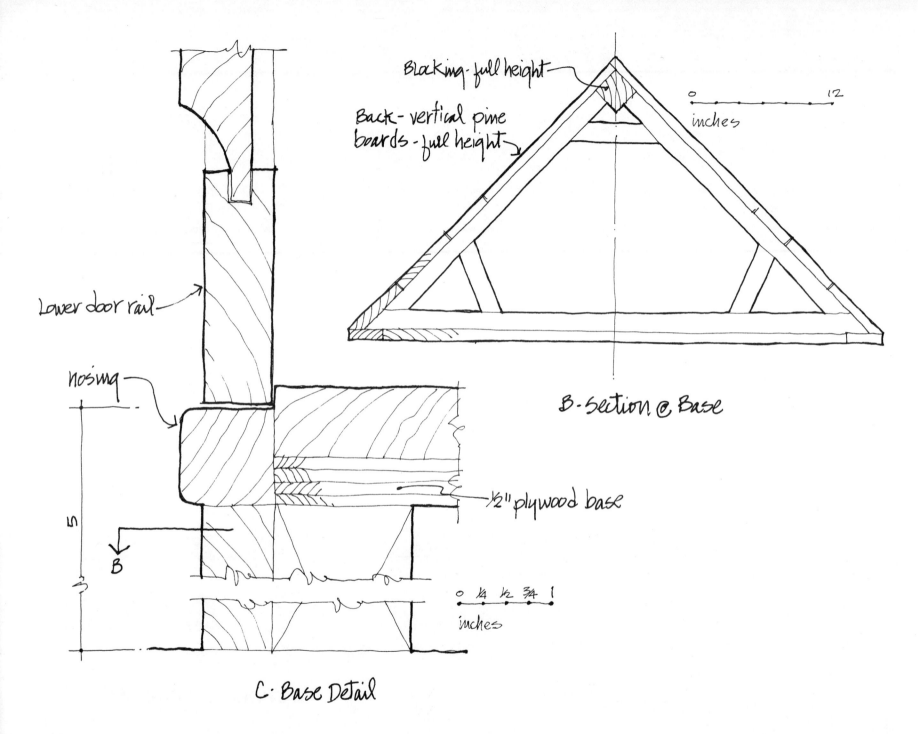

Blocking - full height

Back - vertical pine
boards - full height

0   12
inches

B· Section @ Base

Lower door rail

nosing

½" plywood base

5

B

0 ¼ ½ ¾ 1
inches

C· Base Detail

Candlestand

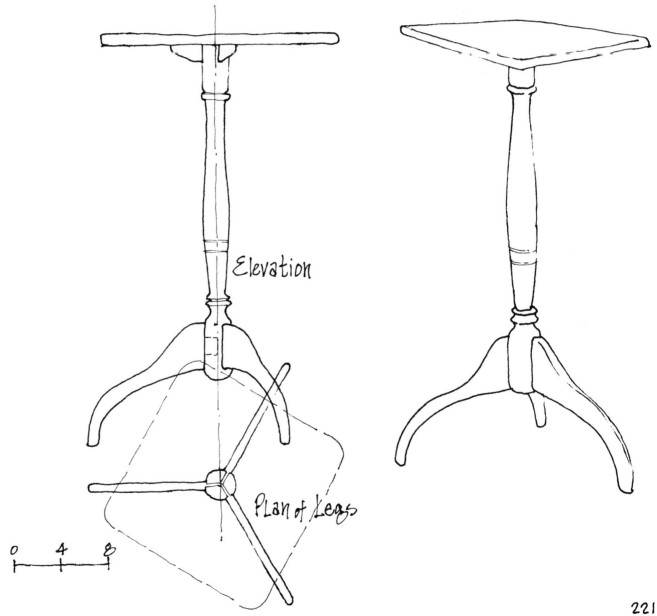

Elevation

Plan of Legs

0   4   8

- Maple Table Seat -

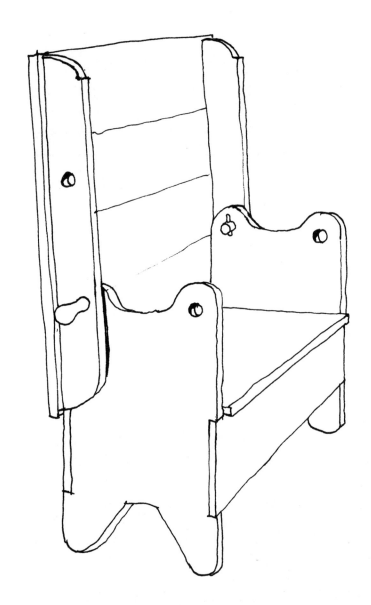

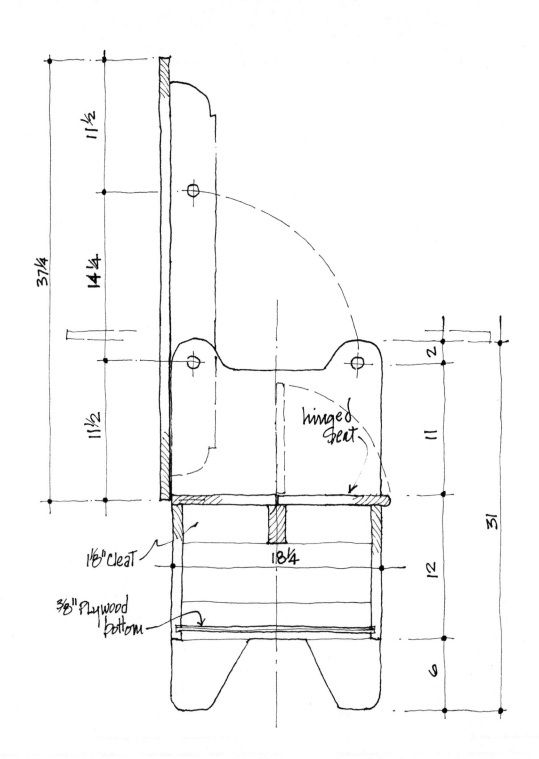

37¼

11½

14¼

11½

2

11

31

12

6

18¼

hinged seat

1⅛" cleat

⅜" Plywood bottom

Maple Table Seat

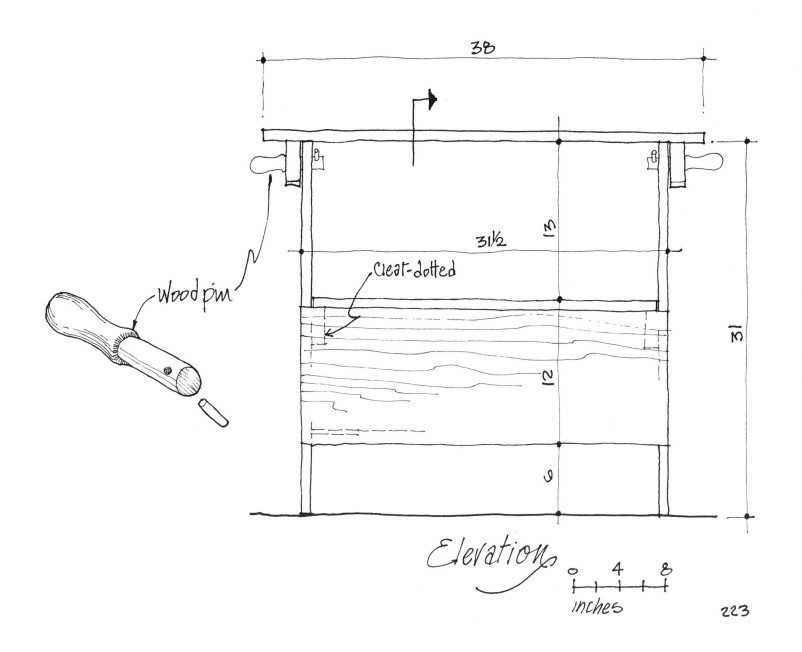

38

31½

13

12

9

31

Wood pin

Cleat-dotted

Elevation

0   4   8
inches

223

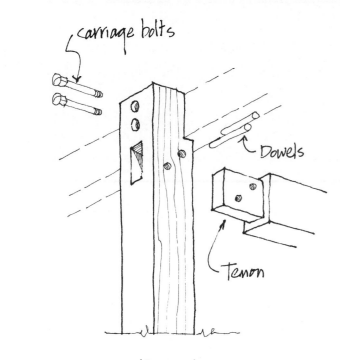

carriage bolts

Dowels

Tenon

· Maple Table ·

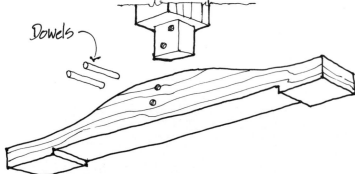

Dowels

Leg Detail

Maple Table

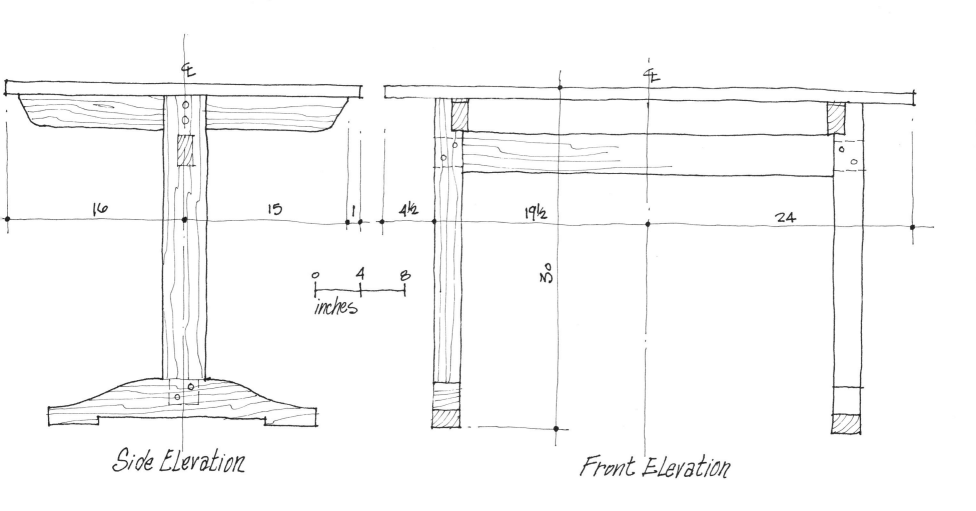

Side Elevation

Front Elevation

16   15   1   4½   19½   24

30

0   4   8
inches

225

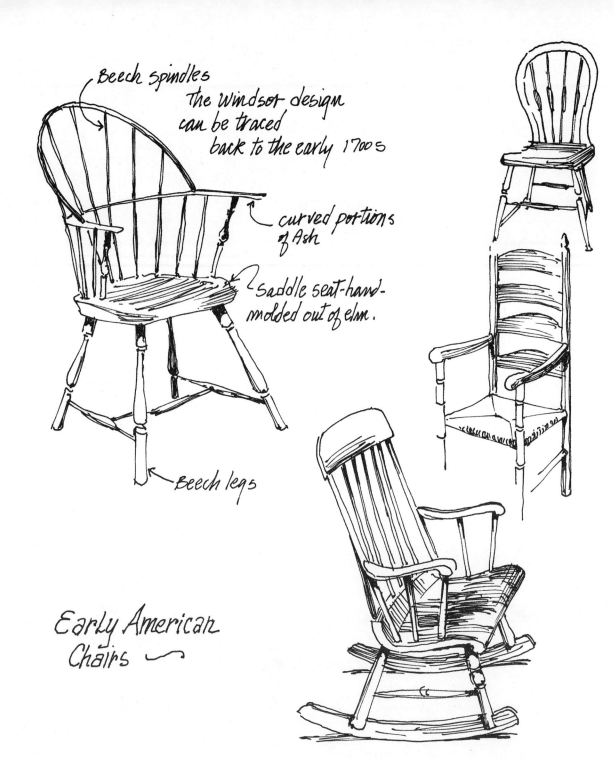

Beech spindles

the windsor design
can be traced
back to the early 1700s

curved portions
of Ash

Saddle seat-hand-
molded out of elm.

Beech legs

Early American
Chairs

Miscellaneous
Entrances

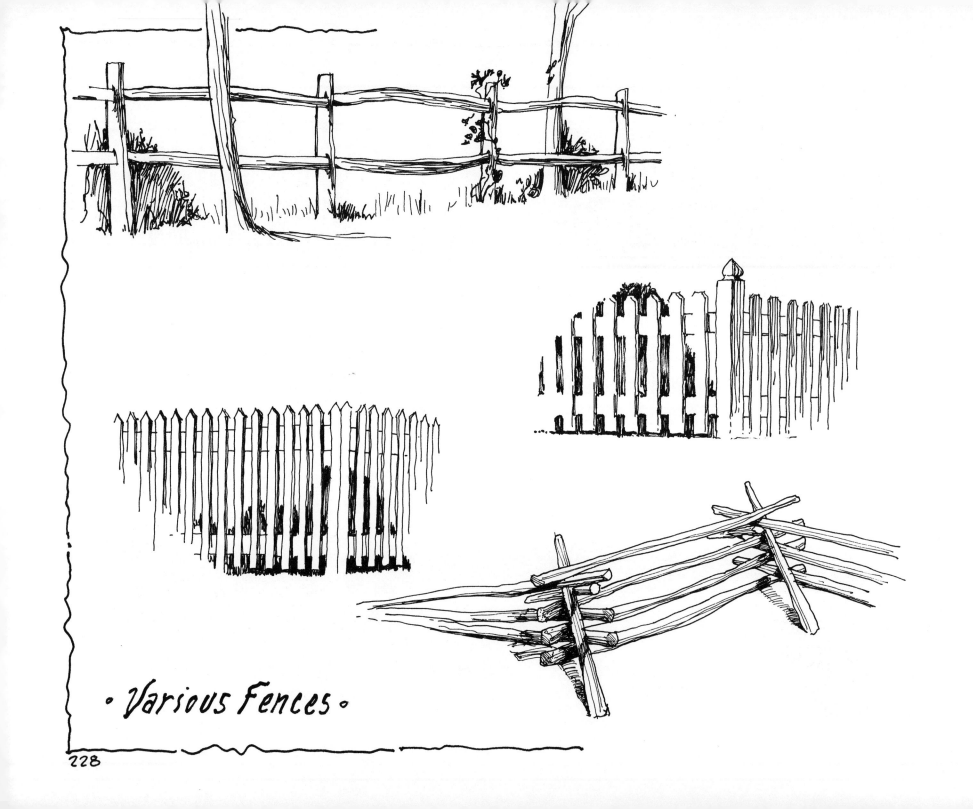

· Various Fences ·

229

Glossary

ADZE – CUTTING TOOL USED FOR HEWING TIMBER.

ADOBE – SUN BAKED EARTH BLOCKS MADE WITH STRAW REINFORCE-MMENT; USED IN SOUTH WESTERN UNITED STATES.

ANIMAL GLUE – A STRONG GLUE MADE FROM ANIMALS BUT NOT VERY WATER RESISTANT.

ANNULAR BIT – A HOLE BIT OR HOLE SAW FOR USE WITH AN ELECTRIC HAND DRILL.

APRON – THE WOOD TRIM DIRECTLY UNDER THE STOOL.

stool

apron

ARCHITRAVE – TRIMWORK AND MOLDING BUILT AROUND A DOOR OR WINDOW.

architrave

ARRIS – THE POINT OF INTERSECTION OF TWO SURFACES – EITHER CURVED OR STRAIGHT.

The intersecting ridge is the arris

Ash dump – THE OPENING IN A FIRE PLACE HEARTH THROUGH WHICH THE ASHES ARE DUMPED.

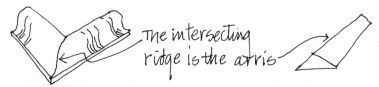

Fireplace ash dump

ASHLAR – SQUARE STONE FACING WHICH IS HEWN AND LAID WITH THIN JOINTS IN COURSES.

ALLOON FRAMING — HOUSE FRAMING IN WHICH THE EXTERIOR WALL STUDS RUN UP CONTINUOUS TO THE ROOF PLATE. SECOND FLOOR JOISTS ARE NAILED TO SIDES OF STUDS.

LUSTER — VERTICAL POST OF A STAIR BALUSTRADE

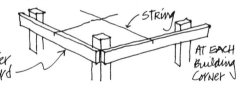

Baluster or Banister

TTER BOARD — HORIZONTAL BOARD AT INITIAL BUILDING FOUNDATION USED FOR REFERENCE ELEVATION.

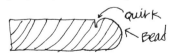

String

AT EACH Building Corner

tter ard

Y WINDOW — A WINDOW PROJECTING OUT FROM A BUILDING BUT SUPPORTED ON A FOUNDATION WALL.

AD AND QUIRK — WOODWORK DETAIL

Quirk
Bead

ARING WALL — MAJOR SUPPORT WALL

BOARD AND BATTEN — FACING BOARDS AND JOINT COVER - USUALLY VERTICAL

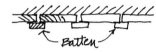

Batten

BOARD FOOT — BOARD MEASURE OF 12 x 12 x 1 INCH BEFORE PLANING

BOW SAW — WOOD SAW FOR CUTTING CURVES

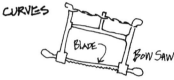

BLADE

BOW SAW

BOW WINDOW — A CURVED BAY WINDOW

BOXWOOD — A HARDWOOD; CLOSE-GRAINED - USED IN MAKING CHESS MEN AND OTHER FINE WOODWORK.

BRAD — FLOORING NAIL; EARLY BRADS WERE HAND-FORGED FROM SOFT IRON.

BRESSUMMER — HEAVY GIRDER AT CENTER OF HOUSE CARRYING THE FLOOR JOISTS; (SUMMER BEAM).

BRICK — BUILDING BLOCK MADE OF BURNT CLAY; COMMONLY 3 COURSES TO 8 INCHES.

BRIDGING — MIDSPAN BRACING OF FLOOR JOISTS

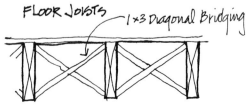

1 x 3 Diagonal Bridging

BROAD AXE — AXE USED FOR HEWING LOGS; CUTTING BEVEL IS ON ONE SIDE ONLY; HAS OFFSET HANDLE.

Broad axe

BROWN COAT — BASE OR FLOATING COAT OF A PLASTER WALL.

BUILDER'S LEVEL — A 'DUMPY' LEVER USED FOR SITING HORIZONTAL LINES.

BUILT-UP ROOF — ROOF FINISH MADE UP OF TWO OR MORE LAYERS OF BITUMENOUS FELTS - FOR LOW SLOP-ING ROOFS.

BULLNOSE — ROUNDED EDGE.

BULLNOSED BRICK

BURR — A HIGHLY REGARDED FACE OR FIGURE IN THE GRAIN OF BEAUTIFUL FINISHING WOODS.

BUTT HINGE — SIMPLE FOLDING HINGE; DOOR HINGES ARE REFERRED TO AS DOOR BUTTS.

CANT STRIP - SHORT SLOPE OF ROOF TO SHED WATER.

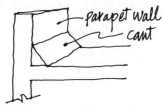

parapet wall
cant

CARRIAGE - WOODEN STAIR SUPPORT.

the two stringers of a stair carriage

CARRIAGE BOLT - A ROUND-HEADED BOLT WITH A SHORT SQUARE SECTION TO LOCK INTO THE WOOD.

CASEMENT WINDOW - HINGED WINDOW; OPENS SIMILARLY TO A DOOR.

CAST STONE - CONCRETE POURED INTO MOLDS; THE FINISHED PIECE LOOKS LIKE STONE.

CAULKING - ELASTIC MATERIAL SQUEEZED INTO A JOINT IN ORDER TO PREVENT MOISTURE PENETRATION.

CHAMFER - 45° ANGLE CORNER CUT.

chamferred Edges

CHECK - SEASONING CRACKS IN TIMBER.

CLAPBOARD SIDING - FEATHER-EDGED WEATHER BOARD HOUSE SIDING.

CLOSE GRAINED WOOD - WOOD GRAIN WITH A VERY FINE TEXTURE.

CLOSED STRINGER -

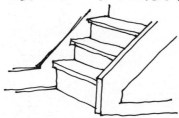

STRINGER THAT HAS A TOP CUT PARALLEL TO THE SLOPE OF THE STAIR HIDING THE STEP EDGE.

COLLAR BEAM -

collar beam

HORIZONTAL ROOF TIE BEAM USUALLY LOCATED AT THE TOP 2/3's OF A GABLE OR "A" FRAME.

COMBED JOINT -

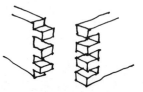

SIMPLE TOOTHED WOOD JOINTING OFTEN USED IN WOODEN BOXES.

COMMON BOND - BRICK COURSING COMPOSED OF STRETCHERS WITH EVERY 6TH COURSE DONE IN HEADERS.

COMPASS SAW -

HANDSAW USED FOR CUTTING CURVES.

CONCAVE JOINT - MASONRY MORTAR JOINT STRUCK WITH A TOOL GIVING A CONCAVE SURFACE TO THE MORTAL.

CONCEALED GUTTER - GUTTER HIDDEN BY THE FACIA OR CORNICE-WORK.

← concealed gutter

COPE - IN WOOD JOINERY - CUTTING ONE MOLDING TO THE SHAPE OF ANOTHER IN LIEU OF MITERING AS AT INSIDE CORNERS.

This piece is coped to the shape of the second piece.

COPING - WALL CAP

coping

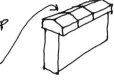

COPING SAW - SAW WITH NARROW BLADE USED FOR COPING MOLDINGS.

CORBEL -

MASONRY PROJECTION OUT FROM THE WALL FACE USED FOR A BEAM OR ROOF SUPPORT.

CORNER BEAD - METAL CORNER WITH ROUNDED BEAD USED AS A PLASTER STOP AT AN OUTSIDE CORNER.

CORNICE -
EAVE OVERHANG WITH ACCOMPANYING DECORATIVE WOODWORK.

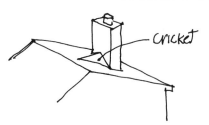

cornice

COUNTERSINK -
BORING DOWN INTO A MATERIAL SO THAT A BOLT OR SCREW HEAD IS FLUSH WITH OR BELOW THE SURFACE.

COVE MOLDING -
CONCAVE QUADRANT MOLDING USED AT CORNERS.

CRICKET - A ROOF SADDLE USED TO SHED WATER FROM BEHIND A CHIMNEY ON A SLOPED ROOF.

← cricket

CROSS-CUT SAW -
A SAW USED FOR CUTTING WOOD ACROSS THE GRAIN.

CROSS-GARNET HINGE -
METAL STRAP HINGE.

CROWN MOLDING - WOOD MOLDING USED AT THE TOP OF THE FACIA AND INSIDE AT THE WALL/CEILING CORNER.

section through crown molding.
← wall

CUT NAIL - A NAIL OF RECTANGULAR CROSS SECTION CUT FROM STEEL PLATE; CANNOT BE BENT.

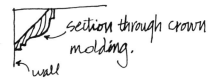

233

DADO - IN JOINERY: RECESS IN A PIECE OF WOOD INTO WHICH ANOTHER PIECE IS FITTED

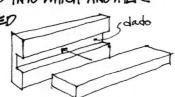

DAMPER - METAL HINGED DOOR IN FIREPLACE FLUE TO CONTROL DRAFT.

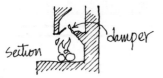

Section — damper

DEAD BOLT -
LOCKING BOLT ON A DOCK LOCK SET IN PLACE BY A KEY.

DECIDUOUS - KINDS OF TREES WHICH LOSE THEIR LEAVES IN WINTER (HARDWOODS).

DELIQUESCENCE - DAMP AREA ON MASONRY CAUSED BY WATER BEING ABSORBED BY SALTS IN THE MATERIAL.

DIAMOND SAW - MOTORIZED CIRCULAR SAW WITH DIAMONDS ON ITS EDGE USED IN CUTTING CONCRETE OR STONE.

DIE - THE TOPS AND BOTTOMS OF BALUSTERS.

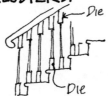

Die
Die

DOOR BUCK - ROUGH FRAME FOR A DOOR OPENING TO WHICH THE FINISHED FRAME OR CASING IS AFFIXED.

DORMER - A WINDOW PROJECTING OUT OF A ROOF SLOPE.

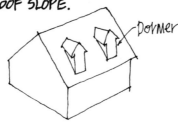

Dormer

DOUBLE GLAZING - WINDOWS HAVING TWO PANES OF GLASS SEPARATED BY AN AIRSPACE.

DOUGLAS FIR - A SOFTWOOD, BUT USED EXTENSIVELY FOR STRUCTURAL FRAMING LUMBER.

DOVETAIL - AN INTERLOCKING JOINT SHAPED LIKE A DOVE'S TAIL.

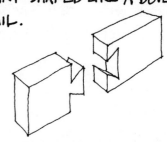

DOWEL - SHORT ROUND HARDWOOD ROD USED IN WOOD JOINERY.

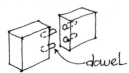

dowel

DRAFTED MARGIN - SMOOTH BAND AROUND PERIMETER OF STONE FACE - OFTEN APPLIED TO CONCRETE SURFACES.

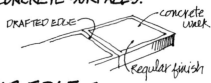

DRAFTED EDGE
concrete walk
Regular finish

DRIP EDGE -
METAL ROOF EDGING.

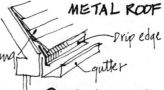

Drip edge
Roofing
gutter

DUTCH DOOR - A DOOR WHICH OPENS IN TWO SECTIONS, TOP AND BOTTOM; A STABLE DOOR.

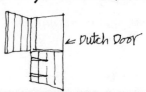

Dutch Door

EASEMENT - A LEGAL RIGHT-OF-WAY WHICH ONE PERSON MAY HAVE IN ANOTHER PERSON'S LAND.

ENGLISH BOND - BRICK COURSING OF ALTERNATING HEADERS AND STRETCHERS.

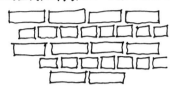

EAVE - A ROOF OVERHANG

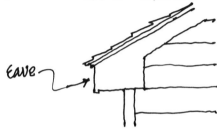

eave

ESCUTCHEON - ORNAMENTAL PLATE AROUND A KEYHOLE.

Escutcheon

EDGE GRAIN - APPEARANCE OF WOOD GRAIN IN A BOARD WHICH HAS BEEN QUARTER-SAWN.

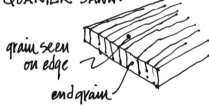

grain seen on edge

end grain

EXTRADOS - THE UPPER SURFACE OF AN ARCH.

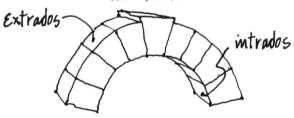

Extrados

intrados

EFFLORESCENCE - SALTS WITHIN BRICK WHICH APPEARS ON THE SURFACE OF WALLS AS A WHITE POWDER; CAN BE REMOVED WITH MURIATIC ACID.

EYEBROW DORMER - A DORMER WHICH PROJECTS THROUGH A ROOF FORMING A CURVED TOP.

Eyebrow dormer

FACE BRICK - EXPOSED, FINISH BRICK.

FAIENCE - TERRA COTTA WITH A GLAZED FINISH.

FASCIA - HORIZONTAL FINISH BOARD USED AT THE CORNICE (EXTERIOR).

fascia board

FEATHER-EDGED BOARD - BOARD WITH TAPERED END.

feather-edged weather boarding

FIBERBOARD - MANUFACTURED BOARD MADE FROM COMPRESSED FIBERS.

FIDDLEBACK - MOTTLED GRAIN AS IN THE WOOD GRAIN OF MAPLE.

FINGER-JOINTED - A COMBED JOINT.

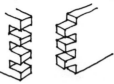

FIREBRICK - REFRACTORY BRICK MADE TO WITHSTAND HIGH TEMPERATURES.

FIRE STOP - SOLID BLOCKING USED TO PREVENT THE SPREAD OF SMOKE AND FIRE.

FLASHING - A MEMBRANE OR METAL USED TO PREVENT WATER PENETRATION.

FLAT-SAWN TIMBER - PLAIN SAWN LUMBER.

parallel cuts

FLEMISH BOND - BRICK COURSING OF HEADERS AND STRETCHERS.

FLITCHED BEAM - COMPOSITE BEAM MADE OF TWO WOOD BEAMS AND A CENTER STEEL PLATE.

Bolts

FLUE - CHIMNEY PIPE.

clay tile flue

FLUSH DOOR - A DOOR, BOTH SIDES OF WHICH ARE FLAT SURFACES.

flush door

panelled door

FRENCH DOOR - TWO GLAZED CASEMENT DOORS.

FROG - RECESSED MORTAR KEY IN A BRICK FACE.

FURRING STRIP - WOOD OR METAL STRIPS USED FOR A NAILING SURFACE.

GABLE ROOF – AN "A"-TYPE
ROOF FORMING TRIANGULAR
END WALL.

GAMBREL ROOF - A ROOF
CONFIGURATION USING TWO DIFFERENT
PITCHES.

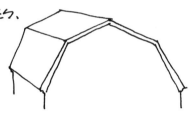

GERMAN SIDING – WEATHER BOARDING
WITH THE FOLLOWING CONFIGURATION.

GIRDER – MAIN SUPPORT BEAM.

GLAZING – GLASS; PLACING GLASS IN
AN OPENING.

GRAIN – ARRANGEMENT OF FIBER AND
TEXTURE IN A PIECE OF WOOD.

GUDGEON – A GATE HOOK; ALSO A METAL
PIN USED TO LOCK ONE STONE TO ANOTHER.

GUSSET PLATE – STRUCTURAL STEEL PLATE
USED IN TRUSSES.

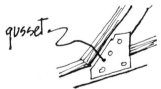

GYPSUM WALLBOARD – MANUFACTURED WALL-
BOARD MADE OF GYPSUM AND COVERED
WITH PAPER.

HACKSAW - HANDSAW USED
   MAINLY FOR CUTTING METAL.

HALF-LAP JOINT - A HALVED
   JOINT:

HALF-ROUND - SEMICIRCULAR
   MOLDING.

HALF-TIMBER - ELIZABETHAN
   HOUSE FRAMING IN WHICH MAIN VERTICAL
   POSTS DID NOT EXTEND IN ONE PIECE ABOVE
   THE SECOND FLOOR LINE; THE WOOD
   FRAMING WAS EXPOSED TO THE EXTERIOR.

HANGING STILE - DOOR STILE TO
   WHICH THE HINGES ARE AFFIXED.

HARDBOARD - MANUFACTURED
   BOARD COMPOSED OF COMPRESSED
   WOOD FIBERS.

HARDWOODS - BROADLEAVED TREES.

HASP - LATCHING DEVICE FOR A
   GATE OR DOOR

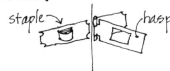
staple   hasp

HEADER - A WOOD BEAM AT RIGHT
   ANGLES TO THE JOISTS OR RAFTERS-USED
   FOR SUPPORT.

HEARTWOOD - HARDER INNER WOOD
   OF A TREE USED FOR TIMBER.

Heart
Wood   sapwood

HEW - TO SHAPE TIMBERS WITH
   AN AX OR ADZE; STONE IS ALSO
   "HEWN".

HIPPED ROOF - A ROOF
   ANGLED FROM ALL FOUR WALLS.

HOLLOW BLOCK - CONCRETE
   MASONRY UNIT WITH HOLLOW
   CORES.

HOPPER WINDOW - A WINDOW
   HINGED AT THE BOTTOM.

HOUSED JOINT - JOINT MADE
   BY "LETTING" ONE BOARD INTO
   ANOTHER.

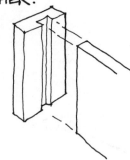

INLAY - SEE PARQUETRY.

INTRADOS - THE UNDER SURFACE OF AN ARCH OR VAULT.

intrados

JACK ARCH - A FLAT ARCH.

JACK PLANE - A GENERAL PURPOSE WOOD PLANE USED TO SMOOTH WOOD.

JAMB - THE VERTICAL SIDES OF A WINDOW OR DOOR OPENING.

JERKIN-HEAD ROOF - A HIPPED GABLE ROOF.

gable-end.

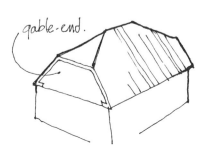

JOINERY - THE ART OF FINE WOODWORKING.

JOINT TAPE - TAPE (PAPER) PLACED OVER THE JOINTS OF GYPSUM WALL BOARDS.

JOIST - FLOOR SUPPORTING MEMBER.

JOIST HANGER - METAL END SUPPORT FOR A FLOOR JOIST.

KEENE'S CEMENT - A HARD PLASTER USED FOR FINISHING COAT.

KEEPER - RECEIVING GUIDE FOR A LOCKING BOLT.

the keeper

KERF - SAW CUT IN A BOARD FOR WEDGING OR BENDING.

KEYSTONE - WEDGE-SHAPED CENTERSTONE OF AN ARCH.

keystone

KILN DRIED - LUMBER WHICH HAS HAD MOISTURE REMOVED BY BEING DRIED IN A KILN.

KING-POST TRUSS -

a simple truss configuration

KNOB-AND-TUBE WIRING - OUT-OF-DATE ELECTRICAL WIRING INSTALLATION USING PORCELAIN KNOB AND TUBE SUPPORTS.

KNOCKED DOWN - A CONSTRUCTION PART WHICH IS DELIVERED TO THE SITE UNASSEMBLED.

KRAFT PAPER - A STRONG PAPER USED FOR LINING INSULATION & USED AS A BUILDING PAPER.

239

LAG BOLT or LAG SCREW - HEAVY SCREW WITH SQUARE HEAD.

LAMP BLACK - BLACK PIGMENT MADE FROM THE SOOT OF BURNED COAL TAR.

LAP SIDING - CLAPBOARDING.

LARCH - TREE OF NORTHWEST U.S. - USED FOR STRUCTURAL TIMBER.

LATH - STRIP OF WOOD OR METAL USED AS A BASE FOR PLASTERING.

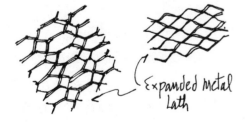

Expanded metal Lath

LATTICE WINDOW - WINDOW COMPOSED OF MANY SMALL "LIGHTS".

Lead "came"

LEADED LIGHT - SMALL PANE OF GLASS USED IN A WINDOW; SUCH PANES ARE HELD TOGETHER BY LEAD "CAMES."

LEAN MIX - REFERS TO MORTAR COMPOSITION WHICH HAS LESS CEMENT THAN NORMAL.

LEDGED AND BRACED DOOR - WOOD DOOR MADE OF VERTICAL PLANKS HELD TIGHT BY LEDGES.

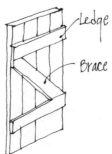

Ledge

Brace

LEDGER - WOOD SUPPORT FASTENED TO THE SIDE OF A BEAM OR WALL.

Ledger

LIGHT - A SINGLE PANE OF WINDOW GLASS.

LIGHTNING ROD - A CONDUCTOR FOR SAFELY TRANSMITTING LIGHTNING TO EARTH.

LINTEL - STRUCTURAL SUPPORT OVER A WALL OPENING.

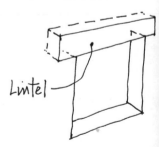

Lintel

MARKING GAUGE – ADJUSTABLE BEECHWOOD GAUGE WITH A MARKING POINT; USED IN CARPENTRY.

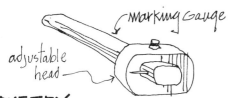

MARQUETRY – DECORATIVE WOOD INLAY

MASONRY NAIL – SPECIAL HARD NAIL USED FOR NAILING INTO MASONRY.

MEETING RAIL – MID-RAIL OF A SASH WINDOW.

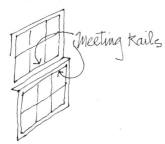

MILLWORK – FINISHED WOODWORK SHAPED OR ASSEMBLED AT THE MILL.

MINERAL WOOL – USED AS AN INSULATION MATERIAL; HAS HIGH RESISTANCE TO COMBUSTION.

MITER – 45° ANGLED JOINT

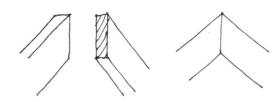

MORTAR – A MIXTURE OF CEMENT, SAND, AND WATER.

MORTISE AND TENON – A WOODWORKING JOINT.

MORTISE GAUGE – A MARKING GAUGE WITH TWO MARKING POINTS – USED FOR MAKING MORTISES.

MOTTLE – DESCRIPTIVE APPEARANCE OF WOOD GRAIN.

MULLION – VERTICAL STRIP THAT JOINS WINDOW LIGHTS.

MUNTIN – A MULLION.

NAIL SET – METAL BAR USED TO SET FINISHING NAILS BELOW THE WOOD SURFACE.

NEWEL POST – POST AT A STAIR SUPPORTING A HANDRAIL.

NOGGING – HORIZONTAL WOOD STUD BRACING. EARLY HALF-TIMBERED HOUSES USED BRICK NOGGING (EXPOSED).

OGEE - AN S. SHAPED CURVE USED IN MOLDINGS AND GUTTERS.

OGEE GUTTER

OILSTONE - A QUARTZ STONE USED TO GIVE A FINISHED POLISHED EDGE TO METAL CUTTING TOOL; THE STONE IS OILED BEFORE USING.

OPEN-GRAIN WOOD - A COARSE GRAIN SIMILAR TO THAT OF OAK.

ORIEL WINDOW - A PROJECTING WINDOW SUPPORTED BY BRACKETS OR CORBELS; SIMILAR TO THE BAY WINDOW.

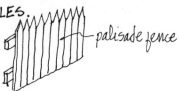

PALISADE FENCE - FENCE MADE OF LONG, VERTICAL, CLOSELY-SPACED POINTED PALES.

palisade fence

PANE - A PIECE OF GLASS; A WINDOW LIGHT.

PANELLED DOOR - A DOOR MADE UP OF STILES AND RAILS WITH INFILL PANELS.

PARGE - A CEMENT MORTAR COATING.

PARQUET FLOORING - WOOD FLOORING PACKAGED IN SQUARES OF 8" x 8" ± AND GLUED DOWN.

PARQUETRY - INLAID WOODWORK OF GEOMETRICAL DESIGN.

inlaid veneer parquetry

PERGOLA - NARROW WOOD-LATTICED ARBOR.

pergola

PHILLIPS HEAD SCREW - A SCREW WITH A RECESSED CROSS SLOT.

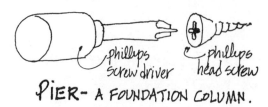
phillips screw driver · phillips head screw

PIER - A FOUNDATION COLUMN.

PILASTER - A STRUCTURAL THICKENING OF WALL; A WALL BUTTRESS.

Pilaster

PLAIN-SAWN - BOARDS CUT BY PARALLEL CUTTING THROUGH A LOG.
End of Log

PLINTH - SQUARE BLOCK AT A COLUMN BASE.

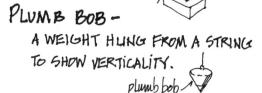
plinth block

PLUMB BOB - A WEIGHT HUNG FROM A STRING TO SHOW VERTICALITY.
plumb bob

POINTING - FINISHING OR REFINISHING (REPOINTING) A MASONRY MORTAR JOINT.

PUTLOG - SCAFFOLDING SUPPORT LOG FOR BRICK MASONS - WHICH IS TEMPORARILY LET INTO THE BRICK - WORK.

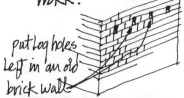
put log holes left in an old brick wall

QUARREL – A PANE OF GLASS IN A LEADED LIGHT WINDOW.

diamond-shaped quarrels

QUARRY TILE – HARD PAVING BRICKS MADE FROM BURNT CLAY.

QUARTER-ROUND – WOOD MOLDING - QUARTER CIRCLE SHAPE.

QUARTER-SAWN – BOARDS CUT FROM QUARTER CUT LOGS.

GROWTH RINGS AT 45° OR MORE - ANGLE TO BOARD SURFACE.

QUIRK – A GROOVE USED IN WOOD MOLDINGS.

Quirk

QUOIN – BRICKWORK OR STONEWORK AT THE OUTSIDE CORNER OF A BUILDING.

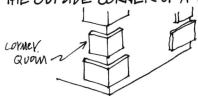
corner quoin

RABBET – A RECESS CUT ALONG THE EDGE OF A BOARD.

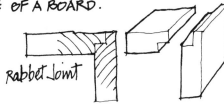
Rabbet Joint

RADIAL SHRINKAGE – TIMBER SHRINAGE AT RIGHT ANGLES TO THE GROWTH RINGS.

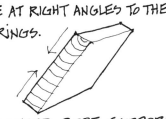

RAFTER – WOOD ROOF SUPPORTING MEMBER.

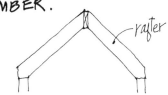
rafter

RAGLET – (OR REGLET) A GROOVE ALONG A WALL INTO WHICH FLASHING IS PLACED.

parapet wall
flashing
Raglet

RAIL – HORIZONTAL FRAME PIECE OF A PANELED DOOR.

Rail

RAKE – MOLDING INCLINED ALONG THE TOP EDGE OF A GABLE END.

Roof Rake
Rake Molding

RELIEVING ARCH – AN ARCH BUILT AS THE MAIN SUPPORT ABOVE A LINTEL.

RIM LATCH – A LATCH AFFIXED TO THE SURFACE OF A DOOR, OPERATED BY THE DOOR KNOB.

RISER – THE VERTICAL PORTION OF A STEP.

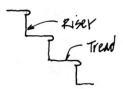

ROOF TRUSS – STRUCTURAL FRAMEWORK SUPPORTING A ROOF.

A simple "W" TRUSS OR FINK

ROUGHING IN – INSTALLING WIRES, PIPES, ETC. PRIOR TO INSTALLING FIXTURES AND FINISHES.

ROWLOCK – A BRICK LAID ON EDGE.

a rowlock course

RUNG – THE HORIZONTAL STEP OF A LADDER.

Rung

RUNNING BOND – A STRETCHER BOND. BRICK WALL FALE OF STRETCHERS ONLY.

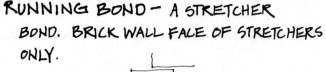

SAFETY GLASS – LAMINATED GLASS WHICH SHATTERS INTO FRAGMENTS TOO SMALL TO CAUSE HARMFUL CUTS.

SAPWOOD – THE WOOD JUST BELOW THE TREE BARK – WHERE GROWTH OCCURS.

SASH – FRAMEWORK AROUND THE GLASS PANES OF A WINDOW.

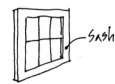

Sash

SAW HORSE – SUPPORT FOR THE SAWING OF WOOD.

SCARF JOINT – A WOOD LAPPED JOINT.

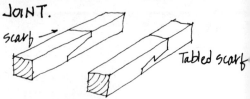

scarf

Tabled scarf

SCISSORS TRUSS – A TRUSS WHICH LOOKS LIKE SCISSORS; HAS NO HORIZONTAL BOTTOM CHORD.

SCRATCH COAT – THE FIRST APPLIED COAT IN PLASTER WORK- SOMETIMES IT IS SCRATCHED FOR BONDING TO THE SECOND COAT.

SCREED – BOARDS USED IN CONCRETE WORK TO MARK THE TOP LEVEL OF A SLAB.

SCRIBE – TO CUT THE EDGE OF A BOARD OR OTHER MATERIAL TO FIT THE SHAPE OF AN ADJOINING MATERIAL.

Board with scribed edge.

Wall surface

SHAKES - HAND-SPLIT SHINGLES, OFTEN MADE OUT OF CEDAR.

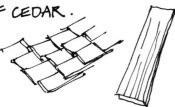

SHIPLAP JOINT - JOINT USED ON WOOD SIDING - EACH PIECE OF SIDING HAVING A RABBETTED EDGE.

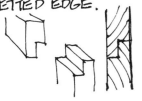

SHOE MOLDING - WOOD MOLDING USED AT THE JOINT BETWEEN THE FLOORING AND THE BASEBOARD.

BASE
SHOE

SLAT - THIN STRIP OF WOOD SIMILAR TO THAT USED IN SHUTTERS.

SOFFIT - UNDERSIDE OF A CORNICE OF BUILDING OVERHANG.

SHUTTER SLATS

SOFTWOOD - TIMBER FROM THE CONIFER GROUP OF TREES.

SOIL PIPE - MAIN HOUSE SEWER DRAIN PIPE. WHICH RUNS VERTICALLY DOWN THROUGH THE HOUSE.

SOLDIER COURSE - BRICK COURSING IN THE UPRIGHT POSITION.

soldier course

SOLID MASONRY UNIT - CONCRETE MASONRY UNIT WHICH IS 75% OR MORE SOLID.

SPLIT-RING CONNECTOR - A METAL TIMBER CONNECTOR WHICH FITS INTO PREDRILLED GROOVES ON EACH PIECE OF WOOD.

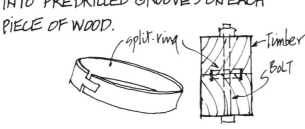

split-ring
Timber
Bolt

STANDING SEAM - A WATERTIGHT SEAM IN METAL ROOFING.

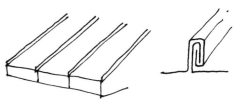

STILE - VERTICAL FRAMING MEMBER IN A PANELED DOOR.

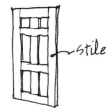

stile

STOOL - FLAT SHELF TRIMWORK ON THE INSIDE LOWER EDGE OF A WINDOW.

stool

STRINGER - SLOPING STAIR SUPPORT ON EACH SIDE OF THE STAIR.

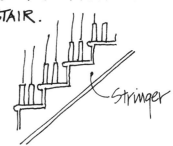

stringer

STRUCK JOINT - A NON-WEATHERTIGHT MORTAR JOINT SLOPING INWARDS.

STUCCO - A CEMENT, LIME, AND SAND COATING PLACED ON EXTERIOR WALL SURFACES.

STUD - A VERTICAL WALL SUPPORT MEMBER.

Plate

Stud

SUBFLOOR - FLOOR SHEATHING BASE FOR THE FINISH FLOOR.

TANGENTIAL SHRINKAGE - SHRINKAGE ALONG THE LENGTH OF A TIMBER, PARALLEL TO THE GROWTH RINGS.

TENON - THE WOOD PROJECTION INTENDED TO FIT INTO THE MORTISE OF A MORTISE AND TENON JOINT.

tenon

mortise

TERMITE SHIELD - METAL SHIELD OVER A FOUNDATION WALL TO PREVENT TERMITE MIGRATION.

Metal Shield

TONGUE-AND-GROOVE JOINT - A COMMON WOODWORKING JOINT OFTEN USED IN FLOORING.

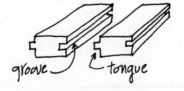

groove

tongue

TREAD - THE HORIZONTAL PORTION OF A STEP.

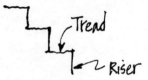

Tread

Riser

TUCK POINTING - MORTAR JOINT POINTED WITH WHITE LIME PUTTY.

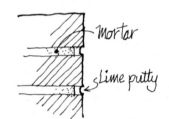

Mortar

Lime putty

VEE JOINT – BOARDS JOINED TOGETHER THAT HAVE CHAMFERRED EDGES TO HIDE SHRINKAGE.

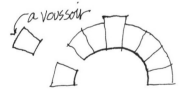

shiplap vee joint

VENEER – THIN SAWN SHEETS USED FOR DECORATIVE FACING OR GLUED INTO PLYWOOD.

VOUSSOIR – A WEDGE-SHAPED ARCH STONE.

a voussoir

WAINSCOT – SOLID WOOD PANELING USED AROUND THE LOWER PORTION OF WALLS IN A ROOM; WALL PANELING UP TO CHAIR RAIL HEIGHT.

WANE – WOOD BARK LEFT ON THE EDGE OF A PIECE OF LUMBER.

wane

WHITEWASH – A FENCE OR OUT-BUILDING PAINT COMPOSED OF QUICKLIME AND WATER.

WIRECUT BRICK – CLAY BRICK CUT INTO LENGTHS BY WIRES BEFORE BEING BURNT.

WYTHE – THE INDIVIDUAL BRICK THICKNESS OF A WALL.

serpentine wall one wythe thick

Wall Two wythes thick

Notes:

Notes:

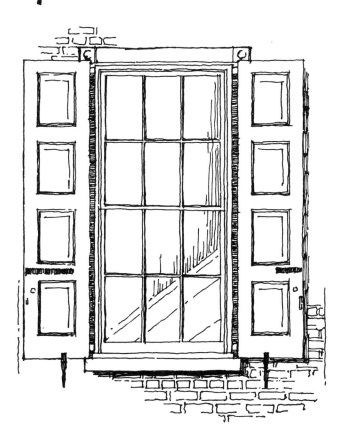

Notes:

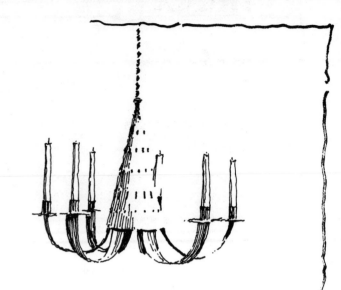

Index

humidity, relative, 93

I

infiltration heat loss, 77-78
insolation, 49
insulation
    areas needed in, 74, 84
    effect on water vapor, 92
    forms of, 82, 86-90
    installation of, 85
    standards, 91
insulation, types of
    batt, 83, 85
    blown, 83, 86, 87, 93
    foam, 83, 87
    granular fill, 83, 90
    rigid, 83, 89
    spray on, 83, 88
inverter, 68, 70

L

land, contours of, 11, 12, 22
landscaping, 14-18, 28, 32, 33;
    see also trees

log cabin designs, 143, 177

M

mailbox support design, 110
mantel designs, 172-173, 175, 176
mildew, 95
moisture proofing, 25, 26, 82, 92, 93
molding styles, 204-205

O

overhang house design, 119-120

P

perm, 94
permeance, 94
plans, floor, 104, 105, 109-110, 113-114, 116-117,
119-120, 122-123, 127, 129, 134-135, 137, 138,
140-141, 152-155, 158-159, 161-162, 164-165, 167, 168
plat, 10, 12

R

radiation, 40; see also energy

253

About The Authors ⌐

Keeler Chapman has been a practicing architect since 1973. The Northern Virginia area where he was raised and the Lancaster, Pennsylvania area where he now works are steeped in Early American architecture and history. During his professional career, Mr. Chapman has sought to impart the human time-tested qualities of the past to today's building technology.

John Traister was raised in the foothills of the Blue Ridge Mountains of Virginia. He became interested in electrical and mechanical systems for building construction during his early college years. The practical ways of his country upbringing have carried over into his many published books and articles on subjects as various as electrical systems and trout fishing.